KNOWING
HERSELF
Women Tell Their
Stories in Psychotherapy

KNOWING HERSELF

Women Tell Their Stories in Psychotherapy

Joan Hamerman Robbins

 INSIGHT BOOKS

PLENUM PRESS • NEW YORK AND LONDON

Library of Congress Cataloging-in-Publication Data

Robbins, Joan Hamerman.
    Knowing herself : women tell their stories in psychotherapy / Joan
Hamerman Robbins.
        p.   cm.
    Includes bibliographical references.
    ISBN 0-306-43430-X
    1. Psychotherapy patients--United States--Biography. 2. Women-
-United States--Biography.   I. Title.
RC464.A1R63   1990
616.89'14'082--dc20   89-26727
                                                                  CIP

In appreciation of the potent impact that special life
experiences have on shaping a woman's character,
the essential flavor of events has been preserved while
names, places, and identifying facts have been fictionalized.

Plenum Press is a division of Plenum Publishing Corporation
233 Spring Street, New York, N.Y. 10013

An Insight Book

Printed in the United States of America

For Bill, my husband and very special friend.

Over and over again, I have practiced with you until I got it: When I speak up for myself and stay firm with my objectives, a vast range of possibilities opens. The way in which you responded enabled us to reinvent our relationship to reflect and respect who each of us really is.

Thank you for always being there during all the experiences that make up writing a book.

"To tell the truth is to give birth to yourself in the world. Again and again and again when you give birth to yourself, you have seized the root powers of your life."

June Jordan, Lecture at Harvard
University, March 1987

"We had the meagerest portions . . . and when things were rare, we went without. That is our lot in life we told ourselves. And we stopped wanting. Only we longed and we grew so accustomed to the pain of longing that we called this our nature. . . . But one day all this changed. On this day we met a woman who was used to getting what she wanted. She ate large portions and her body was big. She let us know there were other such women. . . . We began to dream we were like this woman. . . .
"We began to think we might get what we wanted. Our longings turned into desire. . . . We were alive with desire. And we knew we could never go back to those years of longing."

Susan Griffin, *Woman and Nature:*
The Roaring Inside Her[1]

"If in the middle of a provocative exchange she says, 'Well that's the mother you got, it would have been better with another one, too damned bad this is the one you got,' and I nod, 'You can say that again,' we both start laughing at the same time. . . . We are, I think, equally amazed that we have lived long enough to be responsive for whole minutes at a time simply to being in the world together, rather than concentrating on what each of us is or is not getting from the other. . . ."

Vivian Gornick,
Fierce Attachments

ACKNOWLEDGMENTS

Many people believed in me and encouraged me as I grappled with writing *Knowing Herself*. I deeply appreciate your continuous support and take this opportunity to thank each of you, splendid companions on my journey writing this book.

Special thanks to my children, Rebecca and Saul, who never lost their belief in my ability to do this, even when I wavered.

To my good friends and hearty supporters, some of whom also read portions of the manuscript and offered insightful feedback; your prompt attention to my requests, despite very busy schedules, was always appreciated: Beverly Burch, Erin Dawn, Edith Freeman, Sadja Greenwood, Jane Jacobs, Alan Margolis, Jeff McLane, Lois Talkovsky.

Barbara Claster, Christa Donaldson, Jan Faulkner, and Ann Roth read the entire manuscript with care and generously offered thoughtful, provocative suggestions for which I am grateful.

My siblings Bernice Ward and Arthur Hamerman helped heal old wounds by expressing their interest in what I was accomplishing.

Amy Urdang was the first editor to point me in the direction of becoming a writer. Barbara Rosenblum furthered my writing skill with her thoughtful, gentle suggestions and firm belief in what I was trying to articulate. The major sadness of this undertaking is that Barbara could not see this project completed. She died from cancer in February 1988.

Leigh Davidson had the tough job of helping me after Barbara's death. I owe her much gratitude for her invaluable suggestions and the hard questions she asked that pushed me to clarify what had been confusing, thereby enabling the manuscript to grow in new ways.

At Plenum Publishing Corporation, Norma Fox, executive editor, was especially helpful with her sensitive attention to details and the skillful way in which she gave advice. Frank Darmstadt, editorial assistant, and Susan Woolford, production editor, were both very sensitive and responsive to my desire to be involved in the publishing of my book. I thank both of them for their good advice and patience as we processed decisions.

Before I learned the delight of working on a computer, Debbie Perrin Morrison patiently typed my early drafts.

Very special thanks to all the women whose stories you are about to read. None of this would have been possible without each of you.

CONTENTS

Part III. The Toll of Persistent Disregard

Part IV. Reclaiming Pride

INTRODUCTION

These places of possibility within ourselves are dark because they are ancient and hidden; they have survived and grown strong through darkness. Within these deep places each one of us holds an incredible reserve of creativity and power, of unexamined and unrecorded emotion and feeling. The woman's place of power within each of us is neither white nor surface; it is dark, it is ancient and it is deep.

Audre Lorde, *Sister Outsider*

As a little girl I was fascinated by the many stories my grandmother told of her childhood in Minsk, Russia. Born to poor Jewish parents, her father died of tuberculosis when my grandmother was three years old. The only work her widowed mother could find was as a servant to a very wealthy family who would not permit her child to live on the premises. What happened to my grandmother because of these circumstances was one particular tale I never forgot.

Grandma's mother figured out that the only way she could keep her child with her was to hide the child—in the closet of her room. There my grandmother remained. Hidden. Time passed. She never said, and I never asked, how long she was there. When I think about it now a shiver still runs through my body. Imagine a child hidden in a closet, food sneaked in to her, never being allowed to run around, play outside, or make noise. Her very survival is based on acting as if she does not exist.

For a very long time I did not even realize that an experience very similar to my grandmother's had been mine. It was buried that deeply within me. Even though my mother became the teller of family tales decades later when she visited me and my family, in all the stories I heard her recount, she never said a word nor was there ever the slightest hint about the hardship and misery that surrounded a major event of my early years. I was totally unaware and cut off from a vital part of my own experience because it had been too terrifying and painful to recall.

I would not be able to reclaim this chunk of my past until I had had several years of my own psychotherapy, which grounded me more firmly in my own identity and enabled me to accept myself. Off and on over 25 years, bit by bit, with the help of three different psychotherapists—two women and a man—portions of this life-shaping ordeal have been retrieved.

The time was 1936—in the midst of The Great Depression. My family was poor. My father was employed sporadically and spent his days looking for work. My mother had a part-time job. Suddenly, I became very ill with rheumatic fever. Bed rest was the only treatment; penicillin had not yet been discovered. I was four years old.

Additionally, each afternoon at one o'clock, my mother went off to her job and left me alone in the house, in my crib, for about two hours. Around three o'clock my 13-year-old sister would return home from school. Every day, for about three months, I spent two hours, alone, confined in that crib, waiting—waiting for my sister to come home.

I think baby-sitters were rare in those days, and there was no money for one anyway. Nevertheless, it still does not make sense to me why a neighbor or a relative did not come and stay with me. What about my father? Or teenage brothers? Why were none of them available to watch me while my mother was at her job?

The care of the child is women's responsibility. Men are excused. They go to work or look for work. In any case, whatever they are doing is more important than being involved with the nitty-gritty details of daily family life. Even though my mother was not handling this well she did not ask for help, and my father did not seem to notice what was going on. I never questioned my father's judgment while I was growing up. I respected and obeyed him. I'm sure I also respected and obeyed my two much older brothers. However, they did not respect me as an individual with distinct needs. They were distant—unavailable—when I needed them the most. Now, that feels very sad.

I was fortunate to have an older sister who cared. She wore the nurturance mantle in my family. She already had comprehended her role. Satisfaction and approval both were earned by paying attention to someone else's needs. She did not consider her own.

For my mother to have asked my father to stay with me would have established her as a person deserving of respect and commanding her share of authority in the family. Not only would she have been requesting legitimate help, but she deserved cooperation. She was the major breadwinner. However, such assertion was outside my mother's experience. It also would have been a blow to my father's pride and upset the family balance. That might have had consequences for my mother.

Inadvertently, I paid a large price while my mother subordinated both her needs and mine to protect my father's dignity and a crumbling status quo. I also speculate that my mother, unaccustomed to acknowledging her own needs and finding acceptance for them within the family, could not imagine that mine were being trampled over by her negligence.

Moreover, each time I was left alone I was being devalued and conditioned to dismiss my own experience. This began to train me to mistrust myself and doubt my ability to get what I needed in my family. It also facilitated my retreat into compliant passivity, for which I was rewarded. That was being a good girl. These intimidating experiences that suppressed my spirit were repeated again in the summertime as I began to recover from my illness.

A doctor at a large city hospital who was supervising my recovery suggested to my mother that she send me to a convalescent home for sick children at a nearby seaside resort. He told her, "It will be good for Joan." My mother did not question his judgment. She accepted it. This time, money was not an issue; we qualified for financial aid for families with a sick child. One day that fateful summer, my mother took me out to The Home. She believed she was taking me there to recover. I felt I was being left to die.

Even now, after all the work I have done in therapy to remember this series of terrors, the middle part still remains buried. I have been able to put together the beginning and the end. I recollected being pushed away by my mother. I was clinging to her and screaming. I was terrified of being left. The only way she could get free of me was to push me away from her— into the hands of a matron who walked me down a long corridor. We entered a large room filled with cots. A cot and a metal locker for my clothes were assigned to me. I was handed a uniform and told to take off all my clothes and change into it. I would wear this uniform while at the home. A second profound assault. First, I am separated from my mother. Then, from my clothes. I was thoroughly shaken.

I know I grieved and grieved and could not adjust to what was happening. I missed my family and the familiar surroundings of my own home. I thought I would never see them again. I was frozen in time. Numb. Nothing mattered. My way of coping with all these changes and the inner turbulence they created was to grow quiet, withdraw, and stop eating. Many years later, when I asked, my mother told me that the staff reported this behavior to her and told her to come and take me home. I knew nothing of their treatment plan to help me recover strength and weight, be in the sunshine, and among other convalescing young children. I only knew my own isolation, misery, and terror.

These memories were not recovered while my father was alive. While my mother was still alive, whenever I discussed my memories with her and tried to pinpoint how long I was at the convalescent home, she could not recall the exact length of my stay. She thought it might have been a few days, maybe a week. Maybe longer.

In one therapy hour, I vividly recalled these memories. It was suppertime and we children were all seated at long wooden tables. I glanced up from the table and noticed a side door, open to the street. Suddenly, I noticed my mother walking down the street—*away* from the building. Total confusion. How could I make sense of that? Why was she out there? Why was she going away? Doesn't she know I'm here? Why don't I call out! More terror. Would I ever see her again? Was she abandoning me forever?

Thinking about this now, I cannot imagine how I ever got up from the table that night or went to sleep. The very next day my mother appeared and I was released. Years later, when I reviewed these memories with her, she said: "They wouldn't let me see you the day I came to make arrangements to take you home. They felt it would upset you."

I have never been able to recall my homecoming. I have speculated that I was numb and very wounded from having to cope with experiences and feelings far too overwhelming for a four-year-old child to handle *alone*. I know I was frightened for a long time afterward. I probably did not trust them not to do that to me again. I felt very insecure. I also was very hurt and very angry at my parents for sending me away. It took me a long time to tell that to my mother.

The Healing

I grew up in a time and in a family that was oblivious to the nuances that color important life events. We did not pay much attention to our own or each other's disturbing emotions. We certainly did not discuss them. I know we did not talk over my absence or return. Most likely both my parents believed it was best put aside, now that it was over. It was expected that I would pick up my life as if nothing unusual had happened. I coped with this gigantic nightmare by burying it more deeply. I did such a good burying job that the memories did not even begin to surface—and then only in fragments—until I was in my late 20s, pregnant with my first child. The prospect of becoming a mother, with all its excitement and anxieties, aroused the memories of my most profound childhood experience.

The recovery of these lost parts of myself would have been impossible alone. I needed the support and safety of the therapy process and the special role that each therapist would play as I became ready to unbury my nightmare. Through the relationship that developed with the therapist, I came to trust myself sufficiently to face the feelings I previously could not face alone. Out of the experience of my own reluctance to acknowledge what had been so disabling to me and my resistance to knowing what I feared, I came to understand why the pace of psychotherapy is slow. In time I also appreciated how very fragile a person can feel, as well as how cunning she can be about not revealing herself. No matter how many roadblocks and detours I erected to protect myself from finding out what I had been afraid to know, the therapist's skill and sensitivity enabled me to stay with what was happening. I am deeply grateful. None of this has been easy. For me, it has been very worthwhile.

Each time I have opened up this ancient misery, I have felt the horror of it. The pain was intense and I wanted to flee from it. Despite all that, I have been astounded that I have actually grown from reliving this nightmare. Each fresh excavation yielded both a new tender shard of myself that I had not known was there and released long-denied emotions. A flood of energy also accompanied each reclamation. Once expressed and accepted, these previously discounted experiences yielded new perspectives of myself. I became more expressive of the love and caring I feel for the people closest to me. I felt more complex and complete.

Following the remembering and reliving of the terrifying experience of being left alone in my crib, sick, while my mother went to work, creative energy burgeoned forth. I began to write about women's issues and psychotherapy. I also became active in professional organizations of psychotherapists, especially seeking out other feminist therapists. I later coedited a collection of papers, *Women Changing Therapy*.[1] A vital connection that would become very healing was beginning. As I committed myself more seriously to writing, I gave myself opportunities previously denied to me. I was now taking seriously what I had been trained to discount.

Neither of my parents respected learning. They had not completed the eighth grade, and although school was a luxury they had not been permitted, I think they also were intimidated by educated people. They felt inadequate. Thus, they could not acknowledge or support my intellectual and creative endeavors.

Besides, I was a girl. While I was growing up, the interests I was encouraged to pursue revolved around pleasing and obeying my parents and other people. I was not rewarded for my curiosity and love of learning. For the most part, my interests were ignored. When I tried to gain my parents' approval for my fledgling achievements, they belittled me and my accomplishments; they dismissed me by changing the subject. I felt rejected and neglected by their lack of responsiveness.

I was demeaned for being myself. That felt familiar. It repeated my experience at the time of my illness. I was being conditioned again to discount what I needed to feel good about myself because it made someone else uncomfortable. I was learning that approval was secured by muzzling my initiative and subordinating my needs.

The message to me was the same one my mother and grandmother had received: Girls are best appreciated when they do not actively pursue what creates discomfort in others. Pleasing other people is more important than taking care of myself. My conditioning, similar to the nightmare of my illness, was preparing me to believe that my happiness resided in suppressing parts of myself because others found them unacceptable.

The experience of writing has presented me with many opportunities to rethink the limitations of my upbringing. To write this book, I had to confront terrors and anxieties that felt very reminiscent of those in the past, and affirm for myself what I had been taught to discount. At times these labors have felt very overwhelming. As I lost and regained confidence innumerable times, I was learning to trust the me who had been resoundingly stifled, first by the practices of my family, and later by the values and attitudes of the culture, all of which reflect the generalized disdain of women and their distinct pursuits. In persevering I finally recognized that I was no longer a frightened, resourceless little girl who had been trained to devalue herself. I could trust myself even though I felt anxious as I grappled with the unknown. I could monitor my self-doubt when the going got tough without undermining myself. Although I received consistent support and caring from my husband, my daughter, my son, and a handful of close friends, these labors were mine alone to manage.

The roots of an individual's strengths and limitations are manifold. Appreciating that complexity is central to the healing power of the psychotherapy process. Nevertheless, we remain in the habit of acknowledging certain givens and neglecting others. Much attention has been paid to the interaction involving an individual's nature, fate, and the psychological climate in the family at the time of a child's birth. However, we continue to underestimate the potency of values and attitudes to shape and distort a girl's life because she is different from a boy.

It is my hope that the understanding and appreciation of all women will be enriched through reading about and coming to know the women described in this book. Despite the persistent devaluation of women that has significantly contoured their lives, women have cultivated very special resources that they have used to empower other people. Now, it is time to empower ourselves.

PART I

SETTING THE GROUNDWORK

CHAPTER 1

GETTING ACQUAINTED

It's hard to say I go to therapy because I need a place where it's okay not to be a big person.

Carol

It's very difficult when I feel this open and vulnerable to believe that I'm getting stronger, not weaker.

Kim

Step into the therapy room. This is a special place where the unthinkable becomes thinkable and the unbelievable real. Here, bits and pieces of events, memories, and emotions that have disappeared a long time ago are gradually reclaimed. Everything has meaning. Gestures, comments, incidents that might normally escape attention become noticed. Even though we proceed cautiously, there are constant surprises. Much of what is discovered is astounding, even overwhelming.

Piles of tender experiences have been hidden underground, in deeply recessed crevices. These remarkable, labyrinthine constructions have purpose. They keep each woman detached from her unique collection of damaged, precious possessions. It costs dearly to maintain these painstaking structures, and a long time passes in the therapy before that can be acknowledged. It has been very important that what needs to be known remain unknown.

When ready to dive into the reality of her accumulated pain, a woman will acquire the courage to embark on this immense, personal journey.

The Clients

The many different women whom you will come to know reading these pages were born and raised across the United States, including California and the San Francisco Bay Area. Several women are lesbians, although the majority are heterosexual. Many of them have been married previously and divorced. At present, most of the women are either married or living in a committed relationship with a male or female lover. A few are either single, divorced, or widowed. The majority have children.

Predominately college-educated, many also hold graduate degrees. For the most part these women enjoy their jobs and have been successful in such fields as teaching, the health care professions (including the varied disciplines of mental health), law, computer programming, investment counseling, the creative arts, architecture, scientific research, corporate management. A few are employed at jobs they find dissatisfying, such as retail selling or office work. Very occasionally over the last few years, a woman will become a therapy client who is not employed full time outside the home.

The majority of the women are Caucasian, although several are women of color. Today, each of them would identify herself as middle class. Even though many grew up in the traditional middle-class family of post-World War II America, some women were born into working-class families and, in their youth, were aware that their families were poor and rarely had sufficient money to meet all its needs.

Several Latinas' childhoods were further marked. One woman had never known her father; others knew their fathers, but they had not lived continuously in the same home during the daughters' early years. All the other fathers, whether Asian or Caucasian, resided in the home throughout their daughters' childhood years. Only one father left the family because of divorce, which occurred during his daughter's adolescence.

This particular pattern is significantly different in women in their 20s who have recently come to see me. The majority of them are from divorced families. If visits with their fathers were maintained in their childhood, it was only at regularly scheduled intervals.

The Families of Origin

Depicted as the conventional homemakers of the 1950s, their mothers often had three children within the first five years of marriage. While these daughters were young only a very few of their mothers worked outside the home, primarily out of necessity. As a result of their mothers' employment, several Latin women were raised by their grandmothers. Interestingly, that particular experience was shared by a few Caucasian daughters who, as toddlers, were cared for by a maternal grandmother or aunt during World War II. Their mothers had gone to work while their fathers fought in the war.

Often discussed in flat, colorless tones, their mothers were described as lacking zest for life. Several were depressed. Repeatedly I heard that life at home with Mom had been "bland, boring, and no fun." Although the daughters complained about their mothers, they also yearned for more maternal nurturance.

Their fathers, on the other hand, were primarily recalled with exuberant affection. "He was my universe and my security." Generally, these fathers were successful and provided adequately for the family, sometimes working two jobs at once. They were described as doers: busy and active in the world.

The contrast between how these women perceived their mothers and fathers is a theme that caught my attention early in the therapy and will be fully explored in Chapter 4.

Black and Native American women have not been my clients in the past 10 years. The lack of their stories creates a noticeable gap in a broader understanding of the issues for women that are addressed in this book. The absence of black and Native American women from my practice could certainly be related to economic considerations. However, I think it reflects the revaluing by these women of their ethnic heritage. This has prompted many women of color to prefer to be in therapy with therapists who share their background. Most recently, this has also been my experience with young lesbians.

I am mindful of the privilege of being a self-employed psychotherapist and recognize that this has limited my experience. My observations would have been further enriched by working with a more diverse group of women. Despite these limitations, I believe that the knowledge gained from psychotherapy with this group of clients illuminates many issues of common concern to women.

Revisioning Women's Lives

In the early 1970s a revolution in conceptualization and understanding about women's lives was fueled by the women's movement. The subsequent burgeoning of feminist analyses across all the dimensions of women's lives yielded new information and observations. What had previously been unimaginable could now be perceived. It became clear that the way we had all been trained to understand our experience was not the only way. The ideas, values, expectations, attitudes, language, even imagination each of us—woman and man—had inherited had been primarily founded on men's perceptions and experiences. Basic to this new awareness was making visible the false fundamental assumption: Woman was not the equal of man. Once this was acknowledged, women began to recognize how this conviction had dominated their lives. The wisdom of women had been discounted for so long that women themselves had minimized their strengths and talents. Now they began to see more of themselves.

The subsequent birth of feminist therapy added new depth to the knowledge about women's lives. Over these years the wealth of ideas and observations presented by feminist thinkers, both scholars and clinicians, has contributed to a greater general awareness and sensitivity toward women. For example, we now know that the assumption of female inferiority to males begins at birth and gives rise to stereotypical expectations that train women to subordinate their needs and aspirations to those of men. Moreover, female happiness has been assumed to reside in pleasing others, especially men, which maintains the status quo of male dominance. Daily, this disabling conditioning influences women and has created social and emotional dilemmas for them. My clients, like most other women, have had to surmount incredible hurdles growing up in a world where women are rewarded for discounting their needs, but berated when they consider them.

By focusing attention on the emotional lives of individual women and listening carefully to the detailed, intimate knowledge they share in psychotherapy, we can learn how deeply embedded these damaging experiences really are. In fact, they profoundly shape women's character, promote self-doubt, and undermine initiative. Positive, unequivocal regard vital for self-confidence has been in short supply.

The negative social and psychological consequences of the devaluation of women can be overcome as we broaden our understanding and appreciation of them. The system of beliefs we have inherited has been grounded in men's thinking and dominance. It is time that our fund of knowledge reflect women's experience.

The Therapist

As a child I ran away from witches and other symbols of female power. Now I'm running toward them.

Sara

Although I have acquired much knowledge and training, attended many courses, workshops, and conferences, and read widely in feminist and other pertinent psychological literature, my most meaningful teachers are my clients. I want to acknowledge my appreciation of these women and all that they have taught me over the years. It has been a privilege to be connected to other women's quests to find and support themselves while making the changes necessary to shed self-defeating behavior and unrewarding values.

Also, I have been deeply touched when the women report that in moments of indecisiveness, they recalled words I had spoken to them that provided the additional emotional support they required to stick with new and different behavior. Because I believe in the women and respect what they are doing, I, too, feel their trust and confidence in me. While chance has brought us together to work on some very special and at times difficult undertakings, the process is always nurtured by the mutual respect and warmth that passes between us.

Raised in a family that reflected the cultural devaluing of strong emotions, I was rarely encouraged to express my own feelings. Prior to becoming a psychotherapist, I lacked experience in sitting with disquieting feelings. Like many psychotherapists and most women, I had been trained to do or say something to help other people alleviate the discomfort of their own emotions. I had to work to overhaul this earlier training.

It can be very uncomfortable to sit quietly *and just listen* while someone else expresses the excruciating pain that accompanies reexperiencing past hurts. I have come to realize that interrupting a woman's outpourings, even with words of comfort or appreciation for what she is experiencing, springs from my own uneasiness. She does not require anything from me but my listening to her. No one had ever made it okay for her to express what she is now expressing. We are both learning to *be* with feelings, not *do* something about them.

I have noted from both observing the clients and monitoring my own responses that not only does each person have her own pace and style for handling strong emotions, but several different feelings might be experienced at the same time. Contradictory feelings, like anxiety and excitement, are common. As their expression is allowed they become manageable.

Our bodies are also remarkable registers—if we would only listen to them. "When my back goes out it makes me pay attention to what I usually ignore." "I didn't have any feelings. That's why I'm sitting here with a migraine headache."

While each one of us may be special as well as limited in our capacity to handle emotions, that capacity expands if encouraged. What a powerful sense of adequacy can be discovered as one learns that upsetting feelings are handled by simply being with them!

Constant Vigilance

My own feelings of impatience, frustration, disappointment, and anger have demanded constant surveillance. Since I am not embroiled in the client's emotions, at times it is easier for me to figure out what is happening. By offering explanations or solutions I avoid dealing with my own impatience. Most important, my suggestions can keep hidden the helplessness the client and I might both be feeling. It has taken me some time to appreciate that it does not matter how quickly I put the pieces together— that is an intellectual exercise. The real impact resides in the woman's figuring out for herself what is going on.

Sometimes what I am feeling may be a reflection of what a woman is feeling but not describing. I have practiced differentiating between when it is useful to share my reactions as a springboard, to enable a woman to express what otherwise feels too frightening to declare, and when to remain silent, thereby giving her the time she requires to do it in her own way. On very rare occasions, while sitting with a woman, I have been overcome by enormous, almost immobilizing fatigue. This unusual occurrence has prompted me to monitor what is going on more carefully. I discovered that when clients are struggling to either suppress or express feelings about which they have great uneasiness, enormous quantities of energy are expended. When they do express themselves, they often comment on their exhaustion. I have finally grasped that my fatigue is a clue to what they are handling.

Sitting together in the therapy room working sensitively and intimately, usually over a period of several years, I have come to know many of these women very well. The specialness of the client–therapist connection has produced in me feelings of closeness and caring for the women I work with. Now and then, in the middle of the therapy, a change in life circumstances prompts a woman to move far away. Even though there are feelings of satisfaction about the work we have done, this abrupt departure evokes feelings of sadness and loss. It is poignant to realize that most likely we will never see one another again. The change in our connection is permanent. Even when we are both in agreement that it is time to stop therapy, that ending is difficult. Like the woman, I, too, have become accustomed to our regular meetings. I will miss her.

At other times, the therapy is interrupted because a woman chooses to discontinue. If I disagree with the decision, it is important to explore our different opinions. This brings forward still other feelings. In speaking up for what I believe, I become anxious. I, too, have feelings about putting myself on the line. If we continue to disagree, of course, I have to accept the woman's choice. Usually that feels bad. I have my sights focused on more complete understanding—getting to the bottom of the issues. Many times the clients are pleased to be feeling much better. Sometimes they are angry and do not feel they are getting what they want either from therapy or from me.

Unplanned or conflictful endings are unsettling, arousing my anxiety. Have I done the best job I could? Occasionally, I feel angry too. Instead of diligently following the course we had set upon, the woman is "bailing out." I think she should stay and investigate more fully what is going on, but I will not disclose my anger; it is mine to take care of. This is one response to the feelings elicited when the process is challenged and prematurely halted, a way to deny my disappointment and loss.

After many years I have come to value something I did not originally subscribe to, the importance of the therapist's neutrality. In the sisterhood of the 1970s I participated in the sharing that sometimes went on between some feminist therapists and their clients. Then, I believed that discussing my own experience communicated the range and diversity of options available to women and also demystified the therapist and the therapy process. We were two women working together, one of whom was in need of the services and skills the other had to offer. However, over the years, I have come to appreciate other, more complex reasons for generally not stating my experience or opinion.

Women who come to therapy, like most women in this culture, have been repetitively conditioned to pay attention and focus sensitive awareness on other people. These skills make some women extraordinarily alert to the cues put forth by others. Not only has that been a consequence of female role conditioning, but it has become a survival skill as well. Once that talent springs into operation, many women lose sight of what they want or need for themselves. By my not interjecting my experience, the focus remains with the clients.

Although the ideas developed through writing this book often influence the questions I ask and the comments I make, I rarely share my point of view. Generally, what the women require is not an intellectual understanding but the opportunity to discover and express their feelings.

In the context of a supportive environment, it is up to each woman to figure out what is right for herself. For too long women have allowed other people to determine their behavior. By exploring and coming to know what they want, feel, and think, each woman becomes her own authority.

The Reader

As you read along you may find yourself having a variety of reactions, some of which may surprise you. Whether similar or different from your own, a particular woman's experience can resonate deeply. How you handle that awareness can offer some clues about what the women were discovering or not discovering, as their therapy proceeded.

You may observe yourself becoming very impatient, even annoyed, with a particular woman, thinking, "Why can't she see this or that?" "Go ahead, do it already." Annoyance and impatience are some ways in which individuals distance from or discount the reality of unpleasant emotions. In therapy, women do this regularly, which in part is why it takes so long to unravel what needs to be unraveled. They have not been in the habit of acknowledging the complexity of their emotions. It takes quite some time to become more comfortable with this. "I'm recognizing that my being here for however long it takes to crawl backwards on the outside of the onion, not being able to go in, that's how long it takes."

Staying with your own experience as you read about these women's lives may afford you an opportunity to know yourself better and become more familiar and accepting of a reality that otherwise might remain unavailable. This is what happens in therapy.

CHAPTER 2

THERAPY BEGINS

This therapy gets into all the crevices where the taboos are hidden.

Sara

It's true. Therapy is hard work like keeping on top of stuff in my life is work. Part of what makes it hard is that the old behavior patterns make it tougher to take up the new ones.

Amy

Getting started in therapy, like beginning any adventure into the unknown, arouses a tight knot of emotion. While often relieving to finally be doing something about a problem that has caused much distress, it is also frightening. It is not surprising that at the outset many women, seated in my office with all their discomfort, asked: "Where shall I begin? What do you want to know?" Telling her story acknowledges the pain and anxiety she has been trying to minimize.

Kim had been unable to find a job; her feelings of self-doubt and worthlessness spiraled. She was depressed. It was hard to tell this to me; she handled that discomfort by belittling herself for what she was experiencing: "I feel like a little kid, stupid and utterly dependent."

Laura's son was having difficulties at school and she felt guilty. Were they her fault? This was touching old issues of her own. Long ago, she had been very unhappy at home; she, too, had problems at school. Elizabeth experienced intense grief as a result of her husband's death. It frightened her. Life had lost all meaning. Was it normal to feel so immobilized?

Convinced that it is important always to appear strong, competent, and independent, they voiced comments such as "I can get along without anyone. I've been through this before." "I function quite well; if I learn about my feelings will I function as well?"

Like most women in this culture, these women subscribe to a typical assumption: Competent people do not display feelings of inadequacy or helplessness. Women who might appear weak or inadequate run the risk of being demeaned. These beliefs are so deeply embedded that many women kept their needs hidden by pointing out their strengths. "I can't believe I've done this. For a whole year I lived with incredible stress, and now that the crisis is over, I'm finally coming for help."

The reluctance to reveal what had been concealed for decades was strong. Complex, clever strategies have been developed to protect intense vulnerabilities: "I hate myself when I feel helpless or in a fury. I'm not about to show anyone else these feelings. They're horrible." "Out there I'm running marathons, but inside myself I feel awful." It has not occurred to these women that they might find understanding and acceptance for what they have to tell.

Sara did not appear for her appointment. The previous week we had changed the appointment time, but it was uncharacteristic of her not to appear or call. Puzzled, I waited to hear from her. The day before her next appointment Sara called to say she would keep that appointment.

When she arrived Sara asked if I had received her note. Surprised that I had not, she continued: "Last week I had gotten the time confused. As I was driving here I realized I was going to be very late. I decided to come anyway to leave you a note and a check for the missed hour."

"What were you trying to tell me?"

"I hated myself and felt ashamed for messing up. I never do things like that and I didn't want you to see me that way. I can't believe anyone will accept me when I make a mistake. I can't accept myself when I make mistakes like that. I didn't want any help. I went directly home to be alone. I couldn't call you for several days. It felt so raw."

Deepening the Work

I have developed a funny yearning for this work which belies my desire to get out of it. Doing it makes me feel better as well as bad. The faster I do the work, the better I'm going to feel.

Anna

It's possible to solve big problems in little steps.

Katherine

From time to time the women resemble heroines in ancient myths. No sooner have they overturned one obstacle on the path to self-discovery when another, more cunning one springs forth to take its place. They rush in several directions at once, eager to fix what cannot be tolerated, occasionally "creating fires" in one place to avoid their feelings about something totally different. "I'm trying to run a show no one is interested in." There seems no end to the lengths a woman will go to dodge what she is not yet ready to face. "I should go into the Strategic Air Command. I can really line up the defenses—bing, bing, bing." One woman identified an inner gate that would shut tight when something new or different sneaked through. She then felt confused or wanted to cry. "That's my way of knowing something important just happened."

My respect for the complex strategies each woman has devised to protect her sensitive feelings is fundamental. Nevertheless, while listening, I may wonder aloud why she is doing what she is doing. When I question what appears permanent and steadfast, the notion of choice enters the room. The way things have been is not the only way they can be. What always has felt fixed in concrete begins to move. What has long been devalued gradually takes on alternative meanings. Proceeding very slowly, we plod through difficult terrain. The client has to pass over the same bump many times before she can notice it and acknowledge its importance. Silence, sarcasm, and humor are constant companions.

Common misconceptions about therapy and the release of emotions generally arise early in the work. The woman's anxiety about revealing her inner emotional reality fuels these concerns; it is important to explore this. Because each of us has been trained to fear and negatively judge the expression of intense emotions, the release of pent-up feelings is often confused with losing control. The persistence of these constricting attitudes has encouraged individuals to distance themselves from and deny their emotions. What is rarely understood is that expressing our emotions enables us to better handle them.

These women, like almost everyone else, want to get rid of their "bad feelings" as quickly as possible. Typically, they assume that while it is a difficult and onerous task to pour out their emotions, it is necessary to do that only once. "I have this image of one big session in which I get angry and tear the room apart. Then, it's all fixed." It does not work quite like that. While it is always remarkable how much better it feels to express what has long been denied, some feelings linger. They stand as sensitive sentinels to traumatic events endured in the past.

The therapy process teaches each of us, over and over, about patience, continuity, tenacity, hard work, acceptance, responsibility, and satisfaction.

Although in therapy for some time, Carol often mistrusted that it was really okay to fully express her emotions. In the conversation between us one day, it became evident that the taut patterns that inhibited her expression of complex feelings have also effectively conditioned Carol to believe that something is wrong with her because she has these feelings.

Carol walked into the therapy room remarking: "I've had a terrible twenty-four hours. All day yesterday I was anxious and depressed. Really upset. I'm also premenstrual and I've noticed that about five days before my period I get very upset. This only happens once in a while. I'm fine now."

"Notice how hard it is to tell me that you had a bad day."

"Partly what's so hard is I don't know how to just say it. You know how it was for me in my family. I was never allowed to have bad feelings. Everything was always fine. If I had bad feelings I had to push them down inside myself or else I felt like I was weak, a bad girl.

"I spent a lot of time feeling depressed when I was younger. Maybe I'm afraid of that now. When I have these bad feelings I can't believe they will ever end. I feel out of control—I feel so frightened."

"What's so terrible about telling me this?"

"What keeps me from telling you all this is that I feel like a failure for having such feelings and I'm convinced you will feel the same way about me."

Acquiring Trust

Discomfort about what surfaces in therapy is a continuous issue. "The possibility of another way of being is worse than the feelings aroused." This discomfort is rarely communicated directly. Instead, when anxiety and confusion spiral, many women leap into action. A sense of urgency is conveyed. A decision must be made right this minute. Suddenly a trip is scheduled, a lover arrives, or a crisis occurs at home or in the office.

The woman is scrambling for cover from her inner tornado. "Pieces are coming apart before they can come together." The process is constantly challenged as clients attempt to avoid feeling scared and overwhelmed. Additionally, as a woman takes strides into new behavior, fresh anxieties rush forward. "Sometimes, it's easy to lose the real gut feelings about why I need to do certain things."

Although bargaining for time by adroitly circling their issues, the women really do know what they require if they are going to unlock their secrets.

Anna declared: "I'm housed in this rickety scaffold. It's worked for me for years. It's very familiar and comfortable, but not really very good. Before I can take it down I need to be building a new framework to house me that will do a better job. If I don't do that I'll be with nothing—and I don't trust me to be okay with nothing."

Katherine commented: "I'm surprising myself. All sorts of things are affecting me I never thought would affect me. I have to get out of the way and just let it happen."

It takes a long time to believe that what has been previously denied is now allowed, even encouraged: It is really possible to reveal one's deepest dreads and most tender vulnerabilities and still be accepted. "Can I tell you this and be respected? I feel so alone. I want to know if you'll hold my hand and comfort me."

The therapy bond is continually being tested as trust evolves, not solely in the therapy relationship but—more important—in oneself. "I came wanting help and expected help to be a gift. When that didn't happen I felt pretty disappointed. Somewhere midway it turned around and I realized I was getting help. It was just in a form I hadn't expected—helping myself."

The air in the therapy room is often heavy with accumulated pain and anger. Not only have early demeaning experiences shaped each woman's character, but psychological intimidation and physical mistreatment have also been endured. It takes a great deal of trust in the process before these intensely painful memories can be recollected. They hurt so much that they were deeply buried. As we pick our way through ancient sensitivities and unmet needs, rage at what has always been missing surrounds us.

Once experienced, the power of what previously has been concealed can be awesome. "Who am I if I'm not the person I always thought I was?" The women, like many others both in and out of therapy, are accustomed to denying the disabling consequences of having grown up with a belief system that not only devalues women but also casts aspersion on the full range of their emotional repertoire.

Committed to the Process

> This feels really productive and useful, satisfying. Really different from necessary and life-saving.
>
> Elizabeth

> The simplest, most beautiful things are the hardest to get right.
>
> Laura

As the piles of crumpled Kleenex grow, the craftily hidden, unruly emotions gain expression and respect. One does survive their exposure. In fact, after a while, one even feels better. "If I own my own feelings, I can make choices." A woman's trust in her own capacities grows. "I'm learning, but I'm not doing it well yet. The more comfortable I am with me, the happier I'll be and the less need I'll have to prove anything to anybody."

Accustomed to working very hard on behalf of other people, the women finally begin valuing themselves. "I put myself at the center and paid attention to what I needed and wanted." They marshal both the support and commitment required to give 100% for themselves. "It's great not to be translated through someone else." My positive regard and belief in both the importance of the work *and* the woman's ability to do it blazes a steady beacon of light into the darkness.

No recognizable instrument can measure the time required to work out these issues. An inner rhythm, different for each woman, allows her to establish the momentum she knows she can handle. "I spend my time fighting my feelings and feeling stuck. Probably feeling them would be easier—if I could get to them." This kind of therapy requires a long-term commitment. Even though the frequency of appointments often increases, the pace is slow. A back-and-forth process frames the work.

Delicate transitions influence the pace. The close of each hour, like a vacation, often disrupts the vulnerable mood created as each woman relinquishes her normal guardedness. It always takes some time to come back to where one has left off. For many women, beginning the hour is another delicate adjustment. Shifting from the details they juggle in the world outside the therapy room to a less accessible inner landscape is not simple. Often several minutes are essential to make that transition. Once I understood this I was able to remain silent, thereby enabling each woman to determine for herself how she wanted to begin.

Deeply implanted patterns do not change readily. The clients constantly test whether they can really manage what they are experiencing. "It's frightening and dangerous because I don't know that I'll be all right." It feels like "struggling to get a toehold" in soft sand. One woman had an image of a tightly wound ball of yarn. "You could pull it open from several directions. It's still tangled, but you can unwind it."

Each woman allows her feelings more definition as she finds she can cope with them. "I've found something deep inside myself I didn't know was there. I finally reached in and grabbed my feelings. They're real and they're all mine." One woman likened this to being in a tall building. She had walked on many different floors but had not yet descended to the basement. To move beyond chastising oneself or blaming others—to become aware, tolerate, and be responsible for one's own feelings whatever they might be—is one of the more formidable psychotherapy tasks.

Psychotherapy that embraces a feminist perspective affords women the opportunity to distinguish their complex female identity from the feelings of weakness, helplessness, and vulnerability that they had been trained long ago to scorn. The buried emotions that they believe have made them unacceptable will be redeemed, and the well-disguised yearnings for nurturance will receive long overdue acknowledgment.

I have watched women learn to differentiate between the legitimacy of their own feelings and their cultural training to abhor them, and therefore themselves. It is no longer necessary to deny and distort one's repertoire of emotions to proclaim adequacy as a woman. "I came in here believing I was a bad girl and I found I'm really a good girl. I'll always be grateful for that discovery."

Even though everything cannot be known and made better, many paths are made "a little bit wider." "The old voices are growing fainter. I'll never have amnesia for them, but they don't have the same influence. I can replace them with my own voice." The surprising ways in which some things happen was humbling. "This experience is teaching me that there is more to discover, things I can't yet imagine. That feels very good—in fact, exciting!"

We both came to understand that therapy does not "cure" everything. There is no life without problems. Nevertheless, a woman can acquire a significantly improved and empowering assortment of tools with which to manage the vicissitudes of daily living. One woman put it this way: "I need to feel my helplessness and have that be okay. That's very different from saying I'm going to come here until I don't feel helpless anymore."

There has been a lack of self-affirming models of women taking action on their own behalf and expressing and accepting their vast repertoire of emotions. Two women, client and therapist, work together creating their own models.

CHAPTER 3

AWAKENING
Suppressed Needs and Emotions

I'm a person who wants to do something—and there's not much you can do about your feelings. Am I afraid to be vulnerable?

Jackie

Decades of rebuff, punishment, or ridicule by significant others had conditioned these women to be very tentative about revealing their needs. They had learned to keep their signals dim and garbled. They anticipated that asking for attention would result in the withdrawal of positive regard. "When I try to picture how I would tell my honest feelings, I go blank. It has something to do with not believing that they'd be accepted."

This sensitivity to rejection made it very important that I be nearby, paying careful attention as these women practiced over and over again: "Can I be heard and accepted?" The con-

34

stancy of my presence demonstrated that they were accepted no matter what had to be revealed. We were rewriting an ancient lesson. As girls these women had learned to associate the expression of their emotional needs with the withdrawal of affection. As each girl suppressed herself, her emotional repertoire became distorted.

This became especially disabling because women's role training as caretakers of others has also downplayed their individual needs. The capacity to express their own needs remains underdeveloped in many women. If a woman is not busy paying attention to someone else's needs, she is busy quieting these vulnerabilities because she does not want to be judged inadequate.

Most women were very adept at mobilizing their resources to combat the anticipated derision if they risked expressing themselves. "If I label myself not okay before anyone else does, I cover that base—so to speak." "If I'm hard on myself, their harshness doesn't penetrate." They talked about cops, censors, pessimists, and scolding voices, all of whom aided them in discounting the reality of their inner world of needs, emotions, and yearnings. "A thousand voices are telling me,'You're making it up. You don't have any problems!'" They had been conditioned to accept less to ensure being loved. "All those people in my head don't want me to believe in myself." To act now on their own behalf was to encounter strong emotions.

Needs, Emotions, and Yearnings

At unexpected moments in the therapy when the customarily disguised needs or emotions came bubbling to the surface, the clients would feel very apprehensive. Rather than directly state what they were experiencing, they attempted to escape from their own emotional reality. Sometimes they tried to change the subject; other times they either attacked the therapy or blamed me. Also, they often turned to me. If I could know what they were feeling and tell them what to do next, they could be rescued from their unruly emotions. "I was so angry I wanted to punch you for not assisting me out of my pain. I felt so alone. I wanted to blame you for how much pain I felt." Some fell back on learned archaic shibboleths. A woman—especially a woman therapist—should know what another person needs and supply it. These women did that for others all the time. Decoding these maneuvers enabled both of us to become alert to how sensitive these women were when operating in their own behalf. "I have to stop and tell you how hard this is for me."

Some women expected or waited to be given what they could not give themselves: permission to express their needs and have their strong feelings. "I want you to read my mind, know my feelings without me telling you. It's so scary to open up." Could a woman really be accepted if she expressed what she felt? Told her darkest secret? "Will you like me if I show you these parts of myself? Or will you think I'm exaggerating, trying to get attention?"

In one session Elizabeth was unable to express the feelings of hurt, despair, and hopelessness she had been talking about. She felt tense about this observation and began to belittle and judge herself negatively. We did not understand why this was happening, but right there, in the room, we saw that holding back her feelings was taking a toll on Elizabeth. Continuing to feel stuck and frustrated, Elizabeth revealed that she was angry with me: "Do you know something you're not telling me? Could you make it easier for me? I feel so lost and adrift. When you're silent I anticipate you're being critical. You're too neutral. I want more feedback."

I pointed out that when Elizabeth felt stuck she did not trust herself to find her own way, but assumed that I knew something she did not. I appreciated with her that the grief she was experiencing because of her husband's sudden death in an automobile accident several months earlier exacerbated her lack of confidence in herself. That is a normal reaction while mourning.

Elizabeth acknowledged that her trust in herself was very fragile. Her wish to be taken care of by someone else was stronger. "Jeff supported me so much. I hoped you'd do what he did."

After several months of therapy in which Elizabeth was able to express her many complex feelings about her husband's death, she renewed the trust she used to feel in herself.

After a while, despite the constricting power of the censoring forces, the clients recognized flickerings of other possibilities. By determining what she wanted, each woman was affirming herself. New tools were in the therapy room, although not yet always in her hands. As each woman began to know herself better—accepting the discomfort of her varied emotions and tolerating the anxiety generated by change—an inner neutral observer acquired stamina. Choices appeared. "Lately I have a better awareness of supporting myself. If I get into a situation and overreact, I can stop and say: What's going on?"

Each woman began to handle intense feelings without feeling weak. "When you say time is up with concern in your voice I want to say my capacity to do this has enlarged. Even though I feel awful, I feel better." Most of the women could now experience their emotions and not feel frightened, even if they were not in total control of them. While several acknowledged fear of shedding their old, familiar behaviors, they were doing it. "I envision myself like a newborn calf—all legs. Falling down as I'm trying to walk."

Practicing

I saw you run out of the building and thought, what are you
doing? Don't you know it's almost one o'clock? I need you. If
you hadn't been here I would have been hurt and angry, but
also immobilized.

                                                            Miriam

A multitude of themes and issues were examined over and
over. Although the therapy process was repetitive, each time a
deeper clarity was achieved. Exquisite sensitivity to rejection was
one recurrent theme. When the client and I had a difference of
opinion, despite the problem being talked over and ultimately
resolved, just the idea of disagreeing generated a wide assortment of responses. Most of the women expected to be disregarded. Many were certain that if we were not in accord,
extreme disapproval on my part would follow. Several were very
alert to any differences between us and saw them as threatening.
Others expressed a lot of anxiety that doing what they wanted
to and not what I expected of them would only lead to a disruption in our connection. They believed, erroneously, that I
might discontinue seeing them.

In the context of the therapy relationship, a steady, safe, and
accepting bond between individuals, important new learning
took place as we grappled with these time-worn expectations.
The women learned that the urge for self-expression is
reasonable. It is possible to articulate one's emotions, handle disagreement, and be respected for one's different opinion all at
the same time. Individuals can be in conflict and their relationship can survive. "You didn't bawl me out, be shocked, refuse
to see me again. All the awful things I thought would happen,
didn't."

Testing: Can I Reveal Myself?

One afternoon a carpenter was delayed in finishing up some repairs in my office. I came into the waiting room and asked Lisa if it would be okay to begin a few minutes late. Lisa agreed and no more was said about this. On her next visit, Lisa described a dream she had had during the week: "You have made a mistake about my appointment and I'm angry with you. You won't admit the mistake. Also you've left the door to your office open and I have to close it alone. It's heavy and tricky to close. I don't do a good job.

"Later, a huge, powerful woman comes into the room and knocks you over as if you were a doll. I'm fearful of this woman. She looks crazy. She could attack me. Actually she does hit me, but it's only a light tap."

Lisa's dream provided the impetus for her to tell me that the previous week, although she had agreed with my request, she actually had felt slighted by me. She was very angry; she had even considered stopping therapy. At the same time, Lisa felt she had no right to express her wishes just because they were contrary to mine. Thus, she had complied that day with the delay. However, she also stated that if I had acceded to a request not to wait, that too would have felt awful. Lisa was convinced I would think she was a bad person for wanting something other than what I wanted. Moreover, Lisa was concerned that I would think she was crazy for being so sensitive. There was no way for Lisa to express herself and feel okay.

Lisa's dilemma about speaking up for herself was handled in an interesting way in the dream. It was difficult for her to shut the door alone; it was heavy and tricky to close. She did not do a very good job. Lisa's concern about reprisal was handled more comfortably. The huge, powerful women in the dream gave Lisa a light tap, whereas she knocked me over.

By examining her dilemma out loud Lisa was also testing both of us. Could she really tell me and could I appreciate how hard it was for her to stand up for herself and her different needs with someone who was important to her?

In addition, I learned from Lisa's response that clients have very special sensitivities about their therapy hours. It is important to respect those arrangements.

Tolerating Emotional Discomfort

For the majority of these women, expressing their needs and desires aroused incredible vulnerabilities, which they had been conditioned to conceal. Therefore, requests to modify or change a therapy appointment often provided the vehicle for disguising much more tender concerns: Will this relationship be in jeopardy if I ask for what I need?

As we worked with what surfaced, the women gained practice in articulating differences, handling conflict, and tolerating the coexistence of contradictory emotions.

Early one Friday morning, Carol decided to go to the country. She tried to telephone me to cancel her therapy appointment scheduled for later that day, realizing that she would have to pay for the canceled appointment. Unknown to me, my telephone answering machine had malfunctioned and Carol could neither hear my recorded message nor leave a message of her own. She came by my office to drop off a note that explained her absence.

At her next appointment Carol was furious with me. "Where were you when I needed you! You've told me I could call you in an emergency. When I tried to reach you your answering machine wasn't working." The machine's malfunctioning had made it impossible for Carol to get what she needed—to hear my voice on the tape, as if that would have made it okay for her to "play hooky." Even though Carol carried on with her plans and had made the effort to let me know what was happening, which I later acknowledged, not getting my approval had panicked her. Carol felt abandoned. It took several sessions to untangle these knotted threads.

As it gradually emerged that Carol had also felt overwhelmed by feelings too upsetting to recall, she attempted to dismiss what she had experienced that Friday morning. Carol berated herself, "I feel stupid."

The following week Carol did not appear for her appointment. She "totally forgot," but later telephoned to apologize. As had happened on an earlier occasion, she had retreated after arriving at new understanding, not yet ready to acknowledge what had become known.

In the session following the one she had missed, Carol maintained that she was still angry with me and annoyed with therapy. She did not want to come anymore. "Maybe I'm testing this relationship. I never protested and told my mother what I'm telling you. How much disharmony can this relationship take? I want to do something that gets me free, but I also want your approval."

Investigating this enabled us to understand more clearly that Carol wanted to assert her needs but felt anxious as she did so. "I want my way, but I also want you to approve." Unless she secured my approval she would have to deal with her anxiety. That Friday morning when Carol could not reach me, she felt anxious and alone. It reminded her of earlier situations when, unable to get what she desired from her mother, Carol had to decide what was more important: complying with her mother's demands or sticking up for her own needs? She did not want to recall those upsetting feelings. "If I can't get what I want I'll get revenge. I guess I wanted you to sit and stew like I did that Friday. I could never test that out as a kid. It was too scary to lose what little I had."

By testing the therapy relationship Carol expanded her experience. Could she get something she wanted that I might not approve of while still feeling safe in the relationship and good about herself? To dilute the anxiety created by such unfamiliar behavior, Carol tried to involve me in her plan. When that did not work, strong emotions surfaced and Carol wanted to blame me. It was very difficult for her to tolerate the emotions aroused by acting on her own behalf. She feared being rejected if she did something someone else opposed. It was difficult for Carol to accept her decisions and feel good about them. She admitted, "I now realize that I try very hard to work around things rather than look into them."

When clients tried to involve me in their strategies, they were seeking the approval they required but could not give themselves. The positive regard for self-activation that has been in short supply for many women makes it even more difficult to handle the normal anxieties that accompany self-expression and self-assertion. The expectation that a woman does not make demands of her own but complies with the demands of others further decreases opportunities to practice self-determination.

Masking Fears about Closeness

Ellen walked into the therapy room announcing: "There are lots of pots boiling outside and there's too much pressure on me. I want to cut back my appointments from twice to once a week." I was puzzled by her request; we had been working well on many complex issues. As we explored this, our understanding of some themes we had been investigating deepened. Ellen longed for closeness with people, especially women. However, encased in those yearnings were fears of becoming trapped, which pushed her to break away. Ellen was afraid that if her longings for love were met, she would surrender her individuality and not assert her separate needs. Thus, attachment signaled danger. Ellen, like many other women, had difficulty balancing her desires for intimacy in a loving relationship with the urge to express wants separate from those being met in the relationship.

It was hard for Ellen to affirm her own needs. More accustomed to paying attention to someone else's, she did not believe she could get what she needed and still be loved. Moreover, Ellen feared other people would become angry with her if she asserted her wants and sidestepped theirs. The wish to decrease the therapy sessions was a demonstration of these patterns in operation. Fears about closeness were impinging on self-expression. However, it made Ellen too vulnerable to reveal that. She did not trust that her vulnerable feelings would be respected; hence, she could not comprehend managing her feelings while investigating them. I later came to realize that by decreasing therapy Ellen kept her tender feelings masked.

At that time I disagreed with reducing the frequency of her appointments. The therapy was going well and I believed an interruption in the momentum would affect the work. We discussed our different opinions for a few sessions. Then, in one session, I noticed that Ellen was quiet and somewhat detached. When I commented, she replied she had definitely decided to cut back. I remained silent, accepting her decision. Then Ellen stated that she felt cut off and distant from me—as if she had stopped existing. Finally, she told me she was angry with me for not continuing to protest.

"Can't you know what I want!"

"No I can't. You have to tell me."

Ellen visualized an infant who, while lifting herself up, realized no one was there. In that moment, feeling all alone, the infant was devastated and terrified. She did not cry out but sank back down. We talked about how difficult it had been for Ellen to choose for herself, support her own activation, and still feel cared for.

Memories came forward. "Sometimes my mother was there with a lot of love. Yet, somehow, I'm aware that crying didn't get me what I wanted. I couldn't get her back. It had to be on her terms. No one had time for me in my family. I always felt on the outside, like I never belonged. I felt so alone and helpless."

We cut back to once-a-week therapy. In the following session, Ellen reported that last time it had felt good to be grappling with all those feelings. She appreciated "being in the moment" and trying to figure out what she wanted.

Ellen, like scores of other women, primarily squelched her wants so she would not have to experience the pain of having someone else ignore or trample over them. She also had become alert to signals other people occasionally put forth that indicated they were receptive to hearing her needs. Additionally, to avoid disharmony she waited for someone else to intuit what she required. When none of those strategies worked, Ellen felt isolated and apprehensive.

When I did not respond as Ellen would have liked me to, she was unable to tell me how vulnerable and frightened she was feeling. Not only did it create anxiety to expose these sensitivities, but it was so unfamiliar.

These learned attitudes impaired Ellen's trust in herself to handle her own emotions. When she was in the grip of strong emotions, long familiar feelings of helplessness often triumphed over her expanding her capacity to tolerate what was being experienced. Conflict over the appointment frequency kept these much more complex issues invisible.

Controversy and anger were old disguises for caring that Ellen understood. In her family people fought with one another. "If you'd have fought with me I'd have resisted—although fighting would have meant you cared." Becoming angry with therapy and blaming me for not protesting more than I did masked the confusion and vulnerability that generally accompanied opening up complicated, sensitive issues. To become more vulnerable would also intensify her dependence on the therapy relationship. For Ellen that would have aroused more anxiety than she believed she could handle.

These obstacles are often difficult to overcome, although Ellen and I certainly worked with them. As I understood better what these strategies were about and we were able to address them more directly, Ellen was able to explore more deeply. Nevertheless, about a year later, as we came to stop the work—not a mutually arrived-at decision—Ellen's fears about closeness and trust were still there. "I can't trust. No one is ever there for me. If I do trust them I fear I'll be swallowed up—consumed. I can't trust. It's dangerous to my being as a person."

Again Ellen needed to back off rather than explore more deeply why these issues aroused such intense feelings. "I'm not ready or I'm unwilling to go on now. Maybe I don't want to change. I need to sit with this."

This time I was prepared. While we directed attention at the issues, and I believed Ellen capable of staying with them, we worked within her timetable. Orchestrating the ending of her therapy had immediate consequences. Ellen felt affirmed; she began to take charge of situations in her life that she had been avoiding previously. Our parting was very poignant. There is more work to be done. Perhaps one day Ellen will choose to continue therapy.

As these women activated themselves, their yearnings to be emotionally supported and cheered on resonated deeply within. Moving beyond the protection of loved ones into new experience, or choosing to do one's "own thing" and not comply with the expectations of a significant other, did arouse anxiety, *but* also excitement. That is a normal response. Hesitancy and anxiety are familiar companions to new behavior. Yet each of us has been conditioned to think that anxiety, like anger, is a bad emotion. It must be suppressed. These convictions inhibit our emotional repertoire and do not provide for the reality that individuals can deal with uncomfortable feelings, even though they dislike them. The overvaluing of achieving pleasant and satisfactory experience has not allowed acknowledgment that most people and most interactions really are quite complex.

Grappling with Vulnerable Feelings

I'm angry with you and I didn't even recognize it. I accepted your vacation and planned for it, but now that you're back I feel like picking a fight.

Amy

Even though we are working toward increasing strides into self-actualization, at times, surprising vulnerabilities will surface. As a woman relaxes her guard and more primitive emotions are allowed expression, knowing that I am there, each time, paying attention to her and the process, promotes feelings of dependency. The regularity of appointments further establishes the continuity and security that is essential to revealing one's complex world of emotions.

That continuity is threatened when I announce my yearly vacation, and a bold assortment of normally disguised emotions comes forward. "You can go away. I cut you off long ago so I don't need to let on I'm angry and I'll miss you." Many clients feel quite uncomfortable at having their growing dependence on my presence and support disrupted. "You're not doing your job. If you cared you'd be here."

Although the women certainly try to deny their emotions, as therapy progresses and the alliance between us becomes more sturdy, that is increasingly more difficult. "I used to get pissed in the past. How dare you think I can't get along without you! But this year I'm worried about it." "Last year I concentrated on all the money I'd save. This time I do feel your vacation is an interruption. We've been moving steadily forward. Over the next month I might wish I was coming here."

By and large, anger swiftly masks the mounting anxiety about being left to manage alone. Extraordinarily quick to anticipate censure and rejection for displaying painful emotions, the women try to sweep under the rug their panicky, vulnerable, and dependent feelings. It is equally uncomfortable to admit being angry with someone whom they have counted on and trusted. "I don't have a right to be angry. I can't even give form to such an idea." In their haste to take control over both the situation and their emotions, opportunities to know themselves better are occasionally temporarily short-circuited.

Miriam and I worked together for several years. It is instructive to compare her reaction to my vacation early in the work and, then, much later on. Early on, Miriam's anger overpowered the scarier admission: "I need you. How can you leave me?" In the first year, I responded to her anxiety by offering Miriam the name of a colleague whom she might call during my absence. That was not reassuring to her. It unleashed additional fury. "No, I don't want that. I don't need anyone." The strength of her outburst surprised Miriam.

"It's still hard to feel needy and vulnerable and then tell that to someone else. I'd also like you to feel guilty about leaving me. All right, send me out there."

"Notice what you're saying?"

"Yes, you're still doing it to me and I'm passive. I'm afraid to reveal how much I'll miss you. I'm afraid to show my dependency."

Two years later, her capacity to handle the experience of my absence enlarged, Miriam began to communicate other feelings. She felt cheated, abandoned, and uncared for. As Miriam became more direct her anxiety grew; she then started to cover that by getting angry with me. She became alarmed that I would respond negatively to both her anger and her vulnerability. She would be reproached or rejected as she had been in her childhood. She rescued herself by harshly commenting on her behavior, ensuring that she could not be further hurt by me. "They used to call me a spoiled, selfish child when I had angry outbursts." Vulnerable feelings beat a hasty retreat. Denial was being reestablished.

Between therapy appointments Miriam experienced much emotional discomfort. In the next session, she was ready to abandon the disguise. "I can't believe it's okay to tell you this and take as long as I need to get this out. I'm afraid you'll become disgusted with me just like my mother did and say, 'Oh come on Miriam, that's enough.'"

Finding acceptance for both her anger and her sensitivity to abandonment, Miriam began to look at other feelings she had difficulty accepting: loneliness and unhappiness. As she explored her emotions she again became aware of the emptiness my vacation would create. She began to back off, wishing someone else could make it all okay. She did not want to be left alone to deal with her feelings. However, with new clarity, she stated: "I know this is my hole and no one can ever change it. Only I can wade through it. Of course, your being near is important. It's a comfort to me when I get in this place. You lend me strength to do the work."

Just prior to our last prevacation meeting, a fresh attack of panic caused Miriam to revert to her old tactics: become angry, push me away, deride herself for what she was feeling, and then feel overwhelmed by all these emotions.

"I am furious with you! I wanted to stomp in and bang the door down. How can you go? I'm in an absolute panic. How can I manage? I want you. What good does it do me to express all this? I feel so helpless to change anything. I hear my father saying, 'What's all the fuss about?' I feel like saying don't come back! Just like I felt with Dad when he took that job and moved to Cincinnati. I was never close to him again."

Once having said all this, Miriam recognized that the way she had always behaved did not get her what she wanted. Now she wanted to change that. "I remember being sick one night with an awful stomachache when I was a kid, all alone and miserable. I never woke my mother. I wallowed in all that discomfort and I'm still wallowing in all my feelings. I couldn't ask anyone to comfort me then, but now I want something of yours to hold while you're gone. I also want to deepen this work and find out why I don't get better."

Telling the Anger

Anna's feelings, although similar to Miriam's, have a slightly different cadence. More direct in expressing her sadness and loss, Anna was uneasy about revealing her anger: "I'm bereft, sad, fearful about your absence. Will I be okay? I can really pull the walls in around me, you saw that. When I'm hurt you have the ability to help me open doors and windows and create space around myself that I don't seem to do on my own. I'll miss that. It feels like a real loss."

I appreciated what Anna said. Then I asked, "Are you feeling anything else?" Hesitantly and with uncharacteristic belligerence, Anna continued: "This is coming from the little girl place inside me—I don't like your going away! I didn't like Ruth getting married and leaving me with my parents. Yup. I'm annoyed. It's hard to tell you I'm annoyed because I need you. If you tell someone you need them, they have power over you. That makes me feel so vulnerable. Is there any way to have your needs and not give your power away? All I can come up with is to deny my needs. Or—maybe—I could take care of them alone."

When I announce my vacation dates, antiquated patterns come into sharper focus, opening a window into vulnerabilities carefully secreted within each of us. Being separated from someone whose presence has been central to one's sense of well-being can create intense discomfort; sometimes even panic. "When someone important goes away they'll never come back." To admit those feelings is to acknowledge both one's own fears about being okay while alone and the growing dependence on the therapist, which mirrors earlier dependence on important caretakers. It is still incomprehensible that such delicate, complex emotions can be respected. These women are convinced that both they and their feelings will be trivialized. "It's just dependence. I'm going to be fine, so what's the big deal?"

Miriam and Anna, like the majority of other clients, were reacting to being left to manage on their own. Each presumed she would be belittled for stating not only what she felt but what she wished would happen. They have not yet learned that whether a person can or cannot have what she desires, it is appropriate to declare how she feels about what is happening. Respect and acceptance are not contingent on concealing either the anxieties or the longings.

In exploring her feelings about her own planned two-month therapy interruption, Kim acknowledged that she felt sad and anxious. She was very excited about her upcoming plans, and it confused her to be feeling upset about the interruption. Gingerly, she then stated that she wanted to ask permission to write to me. "You could throw the letters away. You don't have to read them, that would be asking a lot of you. What's important is writing them."

As we explored this, we observed that Kim was more concerned about protecting my time than in clearly putting forth what she wanted. By making sure that she was not asking too much of me, Kim concealed the sensitivities aroused by asking: Would I respond if she wrote to me?

The clients expend great effort to conceal the vulnerabilities aroused by feeling dependent on another person. Trained to despise those feelings, it seemed to them that my remaining nearby was the only way to overcome the anxiety aroused by having such intense, often contradictory emotions. It was very hard for Lisa to tell me how angry she was with me. Many things were going on for her and she wanted me there. As we investigated this, at first Lisa protected herself by stating, "What good will it do to talk about this?" However, slowly she was able to say: "It's hard to tell you this. Then you'll know I care."

It had not occurred to most of these women that feeling dependent is a recurring experience that accompanies everyone throughout life, and that one may be aware of the wish to depend on someone else while handling the separation.

Separation from important individuals is always difficult, calling forth exquisitely sensitive emotions. Often anger erupts—the arch-defense against feeling abandoned. Remembrances of other significant losses and separations are stirred along with overwhelmingly painful memories of helplessness and powerlessness. Many of the women become aware of how vulnerable they have been, when they could neither articulate nor handle their emotions. This fact of early life makes the clients feel so vulnerable that they hasten to deny its impact.

Although expressing anger is both an appropriate response to what is happening and also taking a risk—stating an emotion normally muffled in women—it enabled these women to feel in control of their panic. Even though now strikingly more able than they had been in the past to articulate and handle their emotions, many of the women continued to devalue them. It is difficult to accept the reality of feelings. They dreaded being put down for revealing their vulnerabilities and anxieties. Judging themselves harshly for the intensity of their emotions, they presumed others would do the same.

The control and mastery by oneself of one's emotional life is highly prized in this culture. Everyone has been conditioned to think that the yearnings to depend on someone else are evidence of weakness and herald the inability to manage life and control one's emotions. At one time or another, most of these women also felt that to be accepted they were compelled to quell their anxieties about managing on their own. This conviction clashes with fundamental human yearnings to depend on other people for emotional support and sustenance.

Generally held in check or repressed, these longings some-times "sneak" back into awareness in intimate relationships. The women realized that it did feel good to depend on someone be-side themselves, indicating that a trusting, meaningful connec-tion between people is occurring. Denying needs that one has been taught to devalue may achieve a momentary comfort; how-ever, the price one pays distorts one's inner reality.

CHAPTER 4

REVERED FATHERS/ DEMEANED MOTHERS

Dad was the seat of power in the family and I was drawn to him.

Sue

My mother was a nonperson. She lived through us kids and acted as if her life was a gift from Daddy. Nothing she did counted unless it had his blessings.

Katherine

Born between 35 and 45 years ago, all but a few of the women I have been describing were raised in the traditional two-parent family. Whether they were middle or working class, Caucasian or of color, the typical gender division of roles upheld the presumptions that men were more equal, more privileged, and more powerful than women.

Whether they behaved like kings, nice guys, or tyrants, the women's fathers had visible power and used it. When they spoke, their wishes and demands were met. "Mom taught us to go along with Dad's way of defining things. She said,'Don't get angry, don't speak out. It'll all work out in the end.'"

It was customary for the father's moods, even his idiosyncrasies, to be felt by, and even dominate, the entire family. Some daughters could recollect the isolation they felt when their fathers withdrew into moody detachment. A few "walked on eggshells" when their fathers were displeased.

Others remembered their mothers counseling, "Don't get Daddy upset. Do what you're told." As children many were advised, "Your father's tired, behave." "We had to be quiet while he got a drink and read his paper." It was rarely reported that when the father came home he played with the children or helped to get dinner on the table. These patterns were customary; they were never questioned

Even though many daughters regularly observed their fathers ignore, belittle, and sometimes physically abuse their mothers, it would take much time in therapy before that information could be revealed. What stood out when disagreements between the parents were recalled was the mother's ineffectiveness. "She always gave in."

It was clear that these daughters did not witness the same respect for their mothers that their fathers demanded. "Who'd want to identify with Mom? She's weak, anxious, and ineffectual. She's someone Dad treats poorly. He picks on her. We all heaped shit on her." It was not uncommon to become angry with their mothers for being helpless; however, it was much more difficult to focus on the father's aggressive behavior.

For generations, mothers have taught daughters how to survive in a world dominated by men. My clients' mothers were no exception. They demonstrated that women adjust their wants to assure approval from men; they stifle anger to promote harmony. Women are not encouraged to champion goals of their own or assert their different needs in the face of male opposition. "When I choose for myself, I'm not being a nice girl."

Over and over the majority of women learn that self-assertion meets with disapproval, whereas compliance results in positive attention. "When I asserted my independence it caused me pain. I couldn't be self-sufficient and get cared for." Mothers are expected to model female behavior while society has squelched the full development of womanly potential.

Even though often depleted from their hard work and frequently harassed and unappreciated by both their husbands and their children, many of these mothers were described as "turning themselves inside out," trying to make it pleasant for their husbands if they were grumpy, unhappy, or came home tired from the job. "My mother taught me to scramble around and do everything in my power to please others—especially men. If I'm not pleasing, I won't be loved."

As mothers raise daughters not to think of themselves first, they are instructing them to value caretaking of others above the expression of their own aspirations. "My mother wasn't a good model for me. I didn't see her get what she wanted. In fact, I saw the opposite. She took care of everyone else."

As they pass on acceptable female behavior, mothers simultaneously pass on the assumption that it is appropriate for women to feel deprived in relationships. While these convictions assure that women will bestow nurturance on others, they neglect to spell out who will provide this vital sustenance for women. Like children and men, they, too, require nurturance from others to feel good and worthy about themselves.

Who Is Important

Having grasped who was important at home, many of these daughters also perceived that recognition and approval were not earned by what went on at home, but rather by what one did in the world. Although the daughters did not see their fathers operate in the paid-work world firsthand and did not comprehend the reality of their successes or failures, many were drawn to the accomplishments and power men commanded, and determined to have that for themselves. All of these fathers were employed and many worked very hard; several were quite successful and talked with satisfaction about their jobs. Depending on the father's attitude toward his job, the daily trips to the workplace told his daughter there was a world beyond the home that was exciting and mysterious, filled with important experiences and people. "I loved the excitement he conveyed about work. I couldn't wait to hear all his stories."

It became increasingly evident, as I listened to these daughters recount their different experiences with their mothers and fathers, that stereotypical convictions about women and men shape human behavior and powerfully influence the attitudes we hold.

Consistently expressing dissatisfaction and anger toward their mothers, they primarily adored their fathers. The majority were furious about what had been missing with their mothers, who often were described as "going through the motions" of mothering without communicating much feeling, whereas their fathers could do no wrong.

Repeatedly criticizing the mothers for not being more affectionate, nurturant, and supportive of their self-expression—"No matter how hard I've tried I've always felt misunderstood by her"—for the most part they extolled their fathers. Characterized as "pretty important," these were big, powerful, and special men. "My father is the only person I've known since I was born who has always loved me. He's my favorite parent."

Miriam expressed the adoration shared by many other daughters. "My daddy. I loved him a lot, he was so big and strong. I got a lot of attention from him and was the apple of his eye. I could do anything. We were pals forever. He took me places, taught me to swim and play baseball. I'd wait for him to come home and watch TV with me. He was there for me."

Regardless of the quality and quantity of attention a father bestowed, he remained beyond reproach; the mother's faults, however, were endless. Each woman was encouraged to explore her feelings about what she was recounting; however, what is significant is this: These daughters were so accustomed to discounting their own experiences to secure male approval, which they had been conditioned to hold in high esteem, that they could not appropriately perceive their fathers.

Much exploration was necessary in therapy before these women could reveal that their revered fathers had also been very intimidating, even cruel toward them. The adoration of their fathers had been concealing that painful knowledge.

Moreover, trained to squelch their anger and disappointment, they could not comfortably express these emotions toward men. They were more able to direct these strong feelings toward their mothers because they did not fear their retribution.

The Influence of the Father

In reality, in thought, and in imagination, the influence of "the father" has far exceeded that of any single father. It has been vast, complex, and firmly entrenched. Until now it has defined what we know and what we value. Even the language we speak has fostered the notion that man represents human experience. This reverence for male wisdom and superiority dominates our cultural belief system. While maintaining men in positions of power and authority, it has conditioned women to comply with these arrangements because of their unequal status.

Being in charge has granted men privileges and responsibilities. They have protected as well as controlled the lives of women and children. In turn, men have expected women and children to comply with their demands. Not only have women acquiesced to these expectations, but many believe their well-being resides only in pleasing men. This further extends to women presuming, and men concurring, that women are responsible for satisfying the emotional needs of men. These gender-based divisions of tasks reflect the power differential between women and men. Accepting the role of emotional caretaker, which has implied handling the difficult and unpleasant emotions that everyone has been taught to scorn, has further devalued women. Men, on the other hand, by providing financial and physical protection, have performed more esteemed tasks; they have rarely directly dealt with the messy business of unruly emotions.

The assumption that feelings are "women's business" has insulated many men from both their own emotional needs and those of the people whom they love. Hence, it was difficult for most of these fathers to appreciate what their daughters required to grow into confident, self-affirming women. It was incomprehensible that a daughter had a separate emotional life. Mainly, these fathers relied on their authority to shape and control the family. More finely crafted tools were unavailable and devalued.

The Mothers' Lives

A half century ago, marriage and motherhood were the primary sources of female identity and self-worth, bestowing status and self-esteem on women. Even though men derived their primary status from paid employment, they were also conditioned to expect they would be head of the household and that male prerogative would flourish at home as it always has elsewhere in society.

Encouraged to depend on men, women themselves assumed they had no reason to develop the resources that would have enabled them to more adroitly handle their own lives, whether married or not. There was no need to make independent decisions; marriage and a husband would provide definition and substance to female life. Additionally, for many women the absence of a paid work experience decreased their acquaintance with independent endeavors.

Implicit in these arrangements was the understanding that any ambitions that extended beyond the circumscribed roles of wife and mother, and created difficulties between husbands and wives, would be discounted. Trained to curb conflict, most women chose to minimize their different needs and strivings. They had been socialized to believe that *nice* women did not protest or show anger. They held in or buried contrary feelings; their expression would have created dissension. A *good* wife did not question her place. She accepted it. Women who openly expressed different interests or needs were rare. How could self-determination be valued if social disapproval and unhappiness were the price one paid for being different? These conventions have hampered women's self-esteem. Still no one has appreciated that.

While the attitudes I am describing are predominately associated with the middle-class Caucasian life-style of a half century ago, I believe working-class women and women of color (although often more self-reliant because of economic necessity) also were raised with a similar belief system. Even though their reality might be different, they, too, assumed marriage would provide a husband who supported the family. They believed a wife's place was at home, raising children and attending to her husband's needs.

The Potent Imbalance

When I was an adolescent I didn't want to be a woman. There were all those negative images: my mother's mother, my mother, and her friends. They sat around and talked and ate a lot. They were all fat. I saw them chained to their lives and unable to do anything that was exciting.

Sara

Dad was the center of attention in my family. All three of us girls, Mom, my sister and I, vied for his attention. You could never get enough of it. Dad was everything positive. He heaped a lot of love on us. He was a real king.

Anna

Many women loudly complained that their mothers' love was contingent on their being submissive, well-behaved little girls who cooperated with their mothers' demands. "When I tried to express myself as a child, my mother would undermine my efforts. She'd say, 'You can't mean that. Count to ten and you'll change your mind.'" The conflict and anxiety they experienced if they failed to comply and curb their self-expression was easily recalled. They were much slower to recollect similar feelings about their fathers' demands for obedience.

Although equally sensitive to displeasure from either parent, these women expressed annoyance only over stifling their urges in order to comply with the mother's demands. "At those times when I felt powerful or intact I couldn't get what I needed. I couldn't be an individual—different from my mother." Because they were intent on blaming their mothers for all the discomfort they experienced, their fathers remained protected from similar scrutiny, which is a familiar pattern for many of us.

While their female role model was a major disappointment, the universe revolved around Daddy. This woman was Daddy's little girl: sweet, entertaining, compliant, and devoted. "He sets the measure. I can't let him down." By and large, these daughters felt that their fathers supplied essential ingredients that had been lacking in their relationship with the mothers—loving attention and enthusiasm for their budding initiative. "How I wanted to be whatever he wanted me to be! He was my idol."

Most little girls turn to their daddies whether their relationship with their mothers has been nurturing or dissatisfying. Exemption from more equitable participation in the daily, awesome responsibilities that are part of child-rearing affords the father a special place. His loving, playful energy often represents a certain distinct spark from the one provided by the mother. "As long as Dad's around I know I'll be okay."

Moreover, the presumption that all girls are heterosexual magnifies the significance of the father's love, creating a model for future relationships with men.

This presumption of heterosexuality, which has always dominated our belief system, is another example of the influence cultural values exert on our attitudes. Early in life, each of these girls had learned that tender, sensual feelings invited playful expression when directed toward the father. However, should these good, sensual feelings engendered by early mother–daughter closeness be beamed toward the mother, they were silenced.

Feminist writings[1] have pointed attention to, and remarked on, this significant absence of memories of early, appropriate, affectionate physical contact between mothers and daughters. Vanished, from imagery and recall both, are memories of being held in the mother's arms, fed at her breast, and playfully bathed by her. Aside from the customary inability to remember infantile experiences, the profound scorn attached to demonstrations of intimacy between women has kept those feelings repressed. A positive model for closeness between women—women nurturing themselves and/or one another—has rarely gained form.

Rewards and Penalties

If giving Daddy what he expected made daughters feel lovable, it did not take them long to learn what was required. They were always observing how to "bring joy" to Daddy. Under their mother's tutelage, they developed a keen sense about meeting other people's expectations. Besides, dissatisfaction with their mothers increased the daughters' eagerness to succeed in this new alliance. "I couldn't give her what she wanted, but I could give him what he wanted." The desire to keep this treasured relationship was very strong.

Bright and quick at an early age, many were encouraged to be competent and intellectual. "He told me, 'You've got a brain, do something with it.'" Special attention and glowing approval were the rewards for following the guidelines set forth by fathers who, acting as mentors, orchestrated their daughters' fledgling efforts at self-empowerment.

Believing her father's affection was contingent upon her performance, each girl tried very hard to emulate her father and live up to his model for success—perfection and hard work. "It was quite clear. If I produced, he loved me. So, of course, I produced."

Sue's experiences were similar to what other clients reported. Sue felt like a star when she succeeded at what her father defined as important. It was unthinkable to hesitate or make a mistake because it meant losing his love. "I learned if I didn't succeed I was unlovable. In order to belong I had to be perfect. When I didn't catch on fast enough he'd rush in, take over, and do the job for me. I always presumed he knew best. I was fearful of making a mistake—a colossal mistake. Then he wouldn't love me."

Similar sensitivities present in younger women who are now coming to therapy were heightened by their fathers' leaving the family as a result of divorce. "He left us when I was six, and I felt to assure Dad's love I had to make up a person who would be totally fulfilling in his eyes."

Delighted and grateful, each daughter focused on the father's approval. Not only did it foster self-confidence and esteem and convey a message of love, but it ensured the daughter a place close to this person of influence. Even the few women who did not revere their fathers and were angry with them from the outset of therapy recognized the importance of pleasing this person who exercised power in the family. His opinion really counted. Moreover, several quickly understood that their special place was dependent on giving Daddy *exactly* what he demanded. They had already noted their mothers' different treatment.

Every child is dependent on parental approval and validation for its own sense of adequacy. Yet my clients were stating much more: When outside the glow of paternal love and acceptance, these daughters felt "banished." Their very existence was at stake. "If I don't stay close to him it feels as if I will lose something very important." "If I'm not what he wants he won't love me. Then where will I be?"

Conditioned to believe their well-being was dependent on the father's love and approval, these daughters discredited their own experiences and made excuses when their fathers behaved insensitively. They often replicated this strategy in future intimate relationships with men.

Moreover, an interesting discrepancy remained unvoiced. The daughters did not believe that their adored fathers would love them if their real needs and emotions were known. Keeping this observation outside their awareness served important purposes. It protected the father–daughter relationship from careful scrutiny, which kept concealed the real paucity of paternal support for a daughter's full flowering. Poignantly, although keenly interested in fostering their relationship, the father never quite saw his daughter for the distinct person that she was.

Some Important Consequences

> I'm not a real person to Dad, I'm just an extension of him. He only sees part of me, but I can't be angry with him. He does love me and his love demands that I be a certain way.
>
> Miriam

There is no debate. Paternal approval is essential to children's good feelings about themselves. These women's fathers, however, imparted a far more complex message with impact because it reflected widely held convictions. The daughters were being continuously conditioned to believe that something was wrong with *them* if male approval was withheld.

In the era in which these girls were raised, pleasing the father was a given, the norm. No matter how a father behaved, the authority attributed to his role demanded obedience. "I was expected to do what I was told."

While feisty defiance that supported the fathers' expectations was applauded, the spontaneous expression of ideas or emotions that challenged them was sharply curbed. "If I stood up for myself at school, he was my big supporter. He'd tell me, 'Give 'em hell.' But not toward him." "If Daddy didn't like what I was doing or saying he'd ignore me and walk away."

Some fathers' disapproval of their daughters' inability to "measure up" often included the ridicule or belittling of the daughter. "I could never do grown-up things to please my dad. He was always critical. I was teased and humiliated, told I was acting like a big shot. I hated it."

These daughters rejected their own experience when it did not resonate with their fathers' demands. This unquestioned acquiescence seriously impaired the daughters' ability to discern what was in their best interest. "It's hard to be angry with Dad, he was my lifeline and savior. I never complained. I did just what he wanted me to do. But I was miserable." These daughters

were afraid that if they antagonized their fathers they would
not be loved. "I was afraid not to be or do what he wanted
because then he wouldn't be my friend and love me."

In part, the daughters' compliance with an arrangement that
compromised their needs is a testament to the strength of the
human desire to belong and be loved. Having dismissed the possibility of getting what they needed from their mothers, they
were more dependent on this assurance from their fathers. "I've
always been afraid to do anything rash or get angry with my
father. I'm afraid I could lose everything."

Additionally, either parent's strong disapproval of their
child's spontaneous expression of emotions teaches the child
what behavior is acceptable and what is disallowed. What becomes alien must be altered and banished from awareness. It is
too frightening to defy the parent(s). "It's like a little plant growing—suddenly the ceiling is lowered on it. It has to bend and
conform to get the light."

The idea that differences in thoughts, needs, or emotions
exist between individuals and deserve expression carried little
weight in these families. Moreover, the common practice, especially by the father, of greeting evidences of emotional vulnerability—behavior emblematic of childhood—with ridicule or
banishment drove their expression underground. Displays of
helplessness were definitely scorned. Sara remembered that it
was not okay to show anyone else her feelings of helplessness.
She believed it could lead to abandonment. As she attempted
to describe these very sensitive feelings, she reported a scolding,
derisive voice in her head saying: "You can't say that. Go off
in a corner and hide until you're back in shape."

Lacking positive regard for the vast range of their own emotional repertoire, these daughters did not develop the tools to
appropriately handle their different emotions and feel good
about themselves. "Dad didn't trust me or believe in me
enough to let me try new things." "What I wanted wasn't

what he wanted or liked. So, I learned not to speak up for myself."

A daughter hastened to adapt; unhappy feelings were buried. Her father's approval was at risk. "I wanted to be big and strong and pleasing for my father. I never told him how it really was for me. I didn't want to appear helpless and complaining." Not only was self-confidence undermined, but many daughters doubted themselves because their different needs could not be acknowledged by their fathers.

Unresolved Dilemmas

In cultivating a strong, tough veneer to please their fathers and hide those needs and feelings that had been labeled unacceptable, these daughters also disidentified with their mothers. They had confused the mother's vulnerabilities with her lack of power and esteem in the family. Determining never to appear like their mothers—i.e., helpless and dependent—these women shoveled underground their age-appropriate feelings of vulnerability and uncertainty. Adequacy was perceived as the absence of needs. If disquieting feelings were aroused, they were denied. The keenly felt longings for maternal nurturance were cast off. Asking for nurturance meant that something was wrong with them.

Even if these mothers could have been different, their daughters would still have had to face the profound dilemmas that await most girls growing up in a society that more highly esteems men than women. No matter how an individual mother views herself, the generalized disdain of women prevalent in this society affects every woman.

Although women, mothers especially, have been idealized, they have also been demeaned. Depicted as controlling, they frequently have been powerless. We have chastised mothers for being overprotective and simultaneously admonished them for not being more sensitively attuned to their children. We stigmatize women as weak and ineffectual for revealing their emotions, yet we become furious with them when they have been unavailable to meet the emotional needs of others. It was not surprising that these daughters felt ambivalent about identifying with their mothers.

Unable to comprehend that the cumulative effect of the devaluation of women does create conditions that wound them, the daughters retreated from their mothers assuming that would free them from the conflicts, confusions, and discrepancies that surrounded being a woman.

In search of the possibilities their mothers had been unable to offer—loving support and a respected role model—these daughters turned to their fathers. They identified with them and their style of behaving. They presumed that complying with their fathers' expectations would earn them what they desired.

In their haste to escape from what they had already been programmed to belittle—both the expression of vulnerable emotions and women who express such feelings—these daughters exchanged emotional authenticity for acceptance. The omnipresent and far-reaching influence of the cultural belief system is evident. The ways of the father are the standard for healthy adjustment.

Even though most of these fathers were responsive to their daughters and offered them affection and direction, the daughters found themselves on a path that would become very familiar: pleasing someone else at the expense of knowing themselves.

It is interesting that most of these women acquired some very respected skills as they adapted to the conditions that prevailed. The majority are in intimate relationships and they pay emotional attention to the people closest to them. They work hard and most have been successful. Nevertheless, each of them can feel like an inadequate, weak person when she experiences difficulty handling her varied emotions or declaring her needs. The training to discount herself when she has feelings or needs that have been demeaned has been persistent and severe.

Armored Little Girl

As a child I learned that the key to survival was keeping it all hidden.

Therapy with Miriam, a 26-year-old woman warrior suited up in impenetrable layers of toughness, defiance, and stubbornness, dressed as though for a medieval battle, poignantly illuminated many of these issues. Housed in a castle of protection, surrounded by barbed wit, and bordered by a moat filled with denial, Miriam carried shields marked "I don't care," "I don't need." This armored warrior was clearly determined not to let anyone come close to her. Yet lurking just beyond view were desperate yearnings for love and affection.

Miriam had cultivated a tough, defiant stance to please her loving father. This also effectively concealed her pain and rage at not feeling sufficiently loved by her critical, disapproving mother. She remained in control of her feelings by mimicking the derision she observed her father display toward people who expressed strong emotions. All her life, dark intense feelings had raged within Miriam, leaving her doubting herself and mistrusting her abilities. To express what she experienced would have implied not only that Miriam was incapable of managing her emotions but that she was also behaving like the mother she had been taught to berate.

In her first therapy visit Miriam knew her armor was becoming increasingly difficult to maintain. She announced: "I've been strong, competent, and independent for a long time. Now I may need to learn to be vulnerable." She was alerting both of us to the tasks ahead. Many months passed before we could even identify the problems.

Miriam was brought into the world by a mother who had much difficulty coping with her baby. In therapy, recounting her mother's complaining stories of the pregnancy, Miriam wailed: "Even then I annoyed her. I've never been a source of pleasure." Nothing Miriam ever did was right; she was always too much trouble. Miriam felt she got very little, "not even a loving glance." Cold cereal left out for her on the kitchen table before Miriam rushed off to school symbolized this paucity of nurturance. "I got the bare minimum."

In marked contrast, Miriam's father adored her and offered "unconditional love." Her mother once told her, "He had a way with you. I didn't have the patience." Miriam grew up believing she "could do no wrong" in her father's eyes. However, there were subtle expectations to fulfill to assure his love. Miriam knew her father liked her to be tough and strong. She believed he would not love her if she was weak and emotional—like her mother. "I had to bury any hint of weakness and assume this tough cover. Pretty soon I lost the vulnerable feelings altogether. If I wasn't what he wanted me to be, he wouldn't love me and then where would I be? I know *she* didn't love me."

The Unhappiness

This family of three unhappy people lived in an old, dark house filled with gloom and despair. As a small child, Miriam was the light in all that darkness. "I carried the family on a chain around my neck. It was so heavy I couldn't stand up." The members of this family were locked together by the conviction that nothing could be changed. While they all shared a steady diet of misery, her mother expressed it most directly. Miriam remembered her sitting around the house, depressed and complaining, waiting for someone else to make it better for her. Since he was away at work, the emotional nuances of her father's life were not as visible. At home he displayed a sarcastic derision toward others that effectively concealed his own unhappiness.

In her youth Miriam oscillated between a dispassionate, withholding mother and an adoring, overzealous father. In therapy, she puzzled over this. "I couldn't believe him because of her. What was I doing wrong? He loved me so much, and she criticized me and made fun of his love. As a child I must have felt very bad and been very confused. I still wonder who's the real me?"

The discrepancy between each parent's attitude and their behavior toward Miriam created confusion in her. As a little girl, Miriam found solace for herself in either making surly demands or hastily retreating to the attic, where she hid her unhappiness as she cuddled amid discarded family possessions. These tactics kept totally concealed the hurt, despairing little girl who longed to be understood. "I can't take anything from anyone else because that opens all the old yearnings. I'm terrified of letting my feelings out. It's a tidal wave. It's so huge. No one can satisfy those yearnings—and I'm afraid of them."

Unable to find a more direct way to demonstrate what she really felt, Miriam handled her unhappiness by frequently disrupting the family; she shouted, slammed doors, and screamed at the dinner table. She was trying to let her parents know that she was hurting, but her disguise was so effective they did not catch on. She even carried these tactics to school, where she cut classes, rarely turned in her homework, and became the chief troublemaker in a group of rebellious girls. Here, too, the toughy disguise worked. No one ever deciphered Miriam's pleas for help.

Miserable and lonely for many years, Miriam desperately wanted someone to realize her plight without articulating her emotional needs. Not only did she believe she would lose her adored father's approval if her well-disguised needs were made known, but Miriam had been conditioned to harshly judge any evidence of her vulnerabilities: That meant she was like her mother.

Until Miriam came to therapy and began to unravel these issues, this no-win situation kept her trapped in unhappiness.

PART II

EXPANDING THE ISSUES

CHAPTER 5

THE YEARNING
FOR NURTURANCE

I was pushed out of the lap at an early age to make room for
the next baby. There were six more.

Katherine

In the habit of presenting themselves as strong women who did
not need anything from anyone, these clients totally masked their
colossal yearnings for nurturance. Routinely, they wished I could
intuit what they required. They wanted to be taken care of
without having to voice either their needs or their feelings. "I
really want to know I'm special to you, but I'm afraid to tell
you this because it'll show you how needy I am."

It was dangerous to ignite those hidden yearnings. It hurt
too much to admit what had been missing. "I want so much to
be taken care of, but that part of me has never gotten enough
attention." When the interaction between the client and me
touched this vulnerability, the responses were often contradic-

tory: "I don't like the look in your eyes when I tell you I feel sad. It's too caring."

To disclose their longings was to reveal inadequacies. It was embarrassing to express the wish for more; it was also taking a big risk. The anxiety created by acknowledging these feelings, when coupled with preparing for the anticipated disapproval, was extreme. "If I open myself up, I'll be hurt. I'm afraid you'll reject me if I tell you that I wish I had a mother like you." These sensitivities, rather than being voiced, were discounted. In these women's heads old tapes scolded: "You're too big for that now; stop acting like a baby."

Anna was late for her therapy appointment. She announced that she had had a drink before therapy, most unusual behavior. "Maybe it's because I don't want to go back to the bad feelings of last week. I can't remember anything. I don't want to remember. Tell me."

Resistance to proceeding was always present. Anna was protecting herself from experiencing the unpleasantness that often accompanies opening up old wounds. If she could involve me in remembering what she needed to remember for herself, she could avoid experiencing her feelings.

I remained quiet. After a long silence Anna began to remember. She had been feeling very vulnerable at the end of her last appointment and had not wanted to leave. "It's hard to go out there and be. In here I can be anything I want to be—I know it's okay."

Suddenly the tone of Anna's voice altered. She became angry with me "for making" her "go out there." During the previous session, even though upset, she had not wanted to stop. Besides, she was reluctant to tell me that this work was unpleasant; she wanted reassurance and support from me to enable her to manage her vulnerable feelings. If I could have known this without her saying anything that would have meant I cared. It also would have protected Anna from revealing just how sensitive she did feel. "I did want more that night and I didn't tell you. Instead I made up a dialogue in my head about why it's not possible to have more time. Maybe I'm angry. I don't know. But I covered both sides in my head so nothing else happened. I told myself I can't stay longer because you see someone else after me. You need the minutes in between. Anyway, I can get up and go on. I'll be all right."

Taught to minimize the reality of her emotional needs, Anna, like many other women, assumed that they had to be concealed. That assumption hampered her communicating what she needed and thus robbed her of an opportunity to express what was happening.

Survival

> I was taught that if I'm not happy and smiling I should go away from everyone until I was.
>
> Elizabeth

Long ago, like many other little girls—and still happening, since women in their 20s report similar experiences in their therapy—each of these daughters quickly came to understand that acknowledging their needs—expressing dependent and helpless feelings—announced weaknesses and inadequacies they were being trained to scorn. "I was taught to deny my feelings. Although I had them anyway, they weren't okay. 'Don't be such a crybaby' must have been a very powerful message."

They hid their unacceptable emotional needs both from themselves and from everybody else to avoid unfavorable responses. "It's very hard to put these feelings out straight because I can't be loved if I'm helpless."

The yearnings for more love, comforting, and attention than they had received slowly receded. If reminders ever poked through, they would beat them back by berating themselves for such indulgences. "I'm not allowed to be needy. That means I'm stupid, lazy, no good." These women were determined to demonstrate their self-sufficiency. Women who appear strong, responsible, and in control do not require nurturance. They did not want to depend on anyone; that reopened the old wounds. "I have to manage all by myself. There is no one to really count on." It was extremely difficult and unpleasant to admit that they wanted sensitive attention.

Many women had developed an angry, defiant stance that belied the depth of their yearnings. Nevertheless, at times they could not control, explain, or make their longings go away. They felt very unhappy. "It's like being a plant. You don't get watered. When you complain someone says, 'You're watered, your roots are just in the wrong place.'"

Incredible Sensitivities

When these incredible sensitivities to expressing their needs were explored in therapy, remnants of vivid, chaotic emotions associated with the fragile beginnings of life were also reawakened. Fragments of memories of being totally dependent on the mother's caregiving—wishing to be picked up and comforted, but with no one appearing—were recalled. "I needed my mother to care for me and I'm afraid to think about that. If she didn't take care of me I'd die."

The intensity of these ancient disappointments was overwhelming. "It's awful to feel the pain of what I didn't have. I was always waiting for my mother to love me. I feel sad, angry, hurt. There's a hole inside me."

Often, it rocked the woman's confidence in herself. "I can't hang onto loving myself. I can't give that to myself. Everything feels lost, I have no resources. Instead of trying, I feel helpless to change anything."

Images of food and memories about being fed, basic symbols of nurturance, frequently also accompanied the expression of these long penned-up yearnings. One woman recounted a dream in which she was lost with only a piece of bread in her hand. The sustenance symbolized by the bread enabled her to handle being lost. Another realized that when she was upset a glass of milk always made her feel better. Others remembered not being fed or being inadequately fed by their mothers. "I'm not talking about body comfort or the breast, but the bottle. She couldn't even hold the bottle for me!" Family stories about early eating difficulties were recollected. "My mother told me that when she fed me I vomited my food all over the floor."

Melissa recalled that immediately after her birth, her mother had developed an infection and required additional hospitalization. Reluctant grandparents were called upon to care for Melissa, who, once at home, ate very poorly and developed colic. Melissa became ill. The cry of a tiny baby still evoked very tender feelings in her. She could imagine herself crying, unable to eat. As she recollected this, Melissa realized that sometimes she still used disturbances linked to food, like stomachaches, to gain attention.

These women did not like the reality of their emotions. If *only* mothers had been perfect—met all one's needs—a daughter would not be left to cope with the panic aroused by realizing how helpless she once had been. They could gain strength and control by becoming furious with and deprecating their mothers. Acknowledging that as a child one had been unable to get what one needed, and had been helpless to change that, was immobilizing, terrifying.

Focusing their anger at their mothers' inability to provide everything disguised the daughters' pain. In therapy, as elsewhere in society, blaming the mother has been the most frequently traveled route of escape away from accepting the intense discomfort of one's own vulnerabilities.

It felt terrible to know that something vital to feeling good about oneself was missing. It was a huge ache. "A burning place with no color. It feels so overwhelming." Several women felt bleak and empty, broken inside. "I feel like I have a broken heart. Something is missing. It's what I didn't get in my childhood. I want my mommy." When this pain was touched, a soundless wail reverberated throughout the room.

Sometimes, I too feel intense discomfort as a woman's deeply sequestered hurts throb. As you read you may have a similar response. Your own secret sorrow, silently carried within, may be awakened. We have been trained to distance ourselves from unpleasant feelings, and it can be difficult for each of us to express them. We have also been taught to feel ashamed of our needs, which makes them much harder to acknowledge. "I have to function and be strong. I'm afraid to cry and let on how bad it was for me in my family. No one would listen."

In general, my clients moved back and forth between incredible sadness and rage. It was important for each woman to find her own balance between these two very different emotions. Before finding that balance, a woman raced away from her vulnerable revelations and avoided her rage because she was afraid of it. One of my tasks was to point out what she was doing. Most important, I just listened to these outpourings. No one had ever done that before for them. The women did not require explanations or interpretations, only the opportunity to voice their hurts. Once the memories and emotions were relived, new awareness was possible.

After becoming quite upset and angry in therapy over her mother's unresponsiveness throughout her childhood, Laura reported that the next day her head was filled with images of food and flowers. As she was talking Laura realized, "These are old, old links to the days when my mother functioned better, before I was seven." At present, Laura nurtures herself by cooking and gardening.

The Programming

Like most children, these daughters had been conditioned to expect that a mother would provide a certain quality and quantity of nurturance. Even though the father was usually the favored parent, many persisted in more highly valuing maternal sustenance. "A mother should have an obligation to mother. How was it possible that she didn't know what I needed?" Mothering is synonymous with nurturance. Although some of my clients' fathers did offer "solace and salvation," unless the mother also met her daughter's yearnings for caretaking they remained unsatisfied. "It's not enough that my dad loves me; I want Mom's love too."

The programming to hold the mother responsible and exonerate the father was striking as these intense, unsatisfied longings for caretaking gradually found their voice. "I want to grab her, shake her, and ask her, 'What'd you ever give me?'" "Dad didn't want to hear about my troubles. He wanted a picture-postcard, perfect family. He had troubles enough at work."

Taught to be grateful for whatever attention their big, powerful, important fathers directed at them, they rarely addressed blame or anger at the father. These daughters had been conditioned to have different expectations of men. Additionally, they wanted to believe that their fathers had provided what their mothers had been unable to offer. It was too painful to think otherwise.

Several fathers did soften their daughters' dissatisfaction by providing "some attention." They watched TV with their girls, played with them, instructed them in how to swim, fish, and throw a ball. Jewish daughters, in particular, remembered that while they were falling asleep their fathers patiently sat nearby or offered comfort in the middle of the night when the daughter was restless or upset. "I was told that when I was a baby he used to come into my room and sit with me at night until I fell asleep. If I stirred or cried he would be right there with me." Regarded as exceptional, this behavior was a sign of the father's deep affection. That same attention offered by their mother would not have been recollected as special. It would have been expected.

Furthermore, the training to more highly value attention from men prompted the majority of these women, as adults, to look to men as they originally had turned to their fathers, hoping men would provide the nurturance they longed for. "I know I can get comforting from another woman, but it's like it doesn't count. It's not worth as much, or I'm not worth as much, unless it comes from a man."

Poignantly, however, the women often felt not quite satisfied. Most male lovers and husbands, like the women's fathers, also have been trained to distance themselves from demands for intimacy and nurturance.

The clients' experiences are poignant and sensitive. There is no downplaying the importance of their early wounds; many left long-lasting scars. However, if we continue to view these deficits only from the angle of the mother's inability to provide sufficient nurturance, we limit the picture and postpone seeing reality more clearly. Of equal importance, maintaining this limited scope repeats the very inequities that require correcting.

The Persistent Flaws

Concentration on the mother as the primary source of nurturance has persistently clouded the issues. When women are portrayed as exceptional, with a capacity to nurture that is not affected by either strengths or limitations, that depiction rarely includes the facts.

Mothers sometimes have trouble managing on their own or may be incapable of consistently providing what their offspring require. Besides, no matter how much a mother tries, sometimes her child cannot be comforted. Although she may be pivotal to the survival of her baby, a mother's life has many other demands. Usually an infant has to share her mother with a lover, other siblings, and the intricate arrangements that characterize daily family life. Today, that often includes the demands of a job outside the home.

Most women, nevertheless, want to be good mothers and by and large work hard at this awesome task—to know and take care of all their child's needs while juggling the other responsibilities of their lives. "I forgot my briefcase today in the rush of getting Jenny off to school. Every detail is my responsibility: her lunch, her flute for the music lesson after school, and the consent slip for a field trip tomorrow."

In painful explorations of her discomfort with her son's birthday, Laura said: "I always get upset around Michael's birthday. His birth spelled the end of my marriage and I spent a long time covering that over. I had nothing to live for, but I had to take care of Michael. It was so hard to keep it all together. I had barely enough energy to go to work and pay the bills. I took care of him, but it was only custodial. Later, I thought, thank God I had to put my life back together for Michael. I sure wasn't doing it for myself."

Even with today's heightened consciousness and the awareness of the growing number of single mothers, there is a glaring lack of acknowledgment that mothers require help and support to carry out their tasks. We resist accepting that they are individuals who have needs, rights, and ambitions that can on many occasions conflict with the demands and responsibilities of mothering. This is not evidence of personal shortcomings, but a reality of life.

When a mother behaves like an ordinary person, putting self-interest above interest in others, we rebuke her. But has anyone ever asked who does nurture the mother of six children, the battered mother, the physically challenged mother, the physically or mentally ill mother, the divorced or single mother?

To maintain the illusion that mothers, by doing their job well, can provide all that children require, we have fervently championed unreal expectations. As women have tried to meet those expectations, tormenting dilemmas have been created for all of us. The predicaments and confusion generated by the demands of caregiving are awesome. For generations, left to handle alone these multifaceted responsibilities, women themselves have believed they are responsible for meeting everyone's nurturance needs. "Grandma was my most important role model. She always thought of other people before herself."

Enriched by eons of experience and a vast range of female sensibilities, assumptions about women's talents for caregiving are deeply rooted in their biological capacity to bear and nurse children. As women applied their arts, other people felt good. Women themselves have reaped satisfaction and social approval.

Nevertheless, the conditioning which taught that giving to others would take care of women's own needs has reinforced the false notion that women are not supposed to have needs of their own. "Taking care of them I forgot about me."

The keen training of all women to sense what others want and be responsive to their care-needing signals does shift attention away from the caregiver. "My mother modeled that her needs are second to other people's." Donning the caretaker mantle interrupts a woman's connection to her own needs for nurturance. "I only know how to get my needs met through caring for someone else. That allows me to skip over my own neediness and dependency." Women in their 20s who are currently new therapy clients demonstrate the tenacity of this conditioning: "I give in to other people's need and plow mine underground." "I'm always putting someone else ahead of myself."

These arrangements create a nurturing deficit in each woman. "I come from a long line of unmothered women: my grandma, my mother, and me. None of us got it."[1]

The persistent concentration on the mother as nurturer trains individuals to dismiss the significance of other people's contributions to the infant's well-being: the father, siblings, a hired caregiver, grandparents. Other meaningful factors that shape a specific child's experience—the psychological and economic climate in the family, and the historical moment into which a child is born—have also primarily been downplayed.[2]

Serious Consequences

These attitudes have had serious consequences for all of us, conveniently protecting us from realizing that men have been excused from active participation in the intimacies of daily life. The joys and frustrations that accompany caregiving are outside the male purview. Undoubtedly this has promoted the physical and emotional distancing from intimacy so common among men that women frequently complain about.

Many men have appeared to be, and even believed they were, incapable of knowing how to nurture. Several clients remembered their fathers spontaneously bestowing nurturant attention on them when it pleased the fathers, but not necessarily when the daughter needed or asked for it.

The continuous reluctance on the part of men to spontaneously participate in caregiving, whether at home or at the workplace, maintains the myth that caregiving is gender-specific. This division of responsibilities by gender has kept directed at women the sadness and rage we all can feel at different times about what we have not received. "Maybe we all hate our mothers because they didn't provide the perfect world for us egocentric babies." The desire to deny that disappointment and frustration have always been intrinsic to life is very powerful in each of us.

The entrenchment of strong beliefs that devalue nurturance equally influences men's reluctance to nurture. Caregiving brings too close the exquisite vulnerabilities that are part of life. We do not like knowing that our needs are ordinary and basic— lifelong.

Not shifting blame from the mother to the father, but taking it upon oneself, enables us to identify these flawed beliefs. This is a first step toward changing them.

Other Flawed Convictions

I have to do everything on my own. I can't let anyone help me because that means I'm not okay.

Melissa

Other deep-seated, flawed convictions deserve exposure. Our attitudes, expectations, and mental images of nurturance have been based on the idealization of the mother–infant relationship. We have extolled this special relationship in which the mother has been purported to spontaneously and continuously bestow nurturance as she demonstrates her love and caring for her baby. We have identified unquestioned nurturant attention with this very special population of infants and small children. "I want to be given to just because I exist. The idea of meeting any of this need on my own isn't the same as getting it just because you're born."

Even though this special, deserving group might expand to include individuals who are either sick, aged, or in crisis, a time-limited tone has dominated these conceptions, implying that needs for caregiving are something one outgrows or recovers from. Significantly, these populations that we consider deserving all share some degree of helplessness. This further confuses nurturance with helplessness, casting doubt on the validity of wishing for nurturant attention and curbing that spontaneous expression in most of us.

While we have idealized the nurturance mothers supposedly bestow on their babies, in reality we consider requests for caregiving indications of personal shortcomings. A frequent assumption is that a person who voluntarily asks for emotional comforting must be immature.

Clearly the value system the majority of these women had been raised with was the same, whether their origins were working or middle class, Latin, Caucasian, or Asian. It was common to direct disdain toward individuals who evidenced neediness. Any expression of vulnerability was regarded as a demonstration of personal inadequacy. "I don't want anyone to feel sorry for me. I don't need help or support. I'm totally self-sufficient."

Familiar Patterns

> I saw Mom attend to and give to Dad, but I never saw her get what she needed.
>
> Alice

When the supply of nurturance is short, women go without. Groomed to be caregivers, women are expected to defer their needs. Men, on the other hand, while generally refraining from explicitly expressing their needs for nurturant attention, nevertheless expect women to intuit and meet them. It was no different in my clients' families. "You were supposed to read Daddy's mind and know what he wanted." Fathers who came home tired from work expected and generally received nurturance. "You worked hard to make it okay when Daddy came home because if you didn't he'd holler."

A few women recollected that when they were sitting quietly, reading a book, their fathers would interrupt them and reprimand them. "If I wanted to do something just for me, I was selfish or wrong." Each was told to help her mother. "When I was enjoying myself reading a book, Dad would holler,'What are you doing? Get up and help your mother, your brothers.' It was always someone else. I wasn't allowed to do my own thing." The message is clear: Girls place the needs of the family above their own.

Katherine, an oldest daughter, never questioned whether the demand that she help care for her brother, who was born when she was 10 years old, was excessive. Neither she nor anyone else noticed the loss of her time for herself. What Katherine remembered was how good it felt to "mother him." She felt capable and responsible.

All the women who had brothers noticed that the boys got more attention from both the mother and the father. "Men, brothers, that's who's important. Girls, women, they don't count. The boys always got everything—and there were four of them." Some women who were the only daughters in a family of several sons became aware of their brothers' privileges; they envied their position in the family. The boys definitely were allowed to do more and go more places than the girls, who were often told, "You stay at home with your mother." Boys also got more nurturance. One woman squashed her disappointment by stating, "Maybe there wasn't enough to go around."

Who Does Nurture the Mother?

Occasionally, a daughter remembered her mother turning to her for help and support when in distress. It had never occurred to the women that their mothers might be exhausted from their tasks. Nor had they considered that their mothers looked to them for comfort and sensitive attention because they were not getting it from anyone else in the family.

More commonly, the daughters could not recollect their mothers ever having directly indicated either that they felt overwhelmed by their tasks or that they wanted help. "In my family, asking for help was admitting failure." Acknowledging one's needs diminished one.

Over and over these daughters learned that women suppress their needs by paying attention to others. Many clients, like most other women, developed remarkable antennae early in girlhood that not only picked up and complied with their fathers' desires but also sensitively tuned in to their mothers' needs for attention. "I couldn't say no. I was supposed to take care of her."

In therapy, some of these daughters became aware of their anger; they had felt compelled to comply. Some also felt guilty because sometimes they did not want to. Many realized they felt overwhelmed by their mothers' requests and could *feel* the mother's withdrawal when her needs went unmet.

Several believed that something they had done elicited the mother's behavior; they tried harder to provide what their mothers required in order to ensure their approval. "I was my mother's person and not my own." This provided additional reinforcement for placing their needs second to others in order to secure love. "I got loved by doing what she wanted. I didn't even know what I wanted."

Ellen, as a little girl, sensed that she was expected to know what would please her mother, but was not encouraged to tell her own wants. "I remember wandering around my house, feeling miserable and lonely. Instead of being able to get my mother to play with me, or be with me, I would tell her I was okay. I was afraid to make any demands on her. She didn't want to hear it. I accommodated to her needs. But who cared for me?"

The scarcity of visible, affirming social models who explicitly expressed the emotional ups and downs of everyday life discouraged these mothers and daughters from directly communicating their needs. While there will always be something special and unique about the sensitivity between mothers and daughters that, at times, enables them to intuit each other's wishes, their subtle communications can subvert the importance of direct expression. The recognition and satisfying of these unconscious signals promote the assumption that other people should know even one's unarticulated wants.

Short Supply

When the supply of nurturance was short in these families, the relationships between women suffered, especially the relationship between sisters. This further reflects the persistent belief that women's esteem is dependent on their association with men.

It was rare for the sister relationship to be described as a companionship of mutual respect and delight. "In my family I was repeatedly told: 'It's all fine, we're one big happy family.' It sure didn't feel that way to me."

Older sisters, in particular, were angry at losing their special place and jealous of the attentions showered on the new rival. "She was my dad's favorite. All I got was picked on." One younger sister was quite ill as an infant. Her older sister thought she got the family message: "There isn't room for two babies."

The de-emphasis on women nurturing one another, and the lack of positive regard for closeness between them, deepened the pockets of suspicion between sisters, reinforcing the notion that women are not trustworthy. Many women felt very competitive or angry with their sisters for taking something away from them. "When Maggie was born my reality told me I don't want another sister. We were already three." "My sister and I fought a lot; we didn't do anything together. I was mean to her, but I was probably jealous of the attention she got. Now I can see I missed something—a sisterly relationship."

The demeaning of female closeness failed to provide a valued model of a woman who nurtures herself.

Changing

I have to watch that I'm taking care of myself. There's so much to pay attention to.

Kim

Clearly the beliefs and attitudes one has been raised to value highly influence each individual's capacity to tolerate and accept her own emotional repertoire. It is significant that in psychotherapy, as elsewhere in society, this has received much less attention. Although important goals of therapy include enabling a woman to express and experience the pain and rage of her early losses and to recognize that these losses have affected her feelings about herself, we can no longer ignore this: The stigma attached to expressing one's needs for nurturance keeps these needs hidden.

Initially, these daughters had been waiting for someone to give them what they longed for. They did not know how to go about addressing their needs for themselves because admitting them made the women feel weak and inadequate.

Furthermore, wishing that one's needs could be intuited conceals the shame at having them in the first place. "The old tape is that vulnerable, sensitive, emotional people are limited. They can't function—all the things people say about women. I don't believe it, but it's there and it's hard to change."

In time, we came to understand that to move beyond these original deficits required that they be acknowledged and their validity respected as well. Once her needs gained acceptance, a woman could create her own reserves. "I'm starting to fight for time for me. I have to plan for my needs like I plan for most commitments. If I don't plan I'll forget about them."

As these women began to realize that the nurturance they so deeply desired was not confined solely to the mother–daughter relationship, it became not only appropriate to ask for nurturance from others but also possible to regard their mothers differently. "I realize I've belittled my mother and considered her worthless because that's how I felt she treated me. I carried that around for years. I don't know why; that's just what I did. Now it feels like a city in the desert that no one lives in and no one visits: a relic."

Nurturance could be found in a variety of other relationships; a woman could also feel good about nurturing herself. One client's image was apt: A nice hot rock would accompany her everywhere. It would be warm inside.

New, important learning took place. Previously unable to accept her own needs because that was associated with inadequacies within herself, a woman clung to the expectation that someone else would meet her needs without her declaring them. As their understanding expanded, the women changed. "I still feel needy, but I don't feel bad about that anymore. I still need attention and it's all right to need attention. Nothing is wrong with that."

CHAPTER 6

REMEMBERING
First Steps toward Healing

There were certain feelings you just didn't have, for example: anger, sadness, unhappiness. My mother couldn't deal with them so they didn't exist. So what did I do? I had to cut them off like she did. But feelings you don't express get stuffed inside and feel like a large weight. You carry that around forever feeling like a bad person 'cause you have these feelings you're not supposed to have.

Like most of the daughters described in this book, Carol saw her mother as a damaged, inadequate person and viewed her father as strong, clever, and successful. Although she turned to him for a model to emulate and espoused his beliefs, Carol nevertheless yearned for a nurturant connection with her mother.

When this sensitivity was aroused, Carol associated it with weakness and helplessness, tabooed vulnerabilities she had observed more often in her mother than in her father.

Carol was 24 years old when therapy began in 1976. A newcomer to San Francisco, she was employed as a secretary. Carol remained in therapy for about two years, during which time she primarily investigated her relationship with her father, with whom she was very angry, and her relations with men. Her relationship with her mother was rarely discussed. It was "just fine."

I heard from Carol again four years later when she requested an appointment to explore a transition in her career. After stopping therapy, she had gone to graduate school and studied economics. At the time of her phone call, Carol was employed by a large mutual fund organization and wanted to open her own investment counseling business. Quickly sorting out her anxieties about venturing forth on her own, Carol took steps to open her own firm.

We agreed to continue meeting at irregular intervals for several months. When long-concealed issues with her mother began to surface, we settled into once-a-week therapy; the work, which will be elaborated on in this and the following chapter, continued for six years. During those years Carol expanded her business and married. In the last year of therapy she gave birth to a daughter.

Background

When I asked for a lot I was not okay, but if I buried my neediness I got cared for.

Early in her childhood, Carol experienced a tug-of-war between her own needs and her mother's demands. Unless she cooperated with her mother's demands, she believed that she would not be loved. Expressing her differences meant clashing with her mother's expectations. "If only I knew what she wanted to hear I might have given it to her and gotten love back. But the only thing she wanted to hear sacrificed me. I couldn't be myself and get loved."

Despite their stormy battles during her adolescence and young adulthood, Carol always felt loved by her father. He offered some attention and positive regard. Nevertheless, while she was growing up he was very domineering and argumentative, often shouting at his wife and children. He expected to be obeyed and was not interested in anyone else's opinion. "Life with Dad had its problems too. He's moody and authoritarian, but he's alive. There's meat to him!"

To keep his love, Carol learned to conceal the pain she felt when he was disapproving. His abrasive manner taught Carol to silence herself. She did not examine whether or not his behavior thwarted her self-expression; she accommodated to his demands.

Whenever her longings for what was missing were stirred, Carol felt terrible—empty, bleak, and lonely. Those feelings were often unacceptable to Carol, who had been conditioned to deny unpleasant emotions. She grew adept at intuiting what pleased both her mother and her father, thereby squelching her feelings when she sensed it made either of them uncomfortable. Like most well-behaved daughters, Carol received affection and recognition for placing the needs of others before her own.

Until she was in therapy, Carol had not appreciated that she had been conditioned to distort her own emotional reality. "What hasn't been clear was that I cut off my own arms—or more appropriately my heart—so that I wouldn't feel any more pain. Otherwise, I'd never survive." As Carol gradually displayed her complex repertoire of emotions, needs, and yearnings and found acceptance for them, she acquired increasing trust and confidence in herself.

These issues have been particularly sensitive for many women. Frequently, the absence of sufficient nurturant support, from both their mothers *and* their fathers, for being themselves does create difficulties in generating self-esteem and self-confidence. Additionally, the training to acquiesce to the father's demands for unquestioned obedience further stifles self-expression. The daughter's distinct needs, emotions, and aspirations do not receive the nurturant soil required to grow and flower. Well-worn convictions that downplay women's aspirations and demean them for the expression of their varied needs have prevented these issues from receiving the attention they deserve.

Identifying the Issues

> I'm losing the connection to my feelings. I don't know if I know how to have my own feelings. My mother always wanted me to cry. That was okay. It's okay to cry here too, but that's not my feeling. I feel disappointed, sad, empty, and I don't know if it's all right.

Carol was not in the habit of acknowledging her unpleasant or vulnerable feelings to anyone. It was hard to get started. She would have liked a push from me, preferred that I did the talking. My silence made her uncomfortable. She felt disconnected, alone, powerless, and helpless. Rather than acknowledge what she was feeling Carol wanted me to intuitively know what was wrong and fix it. "I can't stay with the lonely feelings. I can't take responsibility for myself because then I lose the connection to your caring for me." Carol had been taught that love was earned by complying with other people's expectations. If she displayed her own needs and asked for what she wanted, approval might be withheld and Carol's security threatened.

When she became confused and did not know what to do, Carol became upset. However, she could not give expression to her distress, but would mask her feelings with an angry, sullen stance. She was protecting herself from the censure she anticipated if any weakness was acknowledged. "In my family no one accepts me for who I am. No one hears what I feel. Whatever I want isn't important." When she felt vulnerable, Carol would blame me or grow angry with me, blame her mother, attribute her feelings to the other person's behavior, rationalize or philosophize her feelings away—anything—not to accept them as her own. Her fear of disapproval or banishment was disabling. "I can't have what I want. I feel trapped. In prison. No matter what I do it won't make any difference." For a long time these beliefs undermined Carol's ability to feel and accept her own emotions. "To feel my emotions means I have to acknowledge that they and me are important."

Anger was also disallowed in Carol's family. "It didn't exist." As a teenager, when she tried to express her anger, her father would not listen. "He banished me. If I felt angry I was bad." Carol stopped short, suddenly fearful of my criticism. In that moment she also realized that this was what she had done with her mother. "I had to be one way with her and separate off the rest of me. That's what's going on here." I questioned why she would want to repeat that pattern with me. "It's all I know. We're rediscovering and recreating feelings I never was allowed to have. It's confusing and I do run away."

The first time we discussed an increase in therapy visits, these patterns rapidly went into operation. Although hesitantly agreeing, Carol could not tell me that this was making her feel more anxious. Instead she became annoyed with me because I wanted her to open up the "secret parts of herself." To avoid expressing and experiencing her own emotions, which often were overwhelming and painful, Carol projected them onto me. She preferred to think that my actions were responsible for her feelings. After we sorted this out, Carol reported how angry she had felt with me for giving back to her the responsibility for both her own feelings and her therapy!

When Carol felt misunderstood or distant from me, she experienced panic. It was reminiscent of times in her childhood when her mother could not respond as Carol needed her to respond. She felt lost and abandoned. "I have to keep getting supplies from outside. There's no freezer inside. It's all perishable. It doesn't come inside because it was never there.... When you don't catch on or agree with me, I instantly feel lost and alone. I don't like it."

Within two weeks a powerful dream plummeted the issues into therapy. On a stormy night Carol, with the aid of her husband, managed to cross a very rickety old bridge high above a raging river. Safe on the other side, she watched two little girls, about 5 and 10 years old, attempt to cross. The wind was blowing fiercely, and suddenly the younger girl was blown over and dashed to her death on the rocks. Carol's response was surprising. She was upset with the little girl. "She should have known better." That is how Carol feels about herself. "I should have had all the bases covered." This time, however, the feelings of helplessness and sadness leaked through.

Remembering

When Carol was 21 her parents broke a long silence, telling her of their respective escapes from danger. Recognizing the personal danger in 1938 in the virulent anti-Semitism of Nazi politics, Carol's father applied for an emigration visa to the United States. He tried to persuade his family to do the same. Not sharing his alarm, they refused to leave their home. All of them perished in a concentration camp.[1]

Carol's mother was sent by her parents to live with a distant relative in the United States; she was 16. Three years later, just prior to the outbreak of the war, her parents escaped and came to New York City.

Although neither parent endured the psychological and physical devastation and dehumanization that survivors of the concentration camps experienced, they nevertheless sustained many serious losses. Their lives were permanently altered as each of them fled from a world they would never see again.[2] Not only did they leave behind their families and communities, their friends, their style of life, and the special possessions that symbolize home for each individual, but the continuity the past offers to the present was instantly severed.

Surviving any experience that claims the life of a loved one is filled with intense emotions. Surviving an experience that involves the slaughter of millions, including one's entire family and circle of friends, would be overwhelming. We can also speculate that although they themselves were safe, there were many complicated emotions to handle about not knowing what was happening to their respective families in Europe.[3] The impact of these events and the manner in which they were handled by each of Carol's parents influenced them many years later when they sent Carol, at age five, away to summer camp.

To their extreme burdens was added the challenge of survival in a new world. When Carol's mother and father met, they had much in common, making a bittersweet new beginning possible in the midst of their personal turmoil. After they married, the newlyweds lived on the upper west side of Manhattan amidst the refugee culture created by European Jews, also escapees from the horrors of Nazism.

Carol, the second daughter, was born several years after the war was over, in a time of increased stability and material comfort for the family. They moved to Long Island when she was five years old. The family style valued routine and order. "Dinner was always a three-course meal served at six o'clock on a table set with a linen tablecloth and napkins. Until I was six my sister and I ate separately from our parents. We joined them later at coffee and dessert."

Although Carol's parents had long delayed disclosure of the events that profoundly altered their lives, their unarticulated losses were communicated in subterranean ways. Carol had several recurring images in dreams, one of which was of a little girl wandering around with an empty suitcase in her hand. She grew up feeling her parents' fears without their ever having been directly expressed.[4] "Because I'm Jewish I can never feel as if I fully belong. I can never trust that it couldn't go on here."

As Carol recounted her parents' stories, it suddenly became important that I, too, am a Jew. Although we have shared this ethnic heritage all along, we had not discussed it. Now, being Jewish meant I would understand and Carol could safely reveal her thoughts and emotions. She, too, had minimized and denied the impact of these events that had shaped all their lives.[5]

Conditioned by the cultural belief system and the patterns evident in her family, Carol learned to attach more value to men's experiences than to women's. Like many of the other daughters, she was accustomed to perceiving the importance of events external to the family through their effect on her father. She had never considered the effect on her mother, but criticized her teachings: "Nothing is wrong. You can manage. Why are you upset?" It had not occurred to Carol that her mother's coping patterns might be a result of handling the emotional aftermath of having been uprooted from her life at a vulnerable age and forced to immediately adjust to a totally new environment, language, and group of people.

However, she made excuses for her moody, hard to please father and felt responsible, especially as a young girl, for his unhappiness. It was her duty to try to make him happy. "I had the fantasy that I could make Daddy happy. I should try harder, I wasn't good enough. Now I understand he couldn't express happiness."[6]

Uprooted from Home

Following the sharing of this important family history, a previously recounted pivotal childhood event was more fully
remembered. When Carol was five years old, she had been sent
to summer camp with Monica, her eight-year-old sister.
Separated from her mother, and then, at camp, from Monica,
Carol was miserable. She cried so much that the counselors finally placed her in her sister's group. She began to feel better.

Carol attended this camp for many summers. That first summer, while the sisters were away, their parents moved to Long
Island—leaving the refugee culture behind. Carol never saw that
apartment again. "I felt as if I had to give up those roots overnight." Coincidentally, soon after relating this, Carol moved into
a new apartment. She began to feel very upset. At first she could
not understand why. Then, she realized that she had never
mourned these significant early losses—separating from her
mother at camp and moving out of her first home.

In prior recollections, Carol had fiercely defended her
mastery of the experience at summer camp. "I really did make
it, and all other separations from home have been easy." As
camp memories were unburied, however, Carol's emotions also
were unlocked. She acknowledged that it could be hard for a
little child to be separated from her parents. "My mother
couldn't cope so I got sent away—and I can't cope. How could
she do this?" Carol stepped into the darkness. She voiced feeling
hurt, angry, and very needy. It made her anxious to say out
loud, "I did cope, but I paid a big price."

Imagining a little girl with her camp trunk, Carol touched
her panic. "My mother said she told me about summer camp,
but I'm sure she left out that she wasn't going too." Carol began
to sob. She cried for a long time then—until she got into Monica's
cabin. She recollected there were several other five-year-olds. "I
don't know if they also cried. I think not. It makes me feel as

if I failed at the task of being a big girl. I should have made it." At that point in therapy, incapable of accepting that the task was too big for her, Carol still put herself down. Not only did she anticipate being censured, but it was not yet possible to acknowledge how miserable she had felt, left to cope alone with an experience too overwhelming for her to handle.

A few sessions later, more was offered: "I have no choice but to cope. No one is home. My parents go away every summer. Being sent to camp feels like being abandoned. I can't give language to my hurt, it's that vast."

More than a year would pass before Carol could deepen her awareness of her complex reactions to the time spent at summer camp. "Yes, it hurt and I didn't like it, but I turned that around against my mother: I'd show her. I disliked her. For years I went around feeling anxious, but now it's clear. It did hurt. I didn't like it. How could she leave me? It was long enough to feel like forever. I didn't trust them when they came back not to do that to me again—and they did. I'm not going to show my hurt. I stopped caring."

Carol had been unconscious about how much this ancient hurt pained her. However, its presence was betrayed by an exquisite sensitivity to separations from loved ones. Carol did not trust that people would remain close, be there for her. When she sensed a threat to her attachment to important people, she became anxious. Her very existence felt jeopardized. To avoid this disabling dread, Carol relied on survival tactics learned early in her girlhood. Denial and anger protected her from knowing the intensity of her feelings. Additionally, she put much energy into making relationships work. Pleasing others is insurance against abandonment. With such overwhelming threats to her security, Carol could not previously even give form to what she now can say: "It's need. I needed my mother and I never wanted to admit that. This time, it doesn't feel so hard. I don't feel good about myself without her. That's the hard part because I'm getting all confused. Red lights are going on inside. My defenses are up."

The Emotional Repertoire Expands

"You can't be the mother I never had. You can't give me what I want."
"If I can't give you what you never had does that mean you can't take advantage of what I can give?"
"I never thought of it like that."

Having bought the tough, big-girl stance: "I can do it. I'll manage," Carol did not have many options for expressing her emotions. "I don't know how to let on about the fears. I went through a terrible adolescence fighting all my fears and never telling anyone. I felt I had to do it alone." Carol gained her father's approval and respect for her attitude. It also kept her yearnings for nurturance, signs she associated with weakness within herself, at a distance. However, as therapy proceeded and Carol's complex emotional life became more evident to her, she was more willing to examine these attitudes.

Pregnant with her first child, Carol worried about handling the changes the baby would make in her life: her career, her relationship with her husband and with her business partner. She experienced a rush of pressure to fix it all up before the baby was born. Unable to manage on her own the apprehension she was feeling, Carol projected. "I'm afraid the baby will be a chain around my neck and keep me a prisoner in the house."

Becoming clear that she was avoiding feeling helpless, Carol then backed off. "This is big. Too much is happening." She began to intellectualize, a tactic often employed when she was feeling overwhelmed and wanting a respite from the intensity of her emotions. "It still feels like they'll take over and I won't be okay. Yet, as I'm talking, I see I'm just having fears. It's okay to tell them to someone else. It's like acknowledging my feelings." Carol then enabled herself to move deeper into her feelings. "Once when I needed my mother and she didn't come, I felt afraid. I feel scared again, now, wondering how the baby will affect my life."

Finding it difficult to tolerate her feelings of helplessness, Carol subtly shifted the conversation. She expressed concern that handling her feelings by herself could result in "a break in our connection." I responded to this concern, removing the focus from her discomfort, and momentarily Carol was relieved from dealing with her feelings of helplessness. It took one more session for the discounted feelings to gain fuller expression. "That's the biggy. Letting on I need help. That's always been hard for me because it just wasn't done in my family. We lived in an unreal world. There never were any problems or normal concerns, like I might need help. Needing help meant something was wrong with me. I was a failure."

Having articulated this, Carol realized that she was trying to control and organize everything so that she could avoid talking about her fears and feelings of helplessness. She was anxious about having to ask for help during her labor and the delivery of the baby.

CHAPTER 7

ACQUIRING TRUST

Carol does not wear a watch and I do not have a clock in my office; I use my wristwatch to monitor the end of the therapy hour. Early in the therapy, Carol acknowledged that "when the hour is up, it's hard to pull it all in and go on." She asked me to let her know when the hour is close to ending.

As we investigated this concern, Carol revealed: "Your keeping the time feels like you're making a connection to me. It wouldn't feel the same if I did it. I would feel unloved. The thread is breaking when time is up. It's easier to bear if you tell me: 'Time is up.' If I do it for myself it will feel empty. Like you don't care."

My monitoring the hour relieved Carol of experiencing her feelings about *both* being responsible for keeping track of the hour herself and the emptiness she experienced as it ended. Soon after, Carol brought a small clock into the therapy room and placed it beside her. While a significant step toward managing her emotions for herself, this timepiece was also symbolic. It took two years to understand all its meanings.

Very Vulnerable Feelings

Carol's dreams, always sturdy allies, provided access to memories and emotions normally unavailable to her. A series of dreams afforded us rich opportunities to more deeply explore Carol's sensitivities and anxieties about separations. "I'm scared to go away from home. I always have separation anxiety but I never want to admit it. I've never liked going away." A long silence. "I'm not allowed the panic. It just doesn't exist. I don't know how to describe what's going on."

I expressed surprise, "You've just expressed the panic, but it seems as if there's nothing to hang it onto."

A long pause. "That must be it because I can't understand you. I want to be able to have my emotions. Big. Full. Whatever they are, but I can't. Or I won't. Maybe I'm still so angry with my mother for not letting me. Or maybe it's my way to stay connected to her. I wanted closeness with my mother for so long but I guarded against it. It feels very hard to admit that I spent my whole life denying it."

Soon after, aided by a dream, Carol was able to recognize that through her pretense that everything was okay, her anxiety about separation remained concealed. If that was not effective enough, she resorted to anger. Carol reflected: "It crossed my mind that I'm angry with you to avoid my feelings about your vacation. I'm angry about your going. I don't like it. Can that be what's going on with my mother? I didn't like her going away!"

Next time, one week before my announced vacation, Carol walked into the therapy room without her timepiece. She had misplaced it. In exploring what this meant, Carol admitted this was a subtle tug for my attention just before the vacation. "I can say go away, I'll be fine. Then I don't have to deal with this. That's my way of saying I'm angry. When I'm angry it's as if I don't exist. I'm banished."

Then Carol further acknowledged feeling very frightened and upset. My leaving was experienced as banishment. However, unable to stay with that sensitivity, she became angry with me. "Go away. I'll be fine" was protection from her overwhelming emotions. Upon hearing herself Carol recognized her old pattern, fogging over when the feelings were very intense and thus losing them. The anxiety created by feeling banished and telling me she was angry were too much to handle. "I'll be fine" skillfully disguised everything.

After I returned it was safer for Carol to express how angry she had been with me for going away. She quipped, "You're probably sorry you're back. Next time it'll be longer. A lot happened while you were gone. I missed you." Having expressed herself, Carol again became anxious that I would leave her. It was not okay to reveal either vulnerable or angry feelings.

In the following session the pieces came together. "I couldn't handle it. It was too big for me. It's not fair, I was too small. How could my mother have done this to me? I've been betrayed. It was all lies. She never told me the full picture about camp, but I must have sensed she wasn't coming back for a long time."

Carol was sobbing. A long silence. She did not want to feel these feelings. "It hurts too much. It's too big." She tried to get away from them by changing the subject. I remained silent. Carol said: "When you don't say anything, I have to acknowledge these are my issues and I have to do something about them." She continued: "It's the connection to my parents. Being Jewish. Their experiences leaving Europe. Their pain and terror at being uprooted from home, and losing all that was familiar. That's exactly my experience at camp. It's really their experience. Although nothing was ever said, it was all around."

Her childhood years in the refugee culture were recalled. She recollected feeling "shipped off, waiting for something dreadful to happen," when she went to a summer camp that was only for the children of European Jewish refugees. The head counselor was described as a tough German woman, strict, authoritarian, militaristic: "A perfect Nazi." Camp was regimented and disciplined, well planned and organized.[1]

Deeply moved by these memories, Carol declared: "My father tells me never to forget that I'm Jewish. How could I? I'm carrying this around for them. They must have been so angry at what happened. That too was never expressed."[2]

What Has Never Been Expressed

Consider what has never been expressed. Political events in Germany distressed and placed the lives of all Jews in jeopardy. As the Nazis stepped up their campaign to deny Jews their rights and benefits, they were simultaneously destroying the social and emotional fabric essential for individuals to adapt to a crisis. No one knew what might happen from one day to the next when Carol's mother's parents sent her to safety and Carol's father left his homeland. Would this departure from all that was familiar be temporary? Permanent? It was frightening and overwhelming.[3]

There was no time for feelings of sadness and loss. Squirrel them away because they were too much to handle. The moment can barely be tolerated. Sometimes denial of overwhelming anxiety, which may begin as a conscious process, becomes unconscious. That is what makes denial so effective. Moreover, emotional numbness aids individuals in extreme crisis.

The pressure to make a safe plan probably persuaded Carol's mother's parents to discount their emotions. To have appreciated their daughter's anxieties about embarking on a journey to a totally different world, far from her family's support, and to have indulged their own, would have been most unusual. Unaccustomed to scattering their children to foreign lands, these parents faced a terrifying reality. Everyone's existence was endangered.

Carol's mother never mourned the losses endured during those trying years in exile: separated from her parents and siblings, forced out of her familiar life, and then—waiting. Waiting without knowing what was going on back home with the people whom she cared most about created a situation of extreme loneliness and isolation. To cope with those hardships she buried her feelings and denied their import. Because her own feelings were buried, Carol's mother could not appreciate what Carol had to manage at summer camp.

To understand her daughter's experience, this mother would have had to remember her own. Moreover, just as her parents were undoubtedly relieved that they could send their daughter to safety, Carol's mother no doubt thought only that summer camp would be a place where Carol would have fun. Thoughts of "doing the best for our daughter" provided the rationale for not exploring the intense feelings engendered by separations from loved ones—children from parents, parents from children.

Carol's father grappled with different, but equally sensitive, issues. He chose to leave. His family did not. He survived. They did not. This is a very painful and difficult reality. Guilt, a defense against wrestling more fully with mourning the loss of the dead relatives, can also be an expression of loyalty to the dead. According to Danieli, guilt also "keeps both generations engaged in relationships with those who perished."[4]

The enormity of the Holocaust induces pain and rage. It also engenders utter helplessness in people as they grapple with comprehending a catastrophe beyond imagination. Both those who were killed and those who survived have been traumatized. What does one do with such intense emotions? Silence keeps the lid on everything.[5] In denying his own distress, Carol's father could not imagine anyone else's. He, too, was unable to comprehend that summer camp could upset his daughter.

Once Carol revealed her family's history, the magnitude of the forces that wounded both parents became clear. They were equally impaired in their sensitivity to separation and loss; however, Carol made excuses only for her father's shortcomings. Her mother's inability to provide what Carol needed was never linked with her past experiences.

Amy and Jackie, whose stories are told in later chapters, grew up in families that were also importantly affected by events associated with World War II. Although their mothers were significantly involved in key wartime events, only their fathers' experiences were notable to them.

These responses focus attention on an important theme that is often overlooked. Major social and political events equally affect women and men. Nevertheless, the primary medium through which the events are recounted is the experience of men. The discounting of women as individuals is so pervasive that even though they have participated and been profoundly affected by important events, they and their contributions often remain invisible.[6]

The Relationship with Mike

Carol met Mike at a professional meeting; soon they became lovers. They lived together for two years and then decided to get married. Trained by her upbringing to discount her unmet needs because they made others uncomfortable, and conditioned to believe that once she was married a man's love and devotion would take care of all her needs, it was automatic for Carol to assume greater responsibility for making the marriage work.

"I'm supposed to pay attention to the relationship. That's what I saw my mother do."

Any needs separate and distinct from those met by the relationship made her anxious; it meant something was wrong with Carol. By depending on Mike's love and presence to feel good about herself, Carol kept herself from accepting the validity of her different needs and the necessity to express them.

Whenever Mike was absent from home longer than planned, Carol experienced panic. She felt unloved and abandoned. Her sensitivity to, and anxiety about, separation fueled by her joint legacies—a child of Holocaust survivors and her own experience of early parental abandonment—contributed to Carol's denial of her feelings. She did not expect they would be sympathetically received. It had not occurred to her that unless she took responsibility for making her needs known, they could not be adequately addressed.

Mike had a problem with cocaine. A regular user, he had grown more furtive about this habit; it was also very expensive. For a long time Carol denied the extent of his use because it made her very unhappy. Acknowledging the severity of Mike's addiction meant facing her fear that he could not be counted on to take care of her. "It feels catastrophic to lose this relationship. Pieces are missing inside of me and Mike provides them for me. Because of that I'm too dependent on him. I don't know how to do this on my own: Take care of me and love me. Be alone."

When Mike was on drugs Carol would not let on directly that his behavior offended and upset her. "He can't care for me when he's crazy." She was afraid that if Mike knew how awful she really felt, he would not love her. The situation became worse and Carol became scared; she also felt embarrassed that this was happening to her. "I'm caught between a rock and a hard place. No one has ever loved me before and I don't want to lose that. My heart is breaking. I don't want to live without Mike. I wish I had the strength of character to tell him it's me or drugs. But I don't want to lose what I've got."

Months later Carol reported that Mike had stopped using cocaine. Hidden fears now surfaced. "What will I do if he can't maintain this?" It was evident that Carol found it hard to be with Mike when he was on drugs. Yet when he was not, Mike became so quiet and withdrawn that Carol hardly knew him. She felt responsible for keeping him happy. "I live with him. It's my job to keep him happy. If he's not happy it's my fault." Experiences with both her parents had taught Carol that love was earned by adapting to their demands and submerging hers. If something went wrong, it must be because she had misread the signals. Moreover, conditioned as she was to deny her own emotions while trained to pay heightened attention to Mike's, Carol's feelings of panic, helplessness, and anger were totally concealed in taking care of Mike.

Six months later, after a fight with Mike over his use of cocaine, Carol reported: "This time Mike said,'You know, Carol, if I quit taking drugs I may leave you.' I answered, 'I'll take that risk.'" Although feeling blackmailed, Carol stood her ground. New behavior brought ancient fears forward: "There's a little girl place that feels I can't get connected to anyone. Everyone else is connected but me. If you leave or if Mike leaves me I'm afraid. Lost. It's as if I stop being. In those moments when someone is gone I'm in absolute panic. I don't know what to do. I'm all alone until you or he comes back. I can't think. I can't be adult. I'm helpless. There's nothing I can do except hope someone comes back.

"It's my old childhood stuff. I can't get my needs met. I'm helpless and resourceless. Asking for help feels like I've really failed. It has to be real desperate before I can do that."

A few weeks later Carol decided that if she did not tackle the drug problem the marriage would end. We had some conversations about the best way to proceed. At first Carol chose to read a book I recommended about cocaine addiction: Joanne Baum's *One Step Over the Line. A No-Nonsense Guide to Recognizing and Treating Cocaine Dependency* (1985, San Francisco: Harper & Row). Later she talked with a counselor at a community agency that specializes in problems of drug abuse.

Fortified with knowledge and an expanded awareness of the consequences of continued denial, Carol gained the clarity and strength she required. She began conversations with Mike that broke the denial of the problems they had both been practicing. Carol told Mike how she felt and what she experienced because of this problem. She invited him to do the same. Several weeks later, Mike enrolled in a drug rehabilitation program. The situation began to change.

Several months later Mike had stopped his dependence most of the time. Although optimistic, Carol remained very alert. After expressing tender feelings of love for him, Carol became quiet. She was sad, experiencing regret about what had not been possible with Mike while he abused drugs. There was an uncharacteristic long silence. Finally I asked, "What's happening now?"

"I was feeling mad at you. Then I realized I'm not accustomed to being so vulnerable with women. I can't do that with my mother. I'm more comfortable being vulnerable with Mike." A long pause. "In telling you, my own feelings get acknowledged. If I stay quiet I don't have to face them."

Many months later Carol shared her happiness. She felt great! Mike had completely stopped using drugs. Carol appreciated that she had been able to risk a painful loss with the help of therapy. "This is an arena for exploration and change."

Alpine Tundra

I used to think I'd come to therapy and get rid of all my bad feelings, but it doesn't work like that. I'm still learning that I'll have bad feelings all my life.

We walked on alpine tundra during the last months of therapy. Carol wanted my protection because she felt vulnerable and insecure when her intense feelings surfaced. "How can I feel the very feelings I've always carried in the back of my head and felt afraid of?" When she could not manage the strength of her emotions, Carol retreated to old patterns: blaming her mother, blaming me. While very angry about what she never had in the past, Carol still had difficulty in both feeling her anger and letting go of it. She was aware of holding onto grudges and wanting revenge. She was also very sad about the lack of a strong, nurturant connection between herself and her mother. Carol was stuck. She did not want to feel either the anger or the sadness. In the meantime, she clung to the fantasy of a perfect relationship with her mother: She'll do just what I want. Be just the way I want her to be. "If I give that up I have to love and accept myself. I know I can. I have the resources, but when these issues get going I forget that. Just at that moment, when I mentioned giving up the fantasy I wanted to turn to you and ask, 'Will you be there?' Then I realized I have to give this to myself."

After becoming quite angry and yelling at her mother in the therapy room, Carol decided to talk to her. "I'm afraid to tell my mother that she's important to me. Not that I'm angry with her or that I love her, but she's important. Yet as I say it, it sounds stupid. Of course she's important." As Carol contemplated doing this, old anxieties surfaced. The needy little girl who felt she had never been given enough was granted permission to reenter. The burden of being grown up and responsible was too big to bear for a little girl. Carol retreated from both her observations and feelings; she wanted help. "I can't stay here alone." I questioned what was happening. Carol was reaching out to me to mute the intensity of her feelings. This time, I pointed out how this robbed Carol of the opportunity to trust herself to handle her feelings.

Intense yearnings to be taken care of and held by an ideal mother spilled out into the room. Carol sobbed. She realized she never had gotten enough, but actually had pretended and worked hard at not needing anything. "It felt like a weakness to be gotten over." It is difficult to accept the legitimacy of yearnings that might never be filled.

Two weeks later we approached the fear of being banished. "I was ignored or punished for anger. It was terrible. It hurt a lot." Disbelieving that her feelings could ever go away, Carol cut them off. "I've said this all before. Nothing is new." Having said that, however, next time Carol went right on. She was experiencing the pain and felt very alone—abandoned by both parents. Dad reentered, along with memories of his moody, argumentative behavior. He picked on her. Frequently they fought. "I could never argue with him. He was always right. He said a lot of cruel things that hurt for a long time. Anger was never the legitimate expression of an emotion. It was dangerous. I was banished for being angry. I felt powerless and humiliated."

The remembered fights with Dad brought up additional feelings. "My mother didn't help me with him. Why didn't she do anything about it? I was too small to handle all that stuff. I had to deal with both summer camp and his criticisms all alone. He was the judge. He determined my self-esteem. I had none without his approval."

Carol realized that she had built a whole universe to escape this pain. "It's mine and I'm responsible for it. It's like putting on a new pair of glasses. It's the end of childhood."

Trusting Herself

A few days later, still uncertain about managing her emotions alone and wary about acknowledging how difficult this could be, Carol forgot her clock. Monitoring the time had offered Carol protection and control over her intense feelings. By forgetting her timepiece, she could depend on me. I would tell her when the hour was up. Carol was indirectly communicating her anxiety about dealing with her emotions all by herself.

One afternoon soon afterward, aware that the hour was up, Carol felt she would fly apart. She became tearful. "I hate it when time is up." Asking me the time short-circuited her panic. "I can't tolerate that ending and I do many things to cope with it. However, in the midst of those feelings, I did become aware that I could wait. That was very useful."

Now, the underlying feelings of helplessness came forward. They had been concealed in the panic and confusion. Carol then shifted to blaming her mother in her effort to downplay what she was feeling. I commented that she did not seem able to let herself *just be* with her feelings. Carol stopped. "I get it: I can accept my feelings."

Several months later, Carol observed: "Yesterday I didn't keep track of the time and it felt fine. My initial reaction when you said that time was up was surprise. It was really okay. I didn't feel left hanging or confused.

"Afterward, walking down the street, I thought that there has been a fair amount of time-keeping. Trusting you, trusting me, to keep control over my feelings. I guess I can trust me to take whatever comes up here.

"Then I felt a twinge of anger. I didn't want to own all my feelings and separate from you, which now does feel appropriately tender. However, I no longer need to involve you in my feelings. I can handle them for myself."

CHAPTER 8

PROTECTING THE FATHER

Dad was the source of strength in the family. I don't want to know what he can't do. It must be awful if he can't do it. I need to protect and defend my father because he was my foundation. If he's wrong my world will crumble.

Miriam

I loved my father a lot when I was a little girl. He was great! But from the time I was twelve things got bad. He couldn't deal with me growing up, maturing sexually, and having a mind of my own. He tried to squelch me.

Laura

Daughters who had routinely denied that complying with their fathers' expectations had consequences to themselves had much to tell. Experiences and emotions that previously had been dismissed were recalled. "I was tough around my father and he admired me for that, but I covered up how miserable I was a good bit of the time." Memories reawakened and long-stifled

117

disappointments finally found their voice as the clients acquired more trust in themselves and respect for their own emotional responses. "My father wasn't really interested in what I wanted." "I never felt loved by him."

Their highly esteemed fathers turned out to have some rather startling flaws. "I don't recall too many carefree times. He was hollering at us all the time." "I knew all the rules and expectations, and they were not violated. But my father raked my emotions over the coals." Several of the extolled fathers had sometimes not known what was best for either themselves or their daughters. A few had been unsuccessful, mismanaging both their own lives and the family's finances. "I was twenty before I realized that my father was a real failure and took all his frustrations out on us." Several fathers were harsh and judgmental toward those around them, blaming other people for their troubles. "I always heard, 'People are full of shit. No one really knows anything.'"

Some of these revered, hardworking fathers were also miserable, grumpy men who pushed forward with one hand and held back with the other, devaluing their daughters. "He preached, 'Even if you tried, it wouldn't work out.'" These were very stubborn, angry men, some of whom constantly harped on their daughters' faults but rarely dwelled on their strengths. "I wasn't allowed to be a person and stick up for myself. I couldn't even have an idea without his messing it up. So, of course, I think something is wrong with me if my ideas are challenged."

A few daughters remained reluctant to accept that their idol had limitations. "Dad can't fail because it's too scary to realize he can't get me some things." Many wished that it could have been different and became angry with their fathers for not being different. "While Dad was always optimistic, hoping to make it better, in reality nothing changed."

The fathers demonstrated the consequences of overvaluing a tough veneer, so common among men in this culture. Stifled, the vulnerable and unpleasant emotions that are part of daily routine could not find an appropriate outlet. This not only reduced the father's options for self-expression but also forced him to disguise the full range of his emotions. Daughters who cultivated that same style to mask their sensitivities also disguised their complexities. Although that might effectively conceal the pain at having been discounted, that pain did not go away. These survival skills presented obstacles to a woman seeking an appropriate balance between revealing her emotions and containing them.

Anna, who worshipped her father as her hero, later revealed that he was also a scared, anxious man. He had cautioned her: "Don't go beyond the immediate neighborhood. That's all that's safe." His attitudes had strongly affected Anna. "I've always been terrified of taking risks even though I've acted as if I wasn't."

In examining this, Anna became angry with her father for not presenting a more adventurous stance. "My self-effacing father couldn't stand up to anyone. He taught: 'Wait. Don't make waves. Opportunity will come to you.' But it hadn't come to him." Anna remembered that when her father did not get a deserved promotion, he did not protest. He absorbed it all. "As the token Jew it was his fault."

Then Anna recollected an incident that her father had told her about his boyhood in Europe. With just the clothes on their backs he and his family fled from a pogrom that destroyed their entire village. Her father had learned then that being Jewish "made you afraid of the world." It could be dangerous.

While often wanting to protect their children from what they had experienced, some fathers misdirected their anger and unarticulated pain at the family. That made it even more impossible for the child to understand that her father was suffering himself.

Amy walked on eggshells throughout her childhood. She was trying to make it okay for everyone in the family so that her father would not rage at them so often. She barely disguised her own unhappiness, severe anxiety, and anger. "If I gave in to how unhappy I felt I'd have been destroyed."

One day, in therapy, she discussed a letter she had recently reread. This letter had been written by her father to his boss describing their life in the relocation camp.[1] "When I used to read that letter I felt pleased at how articulate my father was. He was taking care of business. Now, rereading it, it broke my heart. I never focused on his anxiety. If you read between the lines, he's anxious as hell about our safety and health. He was keeping a smiling face, but he was afraid. He swallowed his pride. It damaged him."

Don't Get Daddy Upset

If you didn't see it his way you were blasted.

Alice

I could never stand up to my dad and win an argument. *Never.* Not once.

Laura

These daughters had always paid close attention to their fathers' lives, often describing them in much richer detail than those of their mothers. I came to understand that they had paid careful attention to their fathers because it was dangerous not to. Many of them were frightened of their fathers and tried to steer clear of their unpredictable, volatile behavior. Even though it frequently disabled the entire family, everyone had accommodated to the fathers' behavior. It was never questioned. "It was like the air you breathed. That's what I knew."

When there was a disagreement between a daughter and her father, the majority of my clients reported that the father had used anger to uphold his authority. For the most part, a daughter's different opinions or ideas were resoundingly dismissed. A thoughtful discussion of their differences was rare. "If you spoke back he'd punish or belittle you. So you shut up." Rather than run the risk of provoking the fathers' anger, which was described as unyielding, cruel, and devastating, these women blunted their initiative and curtailed their self-expression. "I never found out what I wanted. I was too scared not to do what he wanted."

Only the father was allowed to be angry. If other family members expressed anger they would be cut short, belittled, or punished by the father. "He used to call me Miss Malcontent. I didn't know what it meant, but I knew it was bad." Several fathers relied on derisive name-calling to keep their daughters in line. "He called me 'commie' just because I didn't like his ideas." "I was a tramp for disagreeing with him." Some got banished from the family for being angry. "When I was an adolescent Dad wouldn't hear my outbursts. I was told, 'Those aren't your feelings. You're acting like a baby.' Then I was sent to my room."

In general, the father's opinion settled the matter and closed the conversation. "My father was an autocrat. He decided everything." The daughters quickly learned it was pointless to pursue their own agenda. "You could never argue with him. He was always right."

Most of these daughters never had a chance to learn how to actively disagree, have the right to a different opinion, or tell their fathers they were angry and have that anger respected. "I was trained by my father in how never to win an argument."

Occasionally a father withdrew in stony silence, leaving the daughter feeling guilty because she had "ruptured" their alliance. "He'd walk away and not talk to me. I felt annihilated right in the room." Not only were disagreements very uncomfortable, but they threatened to sever this important connection. Whatever tactics these fathers employed, they all conveyed the

same message. "Don't get Daddy upset. There will be consequences."

Typical Incidents

Alice loved her yellow jacket. It was the only new jacket
she had ever received. "It was very special to have something
for myself." Soon afterward she overheard her father yelling at
her mother for having spent so much money for it. Alice never
wore her jacket again. "He spoiled it. I knew it made him so
angry."

Sara was 16; she was sitting in the kitchen trying to tell her
father something. "He wouldn't pay attention. So, I stuck my
hand over the flames on the stove. He still ignored me. Later I
told myself he ignored me because I had frightened him."

Even though both Alice and Sara knew that their fathers'
lack of responsiveness to them was upsetting, each denied her
own feelings and focused her attention on her father's discomfort. That action protected both the daughters and the fathers
from dealing with the daughters' sensitive feelings. The conditioning that trained daughters to regard their fathers' well-
being more highly than their own also instructed them to believe
that preserving relationships was more important than articulating one's needs—as if the two were incompatible. Self-expression
was definitely quashed in both daughters.

The fathers' lack of sensitivity fueled disappointment and
anger in their daughters. Yet these daughters made excuses for
their fathers' insensitivities. Women have been trained to adjust
their expectations rather than provoke conflict.

Besides sidestepping conflict, without her father's prompt-
ings neither daughter could acknowledge that her feelings were
hurt. That would have been an admission of weakness that each
assumed would be disrespected. The daughter's silencing of her

vulnerable feelings allowed her father to remain oblivious to what really went on. These daughters paid large penalties to uphold such disabling beliefs.

Terrifying Experiences

I know it hurt a lot but I don't feel any physical pain. I don't hear my cries, I only hear the strap.

Kim

As young girls, what several women witnessed was so terrifying that it had to be buried. Uncontrolled anger is not only frightening, it can also be very dangerous. Many of these fathers gave vent to terrifying outbursts of anger, which often led several of them to physically abuse family members. "Daddy is hollering at Mom about us kids, the fighting increased. He hit her. Then he knocked her down. I'm scared, puzzled, bewildered. I knew I wasn't supposed to see any of that."

A few of these women were clients for several years before they were able to tell me that they had been physically abused as children. "It's hard for me to own having been an abused child; although I have a lot of rootedness in that, I don't want to spend time on it now." Once reawakened to their own suffering, several daughters questioned their father's power over the family. "Who gave him the right to treat us like his property?" "How could one person have so much power?"

While it is definitely very upsetting to reveal these extremely painful experiences, some dread lingered that the father's power could still be hurtful. "If Daddy were alive I don't think I'd be able to open this up. This is the family that didn't have any problems. No one ever talks about this—yet all of us were beaten."

Some of these women are currently in relationships with men who verbally or psychologically abuse them, though none are physically abused. The training to discount the validity of their own experience has been so thorough that it required sensitive, persistent questioning by me to ferret out whether there was cause for concern.

Incidents with either male lovers or male bosses do often provide the key to unlocking ancient memories of abusive experiences. "When a man yells at me all the buttons get pushed. I assume I'm really in trouble. A reflex occurs which makes me unable to communicate very well or deal with my feelings. I tap into the fear of my father. It's real heavy and scary."

It was especially interesting that whatever was going on right now was not perceived as frightening or dangerous; that did not arouse anxiety. The fear arose from the past relationship. Prompted by my questioning if she had told her husband just how frightened she became when he screamed at her, Kim reported in her following hour: "I was absolutely serious when telling him how frightened I was. I made sure that he got the message that I was scared when he screamed like that at me.

"Yet as I was telling Ralph this, I realized I wasn't afraid of him. I have no doubt that there is nothing to fear from him. The fear I have is very old. It's about my father's explosions."

No hurt equaled the one endured as a child. "I never understood why those things would happen. I know that whatever I did or said was innocent. I wasn't trying to be bad or mean."

Survival Strategies

Trained to survive in disabling conditions by not questioning them, my clients concealed their panic about what had occurred in their own homes. Despite the variety of different abuses endured, they all assumed it was their responsibility to handle these complex, explosive situations.

By being hypervigilant around their fathers, a few fought battles for the mothers. When Ellen's father began to viciously verbally abuse her mother, she felt called upon to intervene. In therapy she was able to recall feeling panicked, riveted to her chair. These repeated demeaning attacks generally happened at the dinner table at the end of the meal when Ellen's father had had too much to drink.

While Ellen's mother handled these outbursts by withdrawing in stony silence, Ellen often found herself trying to be helpful. "I was afraid that if I didn't do my part they would get divorced. I worked so hard to fix it, but it wouldn't fix."

By becoming responsible, rallying around the mother, comforting or playing with a crying sibling, several daughters bridled their own fears. Melissa grew up believing it was her responsibility to stop her father from becoming violent and battering her mother when he was drunk. Melissa's terrified mother used her and her older sister as shields against the father's violence. "Sometimes if we stayed close by he would leave her alone. Other times he'd push us out of the way or take her into another room and start hitting her."

As she talked, Melissa became aware of the heavy burdens she had carried and the dangerous role she and her sister had played trying to keep their father from abusing their mother. She experienced "avalanches" of panic and helplessness. "I can now feel the dread of never knowing what was going to happen. I feel battered and freaky, like something is wrong with *me* rather than with them. It's hard to admit my family was so crazy."

Other daughters could not recall their own fear. "I never thought of it." However, empathy for their brothers who were the more frequent targets of the fathers' wrath was typical. One woman remembered that after her brother had been beaten by her father, she went to her room and slammed the door as hard as she could, "to shake them up." Another woman noticed that her mother was browbeaten by her father's verbal abuse, but did not recognize that having to continually tiptoe around to assess her father's moodiness had any consequences for herself. "I thought I was protecting myself so he wouldn't get to me—but obviously he did."

Sometimes, they reproached themselves for not being more effective at halting the father's abuse. "I berated myself because I couldn't make him happy or secure so he wouldn't be so emotionally abusive of us." A few felt guilty for their strong feelings. "You're not supposed to hate your father." The training to associate their collection of intense emotions with shortcomings in themselves made acknowledging them even more difficult.

The Father Is Central

When Katherine was 16 she and her family had to face a disaster. Her father developed a brain tumor that required prolonged treatments in the hospital. She spent quite a few therapy sessions detailing the crises that accompanied her father's illness. "Here was this man, big and strong, provider and protector, who couldn't do anything for himself and it went on for months. It was so upsetting. I closed off to everything. I couldn't bear the burden. I wanted to be a rock so I wouldn't feel anything. It was so scary then. There was no money for food or rent. Our survival was at stake. It was awful and I was old enough to realize that."

Following the hospitalization her father was bedridden at home for many months. Several times the family thought he would die. He would never again work full time.

There is no question that these daily encounters with illness and death and the sudden change in the family circumstances, which necessitated applying for public welfare, deeply affected Katherine. It took another year of therapy, however, before she could recollect that this same father, whose suffering elicited much compassion in her, had regularly beaten all the children. "When my father was ill his helplessness was even more scary than ours. This man who beat all of us couldn't lift a finger."

She readily recalled that her father's illness changed the family's circumstances and profoundly affected her. "I was in high school, burgeoning forth with all sorts of possibilities, and there wasn't enough food at home. I had to have a stiff upper lip and be brave. I did without a lot of things. Dad getting sick, losing his job, and us growing poorer didn't help my self-esteem. It hurt a lot."

It was much more difficult to remember that the beatings had also damaged her, made her feel bad about herself and question her abilities. "It's taken a long time to see how my bad feelings about myself go back to those beatings."

Everyone relied and depended on this father for their sense of well-being. During his illness and convalescence, the family felt "lost without him." Waiting for her husband to resume his place as head of the household, Katherine's mother was reluctant to fill that role even temporarily. "I went around feeling helpless and powerless—lost. She must have too. It wasn't that Mom couldn't mentally and physically fill his role; it was emotional. She just couldn't take his place. All eight of us were lost."

Katherine's father had taught her to act tough and strong, as protection from the vulnerabilities that life dished up. That stance was so effective that it enabled Katherine to remain unconscious about how much the beatings both pained and terrified her.

Once she recalled her feelings, Katherine could no longer ignore mistreatment. She began to respond actively when either her boss or her lover, both of whom had volatile tempers, became verbally abusive. She realized that she did not have to wait for other people to change in order to change her own experience.

Perturbed with Their Mothers

A familiar tactic employed by many daughters of abusive fathers was to become very perturbed with their mothers. That enabled them to disregard the violence they witnessed and, sometimes, felt on their own bodies. "I've always wanted my mother to pick herself up and fight back. How can the world be okay if your father is beating your mother?" They wanted their mothers to have handled the fathers' outbursts more effectively. "My mother just took that crap. She didn't tell Daddy to lay off. She had power. He adored her. She could have made him shut up."

However, no mother was effective against the fathers' unpredictable explosions. "Mom was helpless and all three of us girls were helpless to confront my father's anger. She didn't seem to know how to do anything different. None of us did. We were each alone against him."

Criticizing the mother replicated familiar patterns. When something is amiss in the family, the mother is at fault. When unpleasant emotions erupted, the fathers usually vented their intense emotions on their wives or the children. What was really troubling them was never disclosed; their inability to manage their impulsive behavior was never addressed.

Typically, the majority of these daughters were able to express strong feelings about their mothers' passivity and powerlessness. "I could hate Mom because I wasn't afraid of her, but I couldn't hate Daddy." Their mothers provided a safe outlet for their anger. However, the daughters were never able to confront their fathers with their varied feelings. For the most part, the fathers remained unaware that their vicious behavior had deeply affected their daughters.

Although several fathers are now dead, intense feelings have remained very much alive within their daughters. "I feel sad and angry that one person had such power over a kid—to make you feel so crummy and for it to last so long in your life."

To have identified with their mothers' handling of these tense situations would have meant the daughters had acknowledged their shared predicament: the terror and helplessness experienced by both women. After reclaiming the memories of her father's physical abuse of her, one woman said: "My mother was weak as mothers traditionally are, and I'm angry with her for not intervening with my father. But she couldn't have done anything short of removing herself and us. My father was totally nuts."

Even if these mothers had been able to respond differently, and could have demonstrated choices for their daughters, they are not responsible for the fear and intimidation aroused by the fathers' behavior. The fathers are. Their inability to handle and control their anger tyrannized and disabled the entire family. "My bad feelings about myself go back to those beatings. I never understood what I'd done wrong. I felt so ashamed and guilty." "Dad's anger was horrible. He said many cruel things that hurt for a long time afterward. I hated it. The whole family was broken up over it."

Abusive behavior creates intense fear, which is immobilizing. It is extremely difficult to think strategically and act decisively while being mistreated. Also, if prior experience demonstrates that expressing oneself leads only to more abuse, silence may be a prudent survival strategy.

Complex Problems

The failure of these mothers and daughters to see the commonality of their struggle, and to join together to tell the fathers that their behavior was terrifying and totally unacceptable, attests to the intimidating effects on women of men's power. To safeguard themselves, women have learned to minimize their experiences and turn their attention to preserving harmony in their relationships with men. Many daughters had not realized how much they distorted their reality to keep the peace. "I see now how I can make nice when it isn't."

Even though many fathers behaved inappropriately, the majority of their daughters had not realized how damaging that had been. It had not occurred to them that they had the right to be respected and receive fair, safe treatment. When I questioned what else could have been going on to interfere with realizing that, a woman usually then acknowledged her terror. It could descend without warning and be experienced all over her body. "I was in physical pain, afraid, and crying. I couldn't control it."

These are very complex problems, and that complexity has been accentuated by the acceptance of violence to settle conflict. Men's privileged status and the power and influence that they have commanded have permitted that standard to exist unchallenged until recently. The minimizing of more finely crafted communication skills, which require practice to be effective, has enabled men's abusive treatment of women and children to continue. The institutions of law and order have protected male privilege rather than enforcing justice.

When women have dared to challenge this injustice, they often have been made to feel responsible for men's abusive behavior. That not only discounts the women's experience but also undermines their self-assertion. The institutions we have been trained to revere have not offered women protection and support for speaking out. It is not surprising that many have kept silent about their suffering.

No Model for Dealing with Anger

I learned how not to be angry. The only way I can be angry is
to cry. I never confront. I know how to sweet-talk and can be
very good at that. That's not very direct.

Carol

The more a daughter had witnessed violent and abusive behavior, the more frightened she was that she, too, would behave
similarly when angry. "Will my own anger turn to violence right
away because of the fighting I saw between my parents?" A
few women were thoroughly convinced that their own not very
"feminine" anger must be suppressed at all costs. It was too
dangerous. If their outrage at having been mistreated were expressed, could they control it?

Our lack of experience of verbally, directly expressing anger
and handling conflict through mutual compromising, agreeing
to disagree, and cooling off by allowing the situation to remain
unsettled has trained most of us to be fearful of the power of
anger. Lacking opportunities to manage the discomfort of this
strong emotion without either suppressing it or resorting to
physical force, many clients were prompted to resort to other
tactics. "I've had a lot of practice indirectly expressing anger,
not being sexual, being bitchy, snide, cold—but I don't know
how to directly express it." A few realized that it can feel very
satisfying to experience the power of anger—without hurting
anyone else. "Anger is beaming a focused light."

The conditioning of women to fear and shun their own and
another's anger and value accommodation is not enabling. These
women, like many others, did not know that one can acquire
more suitable, safe tools for handling conflict. Amy recollected
that she had never seen her mother angry, whereas her father
constantly "shot from the hip and didn't care what he did. At my
worst, I'm like that too. I hate it, but I didn't learn any other way."

What was most familiar was discounting their own feelings. "I hadn't had an opportunity to explain what was happening and he went into a tirade. I clicked him off. I didn't want to get into a big thing with the children around. I thought to myself, go away, stay quiet, but inside I was angry."

Often, these women coped with, and even made excuses for, their male partner's inability to constructively express anger. They did not believe it prudent to assert their displeasure, stand their ground, and insist that people fight fair. For some, their own feelings of powerlessness and their rage at having to deal with impossible tasks remained diffuse, sometimes turned against themselves. "When I'm trying the best I can and he shuts me down—I'm afraid to persevere. I feel hot inside. Rejected and angry. I don't trust myself not to overreact and I withdraw." "I become angry with myself and accuse myself of being a bad person. I've totally forgotten I'm angry with him."

Expressing Anger

I don't even imagine I can confront a bad situation. I'm stuck. Numb. When I'm angry I don't know what to do about it.

Anna

Occasionally, anger burst forth in the therapy room, but more typically it stole in, surprising the women; they had not realized that it was the emotion they were struggling not to express. Usually tone of voice and body posture announced its presence before the client was able to verbally declare and emotionally connect to her feelings.

In therapy most women learned to recognize and cope with their anger. They realized they were not bad people and did not have to stifle themselves because they were feeling this strong emotion. They could just say they were angry. Like all new behavior, this felt very uncomfortable and took practice to get used to. "Expressing anger is like finding a new muscle—a source of strength you didn't know was there. I was told, and later told myself, I shouldn't be angry. But it felt so good to express it, it surprised me."

The most meaningful test came when a woman felt angry with me and told me. Some were anxious that if they revealed their anger I would retaliate by refusing to continue our work together. That would have confirmed their dread that expressing anger severed important connections. "In my family no one was angry. We discussed and were disappointed. If I'm angry they'll leave me and then there won't be anyone to take care of me." The belief that one could be angry, have that anger heard and respected, and still be accepted for oneself was very fragile.

Managing Painful Disappointments

If Dad isn't my hero anymore, if he's just an ordinary guy, then I can't lean on or blame anyone else. I have to be responsible for myself.

                                                                    Anna

Despite the wide range of feelings about their fathers that came to be expressed in the therapy room, most of these daughters continued to yearn for a way to hold onto the closeness they had once shared as Daddy's obedient little girl. The few women who never had felt close to their fathers longed for the experience. "I'm always enchanted when I see little kids with their daddies. I wanted that so much." Some tried as adults to create what had been unavailable earlier. Often, it did not work out.

When Melissa was 12 her parents separated. A long battle over money, the house, and the children followed. Finally, they divorced. A real, permanent rift occurred between Melissa and her father, who soon remarried. She never felt comfortable again with him or his new family.

While in therapy Melissa was able to move beyond her anger with her father to other tender feelings associated with her father's departure and the breakup of the family. She felt very sad about her father's leaving. For the first time her buried pain found its voice. "I didn't really want that to happen." With tears rolling down her cheeks, Melissa continued: "I didn't want him to go. Why didn't he try harder so it could have worked out for us to be a family?"

The Death of a Father

Several women coped with the death of their fathers while they were in therapy. No matter what the daughter's relationship had been with her father, death reopened tender, unresolved issues that most daughters preferred to ignore.

Miriam's father's sudden death left her bereft. His mismanagement and neglect of his business affairs also bequeathed her and her mother a substantial financial mess. Miriam was furious and deplored his behavior. This prompted her to look more closely at this man she had idolized.

For the first time, she noticed that the way her father had managed both his finances and his health problems confirmed their shared patterns of stubborn denial and avoidance. When things got tough they both denied the gravity of the problems, each hoping the situation would change without taking responsibility themselves to change it.

Miriam's new awareness accentuated her depression. Not only did she have to cope with overwhelming feelings of sadness and loss brought on by her father's death, but she was also asked to help untangle his business affairs. Memories came back of an earlier loss; when she was 14, Miriam had tackled a different "mess." Her father had taken a job that required his being away from home. Miriam was left alone with her mother. "I hated it. I missed him so much, but I never let on. I couldn't let Dad know I needed him because that would have meant feeling the pain of his absence. I was afraid of alienating him. I already felt alienated from my mother.

"I haven't realized until now just how angry I was at his leaving me. I felt abandoned. Why wasn't he there for me? My whole life went into a decline. I had no zest and no social life. My grades slipped. Everything closed off."

Taking her cues from her father's silence, Miriam could not tell him how much this change was affecting her. Pretending that she could handle anything maintained the facade Miriam knew pleased her father. However, her unhappiness, like her anger with him for not being present, remained unaddressed. It was too risky to reveal feelings that her father might demean.

Pleasing him had always been a high priority. Miriam was unaware that stifling her unhappiness compromised her needs. In one therapy session, Miriam realized that even at age 14 she was busy protecting her father's feelings. They were more important than hers. "I worried about him." Of course, that's what she had been trained to do. If he was unhappy she would be too.

While these strategies successfully diverted Miriam from her own emotions, they also kept her father from knowing what was really going on for this daughter whom he loved. Although it might be true that Miriam could not get what she needed from her father, how could she know what he was prepared to acknowledge if she never asked? She was afraid to take that chance. Miriam was protecting herself from the derision she assumed her father would direct at her if she showed him feelings she knew he despised.

Real Painful

Laura and her father went through a long period of dishar-mony. They could not agree about anything. After Laura married and became a mother, she tried to approach her father as a more equal adult. However, he stubbornly insisted on his dominance. This alliance could not sustain a close connection based on mutual respect. "We were never close again."

Soon afterward, Laura's father died. Some months later she had this dream. "We were sitting on the couch like we used to when I was real young and he read to me. We're sitting there, now, as adults. He's old. We're just being there, close, like we used to be. It felt so good. I woke up convinced that he was alive and had come to make peace with me. I wanted to have him accept me as his daughter, an adequate adult. I wanted to love him as my father. But we couldn't do that."

About a year later, Laura walked into the therapy room very upset. A close friend was dying of cancer. Her sadness revived feelings about her father's death. Laura realized that it was hard to let go of important people. "I gave up on my dad long ago. He was never there for me, he never gave me support—at all. Although I stopped trying to please him, there's a hole in my heart. That will always be there. An emotional vacuum. It's not anger, it's pain. Real painful. Sad."

Reconciling Reality

The wish for an emotionally sensitive, effective father who would always be there, providing, is as fundamental and power-ful as the longing to be endlessly nurtured by the all-giving mother. These wishes are basic to the human condition and af-firm the power of that original attachment to our parents, reminding each of us of our dependence on other people to provide what is essential to survive.

The gradual unfolding of the relationships between these daughters and their fathers demonstrates how very complex it is to reconcile the reality of one's experience with the depth of the pull of that first attachment. Although what became known was very painful, it was also enabling. Each women learned to respect and be responsible for her own emotional reactions, a lesson neither her father nor mother had been able to provide.

CHAPTER 9

OBSTACLES TO SELF-ACTIVATION

If only I could harness all the energy I've used to not be, to be. I know I was real strong in not being more. I really worked at it.

Alice

If I took the time to explore what felt good rather than worry about what other people want, I might be more comfortable.

Anna

Most of the women I worked with did not know how to value their own activation. When it came to sticking with something that only they wanted, the majority hesitated, "I can't do it just for myself. That's not enough." There had to be a catastrophe— "real reasons"—to do something only for themselves. Just that they wanted it was not good enough. Because the expectation of critical disapproval was uppermost in their minds, they were often reluctant to acknowledge they needed help or guidance.

Rather than persevere with their own agenda, they found all sorts of excuses, including berating themselves for needing anything.

Although frequently starting new ventures with enthusiasm, when the enthusiasm "fizzled out," many gave up. Some felt if only they tried harder—were quicker, smarter, more tactful—they could overcome the hurdles. "When I have a bad experience I think it's my bad attitude. If I just made this tilt, I wouldn't have this bad experience."

Whichever way they turned, these daughters did not sufficiently trust that they had what it took to manage whatever they were feeling *and* work something different out for themselves. "Either I've lost the map I once had or the map doesn't work in this place. Something isn't right and it feels very scary to find out." They would jump from pursuing one small workable problem to feeling totally overwhelmed. "No wonder I feel immobilized! See, I can't do anything with my life."

Never encouraged to rely on themselves, the women felt crushed before they started and minimized their own ability to handle difficulties. "I don't know how, and that holds me back from getting in there and trying." Although they enabled other people all the time, when it came time to promote themselves they felt without "choices or resources." This further compounded their feeling incapable and defeated. "I'm clinging to a decrepit pier and I won't do anything to save myself. I'll wail and bemoan my fate, blame everyone else, beat up on myself, but I won't save myself."

In one therapy session, Miriam could identify ricocheting from wanting her father to do it all for her, to not wanting to see her mother's limitations in herself. The discouragement Miriam felt was so intense that she wanted to be rescued from those feelings before she would even consider taking a step on her own. She wanted me to push her, tell her what to do. As she spoke, Miriam realized that if I did she would be angry and resentful. "I don't want anyone to tell me what to do. I'll run and hide, blast all over the place tomorrow, but I won't tell you I'm scared and I don't know what to do."

At a similar moment of sharp anxiety, Carol said, "I want to be given to, but I won't ask. When I learned the skills to ask, I was told I wanted too much. Am I being too demanding by asking for what I want?"

Accustomed to keeping their dissatisfaction to themselves, the women had not appreciated the effort they had been expending to maintain unrewarding behavior patterns. "I don't even know if what is happening to me is what I feel or what others expect from me." Convinced there was no way to get their desires met without being either dismissed or censured, some women occasionally tried more wily maneuvers to further their own ambitions. They tried to get what they wanted by subtly convincing someone else that he or she wanted it too.

Sometimes, they hoped their needs would be intuited by others, an art they frequently practiced. The familiarity and safety of diminished expectations felt better than risking conflict and disapproval from others. "When I ask for something and I don't get it, I don't make it clear that this is important to me. I become a martyr. Then later on I use this. It sounds very controlling, and it is. But it works. It plays on other people's guilt and I get what I want. This is insane, but it's easier than fighting."

When some of my clients became dissatisfied with these stifling conditions and asked for more for themselves, both their complaints and their discomfort were ignored. Certain that she could not get what she desired, one woman had an image of empty kitchen cupboards that was particularly poignant. Her intense disappointment remained buried by her not even trying to express what she wanted. These experiences have taught the women to be even more doubtful of their emotional responses and suspect the validity of their own aspirations. "While asking myself, 'Is this good for me?' should be a simple question, it isn't. I feel sad and confused. I'm aware I want a lot. Is it okay to want more?"

Trained to suppress both themselves and the potency of their feelings, when I encouraged them to lobby for themselves the women placed their intense emotions on the line.

Held in Place

> I've been trained to accept that someone else's feelings are more important than my own. I can't move on from that place.
>
> Katherine

> The voice of doubt is keeping me from accepting new possibilities.
>
> Jackie

When Laura has to sustain her energy and promote herself to keep her home decorating business flourishing, anxiety and self-doubt are aroused. "I start out here, meet an obstacle, then run over there, and repeat it there. All the pots are boiling. I never finish anything. I'm putting things off for another time because that's what I've always done." Investigating these patterns yielded accumulations of painful, disheartening experiences.

Laura had been consistently disparaged, primarily by her father, but occasionally her mother also put Laura down when she became enthusiastic about something. Laura learned to curb her aspirations to avoid derision. She was conditioned to believe that the pursuit of something only for herself would elicit strong disapproval. Her father's snide comments further reinforced her feelings of inadequacy. "I felt so unsupported when I was a kid. My father used to say I'd never amount to much." Rather than acquiring trust in herself, Laura gathered mistrust. Doubting that she was capable of doing whatever needed doing, Laura quit trying.

Because she lacked the confidence to sustain her own objectives when others disregarded them, Laura dropped out of college when her husband persuaded her to move to Colorado and help him establish his career. "When Todd didn't validate my efforts I couldn't validate them for myself. I didn't believe I was important enough to do it *just* for me."

The disregard for women's independent aspirations that we have all become conditioned to accept as typical does indeed undermine their fragile hold on self-activation.

Planning to return to college in the fall, Alice began to experience anxiety about not being able to handle the combined pressures of her job and college. She was worried about not being able to motivate herself to get the work done and therefore not do well. I commented on Alice's lack of confidence in her own abilities.

Recalling what it was like in her family of brothers, Alice stated, "I could beat them at whatever they did, so where'd I lose confidence?" Slowly she remembered how they excluded her for being too quick. After she won at cards, her father would not play gin rummy again with her. "There wasn't much reinforcement for doing well."

Her former husband, Alice remembered, was like her dad. Jim was never satisfied with what she did. "I got an overdose of criticism and a lack of praise." As this was being described, Alice began to realize that she had done a lot on her own these past few years. She wondered: "How come I don't recognize that? Why am I always surprised when I do something? Why do I expect I can't?"

As we explored, Alice speculated. "Maybe I'm basically lazy and won't do certain things unless I set difficult goals." When I questioned that, Alice replied, "I'm afraid and I don't want to admit it. I say I'm lazy to cover that up. I don't want to take responsibility for myself. That makes me feel very sad and all alone."

Over the next several weeks Alice had difficulty in keeping her appointments with me. She was backing away from dealing with the feelings that had surfaced in therapy. It was hard for her to accept what she was learning. When old vulnerable spots were touched, the terrain became tender and Alice retreated. Assuming that nothing would work out, Alice ignored her feelings. Alternatives closed off. Everything became either black or white.

"It's like waiting for the ax to drop. Which arm will be cut off. Positive outcomes are a surprise. I think of my dad. He's a black/white, either/or man. Everything is that way. Seeing gray meant conflict."

"Could that be a reason for not seeing alternatives?"

"It could be. Saying no could also feel bad and disappoint other people. Momentarily, it feels better to say yes."

"What about the consequences?"

"I feel pissy all week and don't sleep well."

This interchange illustrates the familiar conditioning of women to pay special attention to what makes other people feel good. Pleasing other people creates a paucity of experience in pleasing oneself. "I can't choose for myself. I give people what they want. That's how I get loved." The essential balance between self-generated and other-generated approval is not acquired.

Moreover, women discount their autonomous needs and downplay the resultant cost to themselves because societal pressures have encouraged them to cultivate external approval to feel good about themselves. "Don't make a big flap if it's for yourself."

Exquisite Sensitivities

Since prior efforts to define themselves had frequently met with derision, these women were exquisitely sensitive to being hurt and rejected again. Sometimes they berated themselves and their efforts in order to forestall anyone else's doing it. Feeling frightened and anxious but unable to express this to me, one woman stated. "I feel stupid—like a fool—for what I'm experiencing. I'm embarrassed you'll think I'm inadequate."

These women were reluctant to make their vulnerabilities known; they did not expect them to be respected. They could not imagine a good outcome to expressing themselves. "In my family I'd argue and get humiliated. I'd cry and get humiliated for crying. I felt totally uncared for—alone. I didn't get what I wanted, so I learned to avoid those situations. Why bother."

Often the women forfeited deciding for themselves because they did not want to reexperience the painful disregard that they anticipated would follow affirming their own desires. "If I don't do it your way I'm not doing it good enough." The careful attention to detail that is intrinsic to the psychotherapy process elicited the pain and outrage at having been trivialized and discounted.

Anna declared: "I feel very vulnerable when I say what I want. Exposed and small. If I really want something I have to cloak it in some excuses that deflect away from me because if I stand up and say I want this—I'll be laughed at.

"When I expressed what I wanted as a little girl, people thought I was cute or funny, not capable. No one took me seriously. They said I couldn't have it. So I stopped saying what I wanted. I guess I got real good at not telling what I want."

The clients longed to be rescued from the intense discomfort of what was being uncovered and experienced. Some wished I would wave the magic wand and make it all better—instantly. I would do and know everything without their ever having to reveal anything. When I commented that those yearnings were keeping the women from trusting themselves to do their own work, they generally became angry. The women wanted neither to look into what was prompting the longings in the first place nor to investigate options. Anger, which often fuels self-assertion, had also been disallowed in the majority of their families. Becoming angry with me was doing something previously not permitted. Silenced and invisible in many other situations, some would now be seen and heard in therapy. "If you have brown hair and you've always been told it's blond, wouldn't you be mad?"

Generally, once this anger was expressed, it became more possible to get to the buried, painful details. "I don't know how to do anything different." It hurt—incredibly—to acknowledge how awful it felt to have been repeatedly disregarded. "Anything is safer than telling them what's really going on because then I have to acknowledge it to myself." This was extraordinarily delicate terrain.

Unused to stating their own needs directly—"I've run away from things in here; you've pointed that out so much. It's hard for me to get to myself"—they wanted repeated reassurance from me before they could comprehend that it was okay, safe. "It's like being fed and diapered; someone knows what you need. I never got enough of that. Instead, I got I'm a bad person for wanting more."

Beginning to Trust Herself

Anna put out great effort to do what other people expected of her, whether realistic or not, and no matter what she felt or thought; she wanted to be liked. In therapy, Anna realized just how hard she worked to acquire the approval and appreciation of others.

Over many, many months Anna began to strip off the veils and fantasies that she had devised to deny her unhappiness and cover up her pain and sadness about never having been appreciated for being herself. As Anna grappled with these changes, inner voices were telling her to discount what she was feeling. Paying attention to and accepting that she had emotional needs would mean trusting herself and making her own choices at every turn. Would she be okay without complying with other people's expectations? "The outside body is the same, but I don't know what I'll be like inside. Where's the real me? What can I trust?"

One evening, Anna came home from work to find a message that drawings for one of her most important clients needed to be reviewed immediately. Telephoning a member of her staff to accompany her, she went back to her office and worked late into the night. Afterward, for the first time, Anna felt a real sense of accomplishment. She also felt tired, calm, good. She had done a fine job.

The next day Anna reported that she had to run the good stuff by me for my approval before she could trust what felt right. This gave us another opportunity to explore her reluctance to accept her own feelings, especially when they were intense. The hesitancy to trust themselves to handle their own emotions has been one consequence of the recurrent training of women to discount themselves. Poignantly, it still interfered with Anna's knowing the satisfaction that could come from trusting her judgment. "I don't yet believe I can do it myself. I built my house from the roof down. My behavior determines my feelings rather than the other way around."

We balanced together on a tightrope composed of many complex strands as each woman was enabled to feel safe and supported while she exposed her delicate feelings. "When I get in touch with my feelings, I feel more; that's reality." This was no simple, straightforward task. "It's hard to keep myself on the straight and narrow. I do like the byways."

Even though I appreciated the rhythm of each woman's own process of self-discovery as well as her way of grappling with her particular assortment of disquieting as well as triumphant emotions, many wanted a pat on the head as they handled these moments of intense emotional discomfort. They wished to be noticed for what they were doing and regarded as special. I do not mean to imply that the women's good efforts went unremarked by me. What was significant was that they could not recognize and validate their efforts for themselves.

Determining Her Own Course

> If I express myself, have needs of my own, want attention or sensitivity from someone else, I'll be ignored, ridiculed, and told that's not how I feel. I'll be made to feel like a bad person for what I'm experiencing.

Lisa first came to therapy 10 years ago when her housewife-mother role was beginning to feel limited. Her children were in school and Lisa wanted something more for herself. Moreover, the family life-style was quite modest. Nick, Lisa's husband, often had problems earning an adequate living as a self-employed gardener. Lisa realized she could supplement their income by finding a job. After some exploration of her hesitation about new experiences and her uneasiness about making changes in her routine, Lisa found part-time work as a receptionist in a physician's office. The hours were flexible and she didn't have to make elaborate child care arrangements. Therapy stopped.

Several years later Lisa and Nick separated. Subsequently, Lisa decided to look for more remunerative, satisfying work. Not only was she desirous of a change, but to adequately maintain a single-parent household she needed to earn more money. As Lisa embarked on her job search, disquieting memories and surprising emotions erupted. Lisa returned to therapy, saying, "If I'm ever going to change jobs I need to be here." Soon afterward she reported a nightmare. "I dreamed I was a small child asleep in a dark room. A window was open and the curtains were blowing in the wind. Someone was hovering over me. While nothing really happened, I felt scared to death!"

Lisa felt intense discomfort and was very troubled by this nightmare. Although it appeared to be the surfacing of a long-suppressed memory of sexual molestation, Lisa could not identify its source. She did acknowledge that making "a serious move out into the world" made her feel very anxious. Old unresolved issues with her father, who was now dead, came up for review. Lisa described her father as an authoritarian, critical man who was very hard to please; she earned his affection by complying with his demands. Doing things in her own way resulted in ridicule and belittlement by him. For Lisa, becoming a more self-sufficient adult was synonymous with forfeiting love and approval. "It goes all the way back to me being a girl. My father used to call me 'Lisa-Lou,' sometimes 'Louie boy.' I think it must have been real confusing, I don't remember. I do know I loved to climb trees. That was allowed. I would also have liked to learn to saw wood, but Dad wouldn't do that with me. I know I should have stood up to all his criticism, but I never did. It hinders me now in making my way in the world."

As we focused on the job situation, Lisa investigated her community's resources and joined a support group for women seeking employment. In therapy, Lisa reported feeling scared and confused after the group meeting. "I want to retire to a desert island and sit in the sun. It's so hard. Things are moving too fast. Now I'll have to do something. I can't do this." I listened quietly and Lisa voiced surprise. She had anticipated disapproval. My behaving differently presented the possibility that Lisa could be respected for expressing her vulnerabilities.

Whenever Lisa had expressed herself in her family, she had been derided. "If I said yes, Dad would say no. It was very confusing. I never got what I wanted." Lisa learned not to ask directly for what she wanted or reveal what she knew. She remembered being humiliated by her father and called a big shot when she corrected what he said in a conversation with another person. Lisa cringed recalling this. "I don't have to like this! I hate it! I want to tell my father to listen when I talk. Don't laugh and don't tell me what to do. It may be different from your way, but it's mine."

Taking steps forward, completing her resume and applying for jobs, brought fresh anxieties. Asserting what she wanted as the job search became more serious created new problems. Lisa would have to renegotiate the child care arrangements with Nick, who was difficult to pin down. She felt bad that she had not done that yet. I pointed out how Lisa did not seem to notice what she did do, but remained focused on what she had not done. We observed her patterns: When it came to choosing for herself and asserting what she needed, Lisa doubted herself. Conditioned to expect that harsh disapproval would follow self-expression, Lisa protected herself by devaluing both herself and her objectives.

At first, Lisa tried to do several things at once and completed none of them. Instead of examining these tactics and rethinking her priorities, she felt stupid and considered stopping her search. In time she became aware that these complicated, outmoded survival strategies reinforced her feeling inadequate. She had to discover new ways. Doing one thing at a time would feel much better.

Even though Lisa often wished for guidance, she found it difficult to ask for help. In the past, asking for help had been an invitation for her father to take over. Now, Lisa did not want anyone to tell her how to do what she had to do. It was important to determine her course and set her own pace. She needed to distinguish between asking other people for advice and letting that influence her actions.

While keeping her goals in focus and working hard to attain them were new experiences that made Lisa anxious, it was also difficult to find enough time and energy to be with her children and pay attention to what she needed herself. Lisa complained, "I know how to do for others and pay attention to what they need, but when it's my turn it's real different. It's hard to be strong for myself." While it definitely felt good to be doing what she was doing, Lisa worried that her anxiety would poison her motivation.

Her early experiences with her father, who had demeaned Lisa's efforts at self-activation and then quickly moved to do things for her, had undermined Lisa's self-confidence. Discouraged from experimenting on her own to find out what worked, Lisa had been trained to assume she was not capable of solving her own problems. Before she could begin to develop a style of her own that she could trust, Lisa had to give up this learned assumption. Moreover, that assumption was protecting Lisa from acknowledging that the ways passed down by her father not only did not work, they also had hurt her.

These issues gained further attention following a good job interview. At first Lisa felt very happy. Soon afterward she began to feel anxious about all the energy and attention she was directing at herself. Charting her own course was totally unfamiliar. Lisa remembered: "As a young girl, I used to wait for my father to come home and make me happy. Now I need to learn to take the initiative and do that for myself. While I'm eager for change and stimulation I keep running up against my old fears and conditioning. I'm used to Daddy doing it for me. The idea of being on my own is very powerful and scary. I feel so vulnerable—alone."

Central Issues

Lisa was grappling with issues central to many women. Within each person the strong urge to be independent is modulated by an equally potent longing to be taken care of by others. Each woman has to find her own balance between these fundamental, divergent pulls. When, as is typical in this culture, a woman like Lisa has been consistently admonished for asserting her distinct wants, that equilibrium becomes damaged.

Additionally, the assumptions that girls are heterosexual and marriage and a family will be their primary life-goals, further undermine the cultivation of the tools that sustain independent endeavor.[1]

Although women in increasing numbers have begun to navigate their own course, many still feel like Lisa. They are uncertain about their ability to handle life-tasks for themselves. The accumulated lack of respect for women's self-determination in both the public arena and the family has effectively wounded their self-esteem and confidence. These social obstacles reinforce the normal anxiety aroused by asserting oneself in new ways.

Sometimes, rather than persevere at what it takes to feel good and adequate, some women fall back on self-defeating, dissatisfying patterns that are nonetheless more tolerable than the anticipation of painful disapproval. Practice, patience, and experience are necessary prerequisites to acquiring the confidence and skills to comfortably manage the hard work of self-activation.

Furthermore, while it is appropriate to want and seek out loving support because it feels very good, these women were raised to believe that the absence of approval placed them or their desire in question. Thus, when positive regard for their endeavors was withheld, they did not stick by their goals. Unprepared to affirm their own cause for themselves, they gave up or amended their objectives to retain approval. They were also unused to looking for emotional support elsewhere—e.g., outside the family. Explorations in therapy enabled them to see that if they looked around, that support was often there and available, just for the asking.

Standing on one's two feet—alone—generates uncertainty and anxiety, normal responses to embarking on new ventures. It is important to learn to distinguish this from the anxiety aroused at being reprimanded for self-assertion. It is equally important to recognize that the merits of one's intentions need not depend on other people's approval, and that taking steps forward does not necessarily result in disapproval.

As often happens in therapy, staying with hard tasks trig-
gers memories and stirs complex feelings. Opportunities to examine things more deeply recur. This was true for Lisa. As she
persevered with her job search, additional fragments of her
nightmare about possible molestation were recalled. While
remembering herself lying in bed in the room where the curtains
were blowing in the window, in a tremulous voice Lisa said,
"Did someone enter the room? Do I know who he is? Is he a
stranger?" Then she became very quiet.

After some time I asked, "What's happening right now?"

In a low, childish moan Lisa replied, "I feel like a small
hurt child. Someone hurt me. I want to tell my mommy."

Lisa abruptly stopped talking. The therapy room came back
into focus and she realized where she was. Lisa expressed relief
that she had been talking *only* to me. "I don't know why, but
it begins to feel dangerous and scary. I can't tell my mommy.
If the person in the room was someone familiar it would be *very*
scary and *very* dangerous." After a long pause, Lisa continued:
"I feel as if a wall just went up around me. I'm afraid I won't
be okay if we get behind this wall. I wish I could do this all
alone and then come back and tell you about it."

I acknowledged the importance of what Lisa had recounted
and supported her setting the pace. Her nightmare did not come
up again for many months.

Working Out of the Maze

Lisa became concerned that she would do the wrong thing
or not follow through as the demands of the job quest accelerated. She did not trust her own judgment. She recalled being
belittled when what she had done clashed with her parents' expectations. Already angry with her father for his outspoken lack
of support, Lisa now declared, "My mother laughed along with

him! She didn't offer me any alternatives. She always focused on what I couldn't do rather than what I did do. I'm afraid to open up or express my feelings because others will hurt me." Lisa began to sob.

Ancient, painful memories returned. When Lisa was three years old she and another little girl went for a stroll away from home; their dolls were their only companions. Afterward Lisa was told that the whole neighborhood searched for them. She could not remember being punished, but recalled being told that if she ever did that again she would be given away.

When Lisa was six, a car stopped along the road one day while she walked home from school. The man inside offered her a candy bar and invited her into the car. Lisa was about to get in when she realized something was not right and jumped back. Then she ran all the way home. "I never told my mother because she would have punished me for doing something bad. She wouldn't take my word; she always believed everyone else. She wouldn't have noticed what I had done."

Lisa now realized that as a child she had turned inward and buried her feelings. They were her secret. Making contact with that feisty little girl who tried but could not succeed at expressing what she needed meant breaking out of old traps and freeing long-stifled emotions. "Finding my own way is like going through a maze."

Some weeks later, frustrated and stuck in her job search, Lisa became anxious. There was danger out there—attack, death. More disturbing incidents were recalled. During her adolescence several men had exposed themselves as Lisa was walking along city streets. She remembered telling this to another woman, who brushed it off and remarked, "Oh, that's how men are. They can't control themselves." However, Lisa could not brush this aside. It made *her* feel like a bad person.

These are well-worn patterns. Even though men behave in-appropriately, the persistent devaluation of women trains them to doubt and mistrust the validity of their own experiences. When confronted with men's harmful behavior, they either blame themselves or make light of the behavior. Not only do women curtail their behavior to protect themselves, but often they also curb their own strong emotions so they are not available for expression.

Of equal importance, repetitive, frightening sexual encounters with men have taught women to flatten their own erotic feelings. Instead of desire being regarded as a pleasurable signal, it becomes a harbinger of danger.[2]

Again Lisa's fragmented memories of possible early sexual molestation recurred. This time she felt certain that it could not be true and did not want to explore this more deeply. What became illuminated, however, was Lisa's dread: Men will hurt me if I am powerful.

Although not every woman has been sexually abused, every woman has been abused because of her sex. Every woman lives with feeling frightened and unsafe both on the streets and in the privacy of her own home. Even though most women consistently circumscribe their lives to deal with the reality of sexual abuse, a continuous nightmare hovers over each woman's life regardless of her race, class, ethnic origin, sexual preference, or able-bodiedness. At this very moment a woman is being harassed or molested. These terror tactics effectively deter activation in women.

To protect herself, every woman has curbed the spontaneous expression of her spirit more times than she would like to know. Not only does this intimidation violate the most elementary principles of decency, but it creates painful vulnerabilities.

By giving voice to what many women have silently endured *and* recognizing the toll on their initiative, everyone can appreciate how pervasive and disabling women's fear of abuse by men is. Keeping the focus on her own initiative aroused these complex sensitivities in Lisa.

Two months later Lisa announced she had found a good job. She was exhilarated and anxious about starting full-time work two weeks later. Her desire to succeed was very strong. In the following meeting Lisa declared that after much thought she had decided to stop therapy soon. She would need all her energy to juggle the job, her responsibilities at home, and time with her children.

Lisa took the opportunity to talk about and acknowledge her mixed emotions accompanying this decision. She was sad as she contemplated moving ahead on her own; she would miss the support of our relationship. Lisa expressed concern that I would be disappointed because she was choosing to retreat from examining more fully some of the difficult, tender issues we had identified and temporarily shelved during the job search. Previous experiences with her family prompted Lisa to erroneously assume that I might retaliate, not be available if she wanted to see me again, because she was choosing for herself. Additionally, Lisa acknowledged her wish that she could stay a little girl and be taken care of by me. It felt overwhelming to realize all she would be doing.

Lisa started the new job. In her last therapy visit she reported with delight: "It's going very well. I'm enjoying thinking on my feet. For the first time in my life I feel very competitive. I never used to care how I did. In high school and college I always got Bs and Cs. Now I care. I want to excel."

Personal Power: Vital to Women's Health

I'm also noticing that when I care for myself, that is when I feel good about myself and respect what I do, other people treat me with respect and consideration.

The work with Lisa provides an arena for reflecting on important themes. Lisa's independent nature was not appreciated.

Her parents could not handle Lisa's temperament, and she was taught to be afraid of her most precious resource: an adventurous spirit. It created trouble for her. Over and over, she learned that to be loved and accepted she must muzzle her spirit. Lisa had survived in these stifling arrangements by warping her nature to fit other people's expectations. In doing this, Lisa lost her belief in herself as a unique person with her own needs, rights, and desires. Simultaneously, she learned that distorting herself brought recognition and acceptance. Under these conditions, self-expression became an act of defiance too frightening to contemplate. Lisa hid from herself how much she disliked what was happening. She detached from her potential and buried it—along with her hurt and angry feelings.

Additionally, both as a little girl and as a teenager, Lisa's sprightly stride along the street was greeted by inappropriate, frightening responses from men. In spite of the fact that she was a little girl, she was regarded as a sexual object for a man's pleasure. He did not think about the consequences his behavior could have on Lisa. Even though recognizing that harm would come to her if she did not protect herself, Lisa became more timid, weighed down by her vulnerability. These experiences taught Lisa to defuse her power; it was too dangerous.

As women unearth experiences of sexual molestation in therapy and describe the incredible fear intermingled with the pain at having the integrity of their body and mind violated, we are slowly coming to realize the depth of what they have endured while coping with these experiences to the best of their capacity—at age 3, 16, or 30.

Feeling suspicious and ashamed of her body effectively teaches a woman to mistrust herself. "I want to turn my head away. I feel so ashamed. Such a bad thing happened. I knew it wasn't supposed to and it did anyway. I couldn't stop him. It hurts. It's wrong and no one will believe me."

The profound consequences that this intimidation has had on women's initiative has yet to be fully acknowledged.

More Obstacles to Overcome

Overbearing fathers and insensitive men are not the only people who control and intimidate little girls. Some mothers, like Lisa's, do not support independent endeavors in their daughters. That is a very dismaying experience. It further undermines a daughter's trust and belief in herself. Nevertheless, the extraordinarily complex task that perennially has faced the mother must be acknowledged. As part of the training of her daughter, the mother is expected to impart that female sexuality, assumed to flower in marriage—a loving, respected, adult relationship with a man—is to be safeguarded. Yet this mother must also prepare her daughter to survive in a world in which some men regularly disrespect and assault women.[3]

The mother and her daughter might be living in a family in which the father, brother, uncle, or grandfather has been rarely, occasionally, or routinely sexually molesting the girl. Outside the family, both women have to be continually alert to inappropriate behavior on the part of men that could lead to physical harm and sexual abuse. Can a mother adequately prepare her daughter for living with such contradictory and injurious practices? Should she? Why is it that when men are unable to appropriately handle their sexual and aggressive impulses we not only blame women but hold them responsible?[4]

We routinely cast aspersions on women's character when men assault them sexually, but we rarely question why men refuse to take no for an answer. While it is always prudent for all women to use their wits and stay alert, that evades the central issue: the condoning by society of men's unwillingness to take control over their life-threatening, demoralizing behavior toward women. How is it possible that we tolerate so little responsibility from men yet demand so much from women?[5]

A mother's implicit cooperation with the rule of the father, especially when it is deleterious to both herself and her daughter, clearly demonstrates the powerlessness women experience both in their family and in society. Conditioned to depend on the good opinion of men for their self-worth, esteem, and economic survival, mothers and daughters both have often failed to support one another's autonomy. They have been raised to value more highly the security provided by male endorsement, which they might risk by affirming one another. This dependence on men keeps the mother–daughter relationship besieged by beliefs that hamper women in supporting one another to take the initiative on their own behalf.

By disentangling female self-worth and identity from male acclaim, women establish the value of their different, independent desires. As women can affirm for each other new standards and values that respect them and their daily life concerns, they are exchanging male-dictated patterns that demean and oppress them for options that promote and encourage women. This is an act of creation, not of defiance.

None of this is easy. In fact, it is extremely difficult and uncomfortable. However, this time, the discomfort is in pursuit of women's self-interest. "I suddenly got the image of being in the water and I have to swim out. I don't know if I can make it. I can't know that beforehand. I have to do it to know."

PART III

THE TOLL OF PERSISTENT DISREGARD

CHAPTER 10

THE WORKPLACE
Split at the Root

A woman with a bold, dramatic, successful career can't be a real woman. A real woman is supposed to be soft and feminine, lovable and admired. She should pay attention to relationships and keep the family together. To be an independent adult woman means being in exile. In Siberia.

Sara

At every turn, barriers are evident that signify the tenacity of social conventions. Whenever a woman is not primarily nurturing and subservient she is inviting difficulties. Women who attempt to enlarge their experience, as they do typically in the world of paid work, often meet with opposition and belittlement. Although it can provide satisfaction and independence, it has just as often yielded conflict and confusion for a woman to choose for herself.

161

Prior to World War II, rigid conventions generally prohibited employment after marriage and most certainly after motherhood. The overwhelming majority of working women were single; a job was something to do until the right man came along. Most women downplayed their ambitions. They had been conditioned to believe that independent endeavor was selfish and egotistical, and would spoil their chance for marriage. Besides, incentives for women paled when compared with the economic opportunities offered to men. The most available jobs were in the area of domestic and personal services. A long-term commitment to a career was exceptional.

Furthermore, it was rare for anyone to consider that an older, single working woman might enjoy her work or be a lesbian. "My aunt was a spinster and did what she wanted, yet everyone in the family viewed her negatively." An unmarried woman was thought to be unfulfilled.

Additionally, a wife who stays at home and is supported by her husband is at the heart of the dream of a Caucasian, middle-class life-style. She is a source of status and pride both to herself and to her husband. Although this has been a central concept in our belief system, when husbands' low wages required supplementation for the family to survive, married women have worked, especially women of color, and generally at the most menial jobs.[1]

The Dress Rehearsal

World War II created a temporary suspension of the restrictions placed on all women in the labor force, regardless of their background. Social conventions relaxed as the pressures from the war industry, the government, and the media positively encouraged women to reorder their priorities. Many women put their energy into the war effort by joining the labor force. This was a significant departure from the practices that had persistently curbed women's initiative.

Jobs opened everywhere because women's labor was essential to win the war. Women built battleships and bombers, operated cranes, drove locomotives, announced the news over the radio, and traded on the floor of the stock exchange. Commonalities among people were emphasized, differences downplayed.

In 1942 it was "patriotic" for women to leave their homes and children and go to work. In acknowledgment of the importance of adequate child care to a working woman's performance, Congress appropriated funds to establish day care centers. However, once the war ceased, so did the funds.[2]

On the surface it appeared that World War II had altered convictions about women, paid work, and the family. Hardly. Once the war ceased and the men came home to resume their civilian lives, their reemployment was the priority. Millions of women were abruptly laid off from jobs they had been competently filling. Whereas women's labor and ingenuity had been taken seriously during the war, once that crisis abated, old patterns instantly sprang back into position.[3]

The competence many women had demonstrated in handling their jobs, living alone, and managing household and personal responsibilities was dismissed. Although many women had been profoundly altered by their wartime experiences, "Doing something, being somebody yourself, not just existing in and through others" (Friedan, 1963, p. 40.), their accomplishments were quickly consigned to subterranean quarters.[4]

In the postwar exuberance to reestablish normalcy and avoid the overwhelming, complex problems created by an atom bomb victory and a cold war peace, the solace and security attributed to the home and family were loudly reaffirmed. Women's true fulfillment resided in being at home taking care of their spouses' and children's needs, while men provided for them by earning a living. Significantly, those values excluded independent aspirations in a woman, such as the desire for a higher education and/or a paying job.

Influenced by the beliefs that dominated those postwar years, the mothers of my clients listened as most women do to the voices of the experts; they paid attention to the images created in the media (as exemplified by June Cleaver and Donna Reed), which applauded women's femininity and invited them to cultivate happiness through devoting their lives to a husband, maintaining a clean home, and raising well-behaved children. Not until the advent of the women's movement in the early 1970s did women begin to question again why they had suppressed the expression of their initiative.

The Absence of Choice

My mother couldn't give me what I needed. She wasn't a whole person—a person who has opinions of her own, believes in herself, and is a not an appendage to her husband. My mother wasn't enough for me because she was so anxious and fearful of making a mistake and not doing what my father thought was right.

Carol

I desperately wanted my mother to be a role model for me. I wanted her to do something, be somebody so I'd know what that was all about.

Anna

When my clients were young girls it would have made a significant difference if other women—Caucasian or of color, single or married, with or without children—drove heavy equipment, practiced medicine or law, repaired faulty telephone lines, participated in competitive sports, ran for vice-president, sat on the Supreme Court, or pioneered in space. Such models affirm options for women.

This glaring absence of women in positions of authority outside the home, which earned them respect and admiration, seriously curtailed all women's choices. It also blunted their imaginations.[5] An individual must be able to imagine doing something different before she can do it.

This scarcity further severely penalized women by conditioning many of them to presume that adequacy lies in imitating male standards for worldly achievement. In turn, that has trained women to discount their differences to assure social acceptance. They have been programmed to believe the two are incompatible. Although noncompliance might have spelled trouble, conforming has undermined women's spirit and the full development of their potential.

While many of these daughters forged forward alone, creating options for themselves where before none had existed, their burden might have been lightened by a wider range of possibilities for women. That would have clearly demonstrated that a woman need not compromise acceptance and affection because she does something different from, or in addition to, what her mother does.

The clients' mothers, limited by their experiences, could not conceive of themselves or other women as having a positive identity that was separate and distinct from the one bestowed by their role in the family. Lacking a respected model of a woman who displayed a comfortable equilibrium between independently oriented goals and relational skills, they were unable to provide what their daughters strongly desired while growing up: a mother who championed their initiative and instilled confidence in their ability to take charge of their lives. "My mother didn't encourage me to do well, be my own person, or be proud of myself." At that time, it would have been a most unusual mother who was able to positively envision what she did not know and encourage her daughter to go after what she wanted. That could produce conflict and disapproval. What mother would willingly create difficulties for her daughter?[6]

Unable to comprehend that social conventions and attitudes about women's place in society actually have determined this paucity of respected options, many daughters presumed that the difficulties revolved around their mother's shortcomings. They became furious with them and determined not to be like their mothers. If they did not have *her* life—stay at home all the time and have babies—the problems would evaporate. "I don't want to be identified with her. I want to run the other way."[7]

Forging Forward

> I don't have a value system of my own. I have my mother's values. It's like moving out of the house. I have to start from scratch—I need everything.
>
> Sara

As they forged forward to create an identity that would be uniquely their own, many of these daughters grasped that moving into new realms would be difficult. Very intense emotions can be aroused by moving beyond what is familiar and into the unknown. Even though creating their own possibilities, they longed to be cheered on by the glow of maternal approval. They wanted a woman to demonstrate how to act responsibly and operate effectively. Such a model would have inspired confidence in womanly resources.

It would have been most meaningful if these daughters could also have had their mother's "blessings" while choosing for themselves—something heretofore reserved for men only. Such encouragement would have implied that the primary goals these daughters had been raised to esteem—being in an intimate relationship with a man and having children—are compatible with the pursuit of other, autonomous objectives.

Moreover, it would have demonstrated that a daughter does not choose to be different from her mother at the expense of that relationship. Despite the conflicts and disappointments with their mothers, later in their therapy most of these daughters realized that they wanted to preserve that bond. "I want to give her what I want for myself—the room to be who she is and for her to let me be who I am."

It is poignant that despite this scarcity of women pace-setters, these daughters very much wanted a shared commitment to change from their mothers. Could this have been a rudimentary precursor to the knowledge that grew out of the women's movement? Women's commitment to support one another's aspirations strengthens each woman. Not only does this endow women with more choice about their lives, it also affirms the importance for women to have models of their own.

Choosing for Herself Is Difficult

Anna is an architect and Sara is a sculptor. Each woman is self-employed and her career is flourishing; nevertheless, they both experience conflict around their successes.

As a young girl, Anna noticed that doing what she wanted felt good; however, it frequently brought disapproval. While doing what others wanted earned rewards, it felt bad. These experiences created insecurity and confusion, which Anna handled by downplaying her abilities and distrusting her judgment.

Although demonstrating considerable artistic ability as a child, Sara was counseled not to take that seriously. She was expected to use her talents, as her mother demonstrated, "to give other people pleasure," not primarily to express her independent, creative spirit. Talent and ambition might conflict with a woman's responsibility to a husband and family. Ultimately each daughter learned that loving approval was contingent upon curbing her spiritedness and superior intelligence.

Each woman perceived her father, whom she greatly admired, as clever, energetic, and "the one who knows all about the world." He and his work were highly valued and respected. Significantly, neither mother received such appreciation, nor was what she did at home respected. Anna complained that everything was always so neat and clean, "I couldn't play or make a mess." Both daughters were critical and unsympathetic toward the mother's job. "I did not find any of that attractive."

Typical of the majority of my clients' mothers, these mothers provided a model of a woman who suppressed her own wants while paying attention to everyone else's. Neither woman imparted the possibility of juggling choosing for herself with the demands of a family. They had never been encouraged to know and value their own resources if they were distinct from family life demands.

Neither Sara nor Anna was prepared for the strong emotions aroused by placing herself first. They experienced anxiety and confusion when they respected the demands of their careers over other people's expectations of them. When these responsibilities isolated them for significant stretches of time, they feared derisive judgments and disapproval. Never encouraged to take either themselves or their work seriously, each woman felt like a bad person when she chose for herself. It is very difficult to step back from the conditioning that admonishes women when they place self-interest above interest in others.

Even though very disciplined, Sara would label her work frivolous and herself lazy in an effort to banish those aspirations and emotions that create discord. She had been trained to believe that disowning parts of herself assured acceptance. Therapy enabled Sara to untangle her feelings from the beliefs she was raised to value.

Recently, Anna had smoothly completed a move to new offices that she designed—a definite statement of achievement. Nevertheless, old conflicts reemerged. Unable to contain those uncomfortable feelings within herself, once Anna got home she began arguing with her lover.

Examining this later in therapy, Anna came to understand that she had picked this fight to avoid dealing with all the discomfort and confusion generated by dreaming about and then getting for herself something she very much wanted. "It was too good. I had to spoil it. I can't have things work out."

Success is frightening. It heralds disapproval from loved ones because a woman is choosing to define success differently from what her mother (and often also her father) expected her to attain: marriage and motherhood. "My mother would ignore me for a long time when I did things she didn't like. Even though I rebelled against her, I needed her approval to make things okay." Previously Anna had not realized that the absence of her mother's positive regard for Anna's curiosity and initiative was an important loss.

Each time Anna moved beyond what her mother could appreciate, which meant into experiences that are new for women, she felt anxious and alone. The strength of her discomfort made her feel that she was unacceptable "just as I am."

In fashioning her own new options, a woman comes to realize that an integral part of her past experience lacked positive, emotional support for being herself. The dissonance between current aspirations and the training of the past is being felt. Deep pain and rage can erupt, often followed by a period of uncertainty and intense feelings of isolation. Intensely uncomfortable emotions and contradictory pulls must be handled.

Therapy enables many women, like Sara and Anna, to become aware that they cannot get what they want without conflict. "I feel as if I'm pitting myself against forces that don't want me to succeed." Facing all these challenges, many queried, "Can I do it?"

Some clients become aware of how much they have been handling. Dealing with disapproval from others, as well as the feelings of isolation that arise when one chooses to depart from the customary path, can be quite taxing. It is never simple to be one's own model. "Each road leads back to my fear of being on my own. Whether I choose to be satisfied or try to make changes, accept what is going on at work or try to alter it—it's all up to me."

Being an individual, autonomous woman who appreciates herself and commands a place of respect in society is a complicated process. "It's like navigating a rapid, avoiding the worst pitfalls and rocks while keeping in charge of the boat."

Becoming Aware

In her first therapy appointment, Sue, who is a research chemist in charge of several important projects at a national oil company, declared: "I don't feel capable or in touch with my skills. My intuition tells me that something is wrong, but I don't know what it is." As we explored Sue's complaints it soon became evident that the model for perfection and hard work presented by her father had had a formidable influence. Accustomed to working hard, long hours like all her male colleagues, Sue tailored her personal life to fit her job demands.

Describing her father as a successful man who was overly demanding and hardworking, Sue characterized her mother as a frail, passive woman who had very few friends or interests outside of the family. It seemed as if her mother was invisible whereas her father's presence was definite, powerful.

Even though Sue's father appreciated her quick mind, he was very critical. Although generally programming what she should be doing, "wholehearted approval" was rarely given to anything she did. Making a mistake was especially frightening because it could bring on his disfavor. Sue worked very hard to meet his expectations. She worried that if she did not excel, his love and approval would be withdrawn.

Disappointed at an early age with her relationship with her mother, Sue distanced from the housewife-mother role that her mother modeled. "Our house was always so neat and tidy, it had no character. I hated it. It seemed as if Mom didn't have anything else to do. I won't be caught in that place."

Upon reflection, Sue thought her mother might have had trouble managing her job well. She was always so busy and seemed to lack the energy to do anything with the four children. There was no time for closeness and affection. Sue remembered that her mother would often lie down for a nap in the middle of the afternoon. Recalling her mother's "if it's too hard, quit" attitude, Sue became angry. That was no model for how to stick with and manage tough jobs. Clearly, Sue felt there was no choice. She subscribed to her father's demands for perfection and hard work to escape from becoming like her mother, dismissed.

At 18, when she was applying to a college away from home, Sue recollected that her father criticized and belittled her choice. Even though money was not an issue, he wanted her to remain at home and attend the local college. Unable, without parental encouragement, to stick up for what she wanted, Sue acquiesced to his judgment. Her father's devaluation of Sue's ability to assess what was correct for herself undermined her self-confidence and interrupted her thrust toward self-definition and self-assertion. When strides into ever-increasing realms of independent activity are not emotionally supported by one's parents, these normally difficult tasks generate conflict and become even more complicated.

Signals of Dissatisfaction

One week Sue walked into the therapy room announcing that she had been promoted. Although this was clear acknowledgment of her superior performance, she felt depressed. It heralded ever-increasing responsibilities, longer work hours, and more deadline pressures. What might have brought her pleasure felt like a burden. This brought forward old anxieties.

Believing that love and approval depended on her superior performance, Sue was afraid that any mistake would confirm that she was inadequate. "If a project fails I'll have to quit. There's no margin for error." The prospect of not having the right answer aroused feelings of panic. She felt frozen—in a very lonely, frightening place. This realization made her depressed.

It was hard to tell me this because disclosing it made Sue feel unacceptable. Would anyone love her if she was not perfect? She became very upset. "I'm wading into feelings of despair and helplessness. I want to get right out. If I were a perfect person I'd have this all figured out by now."

The dearth of womanly standards that command admiration and respect for behaving differently from men increases many women's determination to demonstrate their ability to hold their own using the measures promulgated by men. "I always thought grown-up work meant being challenged and pressured. That was the way my father worked." Often that includes taking great pride in "cranking up" to keep on top of the demands of their jobs, working a 65-hour workweek—pushing, rushing, clenching—then dismissing any body pains or emotional signals that suggest the reduction of stress might be appropriate. "I observed myself at work last week and was surprised to discover that I get terrible stomachaches from the stress. I hadn't realized it's that bad."[8]

Since measuring up to someone else's demands told Sue that she was okay, she pressured herself to meet deadlines whether they were realistic or not. Asking for anything different would reflect negatively on her competence. By demanding perfection of herself Sue ignored the signals of dissatisfaction. The reality of her physical and emotional responses was discounted; honoring her reactions would mean that Sue understood she was doing something that did not feel good. It had not occurred to Sue that she might discuss the overload and renegotiate the timetable.[9]

Meanwhile, the boss, usually a man, remained protected from receiving important feedback about the unreasonableness of his expectations. Of utmost significance, Sue did not set priorities based on an internal measure that realistically assessed her capabilities. She had not learned to trust her own reactions and respect her own needs.

While more carefully exploring these issues at another time, Sue came to realize that men have always had a strong influence on her. Her father, her boss, and her lover have repeatedly told her what to do and how to behave. "I presume they know best." Accustomed to men deciding how things would proceed, Sue has had little practice making her own decisions.

She further observed that when a man tells her how she should behave, she immediately feels vulnerable and anxious: Something is wrong with me. She does not even consider what is going on. Retreating from this confusing assortment of strong emotions, Sue has allowed the men to take over. "I'm afraid to figure out what I want by myself. I'm used to men helping me out."

Having been trained to rely on men, who are in positions of authority, to determine what is correct, and furthermore rewarded with positive regard when meeting their standards, daughters like Sue presume that their distinct, different reactions must be dismissed. These women cannot acquire a measure of their own to trust as long as they believe inadequacies would be revealed if they do not conform.

More Parallels

Sue met Philip, a visiting consultant, at work. She was drawn to Philip because of his high standards and perfectionism. They liked one another and soon their relationship became important to each of them. Philip, like Sue, was hardworking; he was also very demanding and critical. While that inspired Sue to try harder, it also raised her anxieties. She was afraid Philip would find her imperfect. As we talked, it became clear that Sue did not need anyone to push her. She already experienced much tension and strain from the pressures she placed on herself to handle perfectly an overloaded schedule and excessive demands.

Several months later Sue and Philip decided to get married. At the end of the summer they would move to Philip's home in another state and would both work at company headquarters. Interestingly, the marriage prospect raised anxieties parallel to those aroused by the job promotion. Sue was accustomed to men expecting her to comply with their decisions, and Philip was no different. He knew what he wanted and did not hesitate to tell Sue both what he thought and how he would like her to respond. Although Sue liked knowing what Philip wanted, she also felt intimidated by his decisiveness. Not wanting to appear inadequate, she held back her real thoughts and feelings when they indicated misgivings or uncertainty.

For example, Philip wanted to have a child within a year. Sue felt very uncertain about immediately starting a family. Her chief concerns were what effect the move would have on her research projects and making the right connections to ensure her new position. She also wondered what it would be like to live in a new city, work at a new job, and have Philip be the only person she knew. Having always placed great importance on her career, Sue now clung to it for security and self-definition as she prepared for all the changes ahead.

Rather than acknowledge both to herself and to Philip that she felt pressured by his timetable, Sue fell back on her conditioning. She relied on Philip as earlier she had relied on her father to know what was best for her. Philip was not struggling with these dilemmas and was not demonstrating any anxiety. He would make things work out. Men always do.

By assuming Philip knew best, Sue deprived herself of the opportunity to establish her own priorities and figure out what she wanted. Not speaking up on her own behalf distanced Sue further from her own needs. In the habit of judging herself lacking when she felt any uncertainty, Sue found it difficult to accept that anxiety can be a signal that emotional attention is required. The doubt and hesitation that normally accompany finding one's own way in new experiences was confused with feelings of inadequacy and the fear of failure. Relying on Philip buried all that discomfort.

Philip, like many other men, generally concealed his confusion and anxiety by taking charge. His style for circumventing unpleasant emotions confirmed Sue's belief that men are more capable of handling difficult situations. This "in-charge" stance precluded an opportunity to examine together what was going on and disadvantaged both partners.

Once Sue began to investigate these complex themes she realized that having a baby could be postponed. It was very reasonable not to want to add another challenge to the ones she already had to manage. She thought: "Maybe men don't know what's best for me. I need to assert my own ideas."

By our final meeting, Sue was aware of the familiar pull to depend on Philip and bypass her own anxieties. If he could provide what she needed to feel secure, Sue would not have to wrestle with figuring that out for herself. Having stated this, she then voiced how scared she felt about the move and all the changes ahead: "I've always felt I wasn't supposed to be scared. Those feelings weren't allowed. Now I know that when I begin new things, I become anxious. I want to remember it's normal and appropriate to feel this way."

Although Sue's move to another city prematurely halted therapy, she left more able to allow vulnerable emotions expression without condemning herself for being a weak, needy woman. Sue also began to separate the validity of her emotional responses from men's approval or disapproval.

The absence of self-affirming, respected female role models in the paid-work arena has prompted the majority of women to rely on men to provide both direction and models for workplace achievement. This persistent influence on women's behavior is harmful. It has trained women to think that acknowledging their distinct needs is an indication of weakness rather than an example of their differences from men.[10]

CHAPTER 11

CONDITIONED NOT TO PROTEST

Accommodation is an art I no longer want to practice.
                                                    Katherine

The majority of women I saw for therapy in 1975 were married homemaker-mothers; only a few worked for pay, primarily at part-time jobs. All except one of the women described in this book are currently employed full time. Whether heterosexual or lesbian, women of color or Caucasian, in a relationship or unpartnered, graduating from high school or middle-aged, entering the workforce has radically affected these women's lives and changed their vision of themselves and paid work.

It is noteworthy that the occupations of most of these women are different from those they were originally "encouraged" to consider. After several years in the labor force or after their marriages had ended in divorce, most of the women

177

came to comprehend that they might be responsible for supporting themselves for the rest of their lives.[1] When that awareness
became more prominent—as it is today for many women—the majority of my clients displayed much thoughtfulness as they recon-
sidered their employment options. Accustomed to a middle-class
life-style, they also wanted to be well remunerated for their labors.

As they expanded their interests and attention beyond the
family and home to paying jobs, entering this male domain in
ever-greater numbers and with increased seriousness of purpose,
these women recognized within themselves previously unreal-
ized talent, ambition, and energy. Many sought additional
education to enhance their possibilities in the work force. They
participated in job training programs, entered college or
graduate school, and in growing numbers enrolled in law, medical, or business schools.

Employment is more than a necessity for the majority of
these women. Their jobs can be very gratifying, providing opportunities to actualize different aspects of themselves. "I like
my work. I enjoy using my brains." For some, careers began to
seriously challenge the assumption that women should stay at
home and have babies.

Most of the women like their jobs and work hard. The challenges they handle do take effort and the women are beginning
to acknowledge that. "I'm pleased and proud. I've accomplished
something. I'm going forward acknowledging that much pain
and effort have gone into this."[2]

From time to time some feel exhausted and resentful. There
are wistful yearnings to be taken care of and not be responsible
for all that they are now juggling; several wish that it could be
easier. "I'm envious of people who have it all, although I'm
aware that many people are suffering more than I am. I'm right
in the middle of the middle class—and it's hard keeping up."
Occasionally, some yearn for "the good old days," and then
remember they were not such good days.

An individual woman's experience in the workplace can become even more complex when her racial or ethnic origin, class background, level of education, sexual preference, age, or able-bodiedness is acknowledged.

Paid work is a steady occurrence in women's lives and increasingly a focus of attention in therapy. By examining their experiences, these women open windows into unforeseen issues. The conscientious engagement of middle-class women in the work force has currently bestowed more esteem on all working women and enlarged our conceptions about women and paid work. Nevertheless, unfair practices prevail that have always plagued working-class women and women of color.[3]

Entrenched Convictions

Socialized to synchronize their aspirations with the demands of men whom they should obey and respect, the majority of these women assumed, as many other women do, that to reap the benefits associated with competent job functioning they had to adapt to prevailing workplace attitudes. It made little difference that many were employed at work that challenged their intelligence and creativity and were in more privileged and secure positions in the work force than the majority of women. They too faced the same recurring demands for compliance from men as did women in less protected jobs.

The entrenched, stereotypical expectations that have operated in the family are alive in the workplace, in both women's and men's heads. Raised not to protest when conditions are unfavorable, many women are hesitant to challenge male rule. Instead, they adapt and try harder. They know that conflict can be avoided by minimizing their own dissatisfactions.

For their part, men assume that women will resonate to their needs, not have needs of their own. Men further expect that women will continue to make the customary accommodations and in no way should their talents interfere with or compromise respect for the authority of men. No one has been cognizant that complying with these practices undermines women's initiative and interrupts opportunities for them to develop their own style.

Typically, many of the women find it problematic to negotiate their wants with men who are accustomed to dominate. It is difficult to appropriately distinguish between the ingrained habit of compliance and the reasonableness of a boss's request. Some try hard to please moody men. Handling their grumpy fathers certainly taught many skills. Sometimes, however, it feels as if "I'm banging my head against a brick wall."

Furthermore, the repetitive belittlement for speaking up for themselves, which began for many of these daughters with their fathers, still colors their reluctance to assert themselves on the job. The possibility of an unpleasant outcome adds to their anxiety. "I'm afraid to talk back to my boss; he could make my life miserable. Yet I don't like myself for giving in to those fears." Some women felt they would be "shot down" for disagreeing. Others believed they could not affect anything, "so I keep quiet." Fears described by some male employees now also visit these women.

Bosses, like fathers, are powerful and expect their demands to be met. Frequently they are unaware of the effects of their commands. Employers also like hard workers who do not speak up and are satisfied with minimal monetary reward and little recognition. While some men reign by the harsh misuse of their authority, others are nice guys who just by their tone of voice convey that women should remember their place and do what they are told. Their opinions are not invited. The subject is closed. These attitudes make many women very angry. They also feel trapped. Bosses control the paycheck.

Raised to direct considerable energy and sensitive listening toward ameliorating the discomfort of others, the women, by and large, were unprepared for the strategizing that is required to champion their own objectives or stand up to unfair workplace practices. "I can sell myself as what I can do for you, but not what I want for myself." "I hadn't thought about what I want so of course I can't get it."

Many pay attention to the office emotional climate and feel selfish if they are not also attentive to other employees' needs. Some are regarded as good listeners, problem-solvers, and one woman was dubbed the office "den mother."

However, it is rare for anyone, the woman included, to acknowledge the skill and energy it takes to provide these sensibilities. Empathy for personal and social distress is a resource in short supply in the world. Nevertheless, when these noble qualities are out of balance they can become a hindrance, interfering with a woman's pursuing her own agenda. "I'm responsive to too many drummers and not my own."

More Problems

To keep their jobs women have tolerated extraordinary, unequal working conditions. Yet without women's cooperation and attention to detail, the policies men promulgate would have little impact. Not only have their comparable jobs with men been both valued less and paid less, but many women regularly contend with the intimidation created by sexual harassment and men's misuse of their authority. Until recently, women's clamor for more equitable, responsible conditions usually was ignored.

In the event that women experience conflict managing the divergent pulls created by job demands and family demands, it is assumed that those dilemmas are the result of shortcomings within the women. This thinking has enabled the workplace and the men who dominate it to conveniently overlook the problems that actually exist, and to remain aloof from the reality that each working person's life is a complex web of everyday concerns.

Besides, the workplace itself—as well as one's colleagues—can generate emotional tensions of their own. People interact on the job, demands are made, and stress can mount. The paid-work arena is not devoid of emotion. "I don't care what the pressures are, I want to be treated like a human being."

This detachment by men further perpetuates the assumption that emotional responsiveness to people's demands is women's bailiwick alone. Thus, the workplace and male colleagues continue to be excused from responsibly sharing the burdens that do arise in making the paid-work arena more responsive to human needs. Of equal importance, because of the downplaying of important contributions women make on the job as well as to the family's financial security, women are still being penalized for choosing *both* a paying job and a family life.

The therapy experience provides a model as well as opportunities for each woman to practice speaking up for herself. Many now use their therapy hours to plan out and rehearse how to confront troublesome experiences in the workplace and unreasonable demands by bosses. The women also learn, through practice, that the anxiety generated from self-activation can be tolerated.

Additionally, they discover that being prepared pays off. More often than not, they are listened to and their jobs are not jeopardized. "There are increasing skirmishes at work now that I don't want to do any more. I wasn't eager before, but I was afraid to speak up."

Moreover, therapy enables these women to learn that conflict and anger are not bad emotions, but natural by-products when individuals clash over differences in values and beliefs.

By clearly identifying the issues and sticking with them, women are correcting the imbalance that has been created by the absence of public support and respect for a woman's right to actualize herself. Working it out in the paid work arena can present unprecedented opportunities. Each time a woman transcends her own conditioning other people are also enabled to alter their preconceptions.

Double Dose

I guess I didn't think I could get something from someone else unless I gave them a lot first.

Although Amy had worked at part-time jobs throughout the years of her marriage, she had been accustomed to relying on her husband to provide financial security. Divorcing Peter altered Amy's life significantly. Later, she declared: "I need a fire lit under me to make changes. I have a tendency to sit on stuff." One major new undertaking for this divorced woman with two adolescent children was entering the world of full-time paid work.

Amy's willingness to work hard, eagerness to please, and talent for organization quickly earned her promotions; in time she became an office manager. As Amy's responsibilities grew and her job became more demanding, conflicts surfaced. Especially sensitive to the needs of others and wanting her staff to feel good about themselves while on the job, Amy found it difficult to use her authority when it was required.

Conditioned to be sensitive to the needs of other people, Amy would pay attention to a staff member's discontent while ignoring her own. Although her thoughtful listening was appreciated, Amy did not realize that responding to other people's demands in order to keep them happy interfered with knowing her own needs. As we examined these issues Amy exclaimed: "It's easier to fight for someone else than for myself. It's so self-centered to think only of me. I was trained to be nice, tactful, observant, and gracious. I pay attention to everybody else, but I take shitty care of myself."

The socialization to be most concerned with preserving harmony in relationships interfered with Amy's effectiveness at handling conflict. It had never been a priority to develop the skills required for negotiating through troublesome incidents. Amy aptly summed it up: "I feel I have to make it all right for everyone else; sometimes that means not making the best decision."

A snag with Marsha was illuminating. Marsha was a difficult, manipulative co-worker whose job performance was uneven. Furthermore, Marsha's response to discussions of her work varied. Sometimes she would accept feedback, at other times she would become surly or defiant. Generally uneasy about taking the initiative on her own behalf, Amy was further intimidated by Marsha's unpredictable moods. Amy rationalized her own discomfort by stating that she didn't want to hurt Marsha's feelings. However, Marsha's behavior did not change and Amy became annoyed. We investigated her reluctance to act.

Marsha's erratic behavior reminded Amy of her father. One day he would be fine and cooperative; the next, glum and attacking. Amy never knew what to expect. She was often anxious in his presence, afraid that if she did not please him she would encounter his wrath. In talking about this, Amy realized that although she had never told any of this to her father while he was alive, she could talk to Marsha. "I've allowed Marsha to push me around because I've been afraid to use my authority and confront her behavior."

Probing more carefully why another person's feelings would be more important than her own prompted Amy to talk of her upbringing. As a Japanese-American, she grew up in a family where the beliefs and customs of the Japanese culture interfaced with female role conditioning. Raised to be kind, considerate, obedient, and respectful, Amy was trained to be more concerned with other people's needs than with her own. "My mother was the model of a good person. She was always doing something for someone else."

Amy was pressured to excel predominantly by her father, who demanded that his children "be tops" at whatever they did. He also cautioned, "Don't give people anything to find fault about." Keeping up appearances no matter how one actually felt was another family standard. "Try harder, look good, and keep strong emotions hidden" were strategies passed on by Amy's parents. They were attempting to protect their children from the abuses of racism, which had dramatically changed their lives and the life of each Japanese person living in the United States at the outbreak of World War II.

Prolonged Hardships

Following the attack by Japan on Pearl Harbor in December 1941, intense anti-Japanese feelings erupted all along the West Coast. In the spring of 1942, the United States government ordered over 100,000 Japanese-Americans to evacuate their homes and report to assembly centers. Later they were interned in shabby, quickly constructed relocation camps primarily situated in the western United States.[4]

Only Americans of Japanese ancestry were interned against their will. No groups of people from either Germany or Italy, with whom the United States was also at war, were ever evacuated. This was a particularly blatant, demeaning display of racism during World War II.[5]

Amy's family lived in dusty, overcrowded, and inadequate quarters for more than three years in a desolate, wind-blown camp in Arizona. The children were frequently sick owing to the substandard living conditions, which included either brutally hot or freezing cold weather and spoiled foods. Assigned to jobs in adjacent states, Amy's father was often absent. Life was confined to a barbed-wire compound. Soldiers monitored their every movement. Fear for his own and his family's safety put enormous pressure on Amy's father.[6]

I knew Amy a long time before she revealed that she had been born a few months before the family was ordered to the relocation center. Possibly, if I had also been Japanese-American, she would have shared this sooner. She could not recall any memories of the internment. Like her parents, Amy had repressed this bitter, painful experience.

However, she did remember that as a teenager she had pressed her parents to talk about their experiences. They would only say, "It was all right." Although she admired them for being strong, Amy did realize that they also must have been very hurt. In recollecting this painful period, Amy further realized that her father had been deeply humiliated and outraged by the relocation. His pride was gravely wounded.[7]

The Price of Survival

While Amy's father might have been assuring that no one would find fault with his offspring by his unrelenting demands on them for obedience, compliance, and excellence, his behavior was harsh and unpredictable. It created fear and anxiety in the children rather than fostering solace at home. Although training his children to survive in an unequal, unjust world, he exercised his power in an unfair and unreasonable manner.

Amy learned to disguise her own anxiety by becoming alert and watching out for everyone else's welfare, talents extolled in all women, especially Japanese women. Her antennae were always up, monitoring the situation. Her father could be charming and witty to strangers, but at home he badgered the family, hollering a lot. Some days, when she returned home after having been out with her friends, he would be pleasant; occasionally he would tell stories and laugh. They would have fun. Other times, Amy would find her father furious, ready to pounce on her. In her absence he had made it miserable for her siblings.

Like most of my clients' families, this family adapted to the father's unpredictable ways even though they harmed and deeply affected them. His erratic behavior was excused; he had endured much. The wounds to Amy's mother, however, remained invisible even though she was right alongside her husband throughout the traumatic events that led up to and included the internment. Her efforts to safeguard family life to the best of her ability in chaotic times also remained ignored.

This absence of sensitivity to the mother's experience is an example of how we have all been programmed to discount the role women play and the contributions they make in major historical events, thereby assuring that the women and their prescribed roles remain devalued. Asian-American women, in particular, are even further diminished by being stereotyped as submissive and subservient. These learned attitudes deprived both Amy and her mother of the opportunity to identify more fully with one another through the sharing of significant female experiences during this outrageous, unhappy time in the life of all Japanese-Americans.[8]

Despite her popularity at school, Amy was miserable during her adolescence. Caucasian boys would not ask her out. She, who loved to dance and go to parties, was excluded from peer social events. At those times Amy hated being Japanese. Even though she tried to do everything in her power—dress neatly, look pretty, be smart, say the right thing, smile—"it didn't matter. I was still Japanese."[9]

If she showed how upset she felt, her father derided her. She was "a wimp" for not handling herself better. There was no place in this family's vocabulary for disappointment and unhappiness. Her father would chide: "It's always worse someplace else. Being sad is unproductive."

In Amy's family, adaptation to the abuses of racism significantly interfered with recognizing that individual flowering and well-being were also being trounced at home. The deleterious effects of racism have taken hold when the family maintains that the best survival strategy is denying the toll racial prejudice exacts on its members. Solace that can come from acknowledging the oppression and devising strategies to combat it is simultaneously being disregarded. How could Amy develop pride in being different when that uniqueness brought her pain both in the family and in the world? "I was a good kid. I brought honor to the family. We all did. Yet I felt so bad and guilty. I used to think it was all our being Japanese, but now I see it was also that my father was so unsupportive. It was a double dose—right in my own home."[10]

Trying On New Behavior

Accustomed to modifying her own behavior in order to promote harmony with her father and with strangers, who always presented the possibility of a racist slur, Amy was not in the habit of questioning the demands others placed on her. She cooperated. Thus, when Amy's boss, Jack, expressed displeasure with her for not supporting office policy at a staff meeting, Amy was confronted with some difficult decisions.

Jack was critical of Amy for endorsing her staff's wishes over what he expected of her. Although Amy felt bad, it also prompted her to explore more thoughtfully what she wanted to do: cooperate with Jack's expectations or risk defending her different point of view? Investigating her anxiety about standing up for her principles enabled Amy to identify her fears. She recalled the dread she felt when she disobeyed her father. He became tyrannical. Amy anticipated being punished for speaking up—maybe even fired. She did not expect her ideas would be respected.

Amy recollected that when she complained about her father's behavior to her mother, she would respond, "Try to understand." That did not help Amy or alter the unreasonableness of her father's behavior. She now recognized that she was doing again with her boss what she had been encouraged to do with her father—make sense out of his demands rather than let him know when they were unreasonable.

The conditioning to acquiesce keeps concealed the maladaptive aspects of a belief system that encourages women, nonwhite women in particular, to believe that everything will be okay if *only* the women work harder to control situations that generate discomfort, put more effort into pleasing other people, and keep their own dissatisfactions disguised. These attitudes train all women to disregard their own needs in preference to making other people feel comfortable.

When Amy chooses to make her presence known—to speak up for her principles with her boss, engage in social activities with a new group of people, confront curt treatment from strangers, express displeasure at being kept waiting a long time—she is unearthing her pain at being made to feel especially vulnerable because of the color of her skin. "At the root of this stuff is not being taken seriously and treated with respect because I'm Asian."[11]

In a culture that primarily does not respect individual diversity, of race, gender, class, needs, or ideas, it takes additional effort for Amy, and women like her, to acquire a measure of her own that honors her unique attributes as a Japanese-American woman.

In therapy, as a woman breaks her silence and expresses what she has endured in order to be accepted, the woman, and therefore each of us, moves forward to a new level of consciousness: the recognition and valuing of the importance for each woman to be herself. Until we take this knowledge beyond the therapy room its impact is minimized.

Challenges

As women stand up for what they need on the job—which includes respect for their own way of doing things as much as it includes working conditions and policies that acknowledge the reality of women's lives—women will clash with men. The control they are accustomed to exercise is being challenged. Intense discomfort can be aroused when individuals feel threatened, which prompts them to block change.[12] Although conflict generally results, it is both possible and necessary to learn to tolerate it. "If I hang tough it'll change."

The birthing of healthy, womanly measures for achievement and satisfaction is a laborious process, engaging women and men in both joyous and painful experiences. To strengthen their objectives as well as manage the difficulties that will ensue, it is essential that women expand their alliances with other work force members who share similar objectives.[13]

New guidelines and strategies that expand women's possibilities for attaining their different goals would benefit from taking into account the experiences of other groups that have clamored to end oppressive working conditions. Present indications are that the legislative and judicial branches of government are backing up the efforts women are making to correct workplace inequities.[14]

A woman can remain steadfast, move forward with her own interests in mind, and also balance her well-being with that of others. It is also perfectly appropriate for each woman to determine for herself how much challenge she can handle.

A woman who wants more for herself prepares to understand and accept that it is normal to feel anxious about activating herself in arenas that have primarily been unreceptive. "There's no end to the story; it's an ongoing process. Up and down."

CHAPTER 12

INTIMATE RELATIONSHIPS

I gave Jim whatever he asked for because that's what I thought marriage was all about. I believed my husband's needs and feelings came first, I came second. I had been taught you do everything you can to keep men quiet and happy. What no one told me was that if you do that, you don't have a self.

Alice

I bought the dream of marriage, a husband, and being taken care of. That meant not paying attention to the issues.

Laura

In no area of women's lives is it more apparent than in their intimate relationships, especially with men, that the persistent training to discount themselves is disabling. "Last time we were talking about do I take care of other people and lose me. I was so aware of what my lover needed to feel okay, I lost what I

191

wanted. I can't recall anything else. Of course, that's where I always lose it."

Divorcing her husband of 17 years, Amy reflected: "I had ideas and opinions, but I put them down. I never trusted myself. I always deferred to my husband: 'What do you think, dear? You're the more reasonable of us, what's your stand on this issue?' I didn't feel confident about myself. I didn't know what I wanted. I never learned to stand on my own and take care of myself."

Conditioned to believe that their needs would be met through giving to others, all of the women I saw in therapy, regardless of their age, demonstrated over and over again that they were emotionally attentive and expended a lot of energy on their partners, children, family members, close friends, and colleagues. "I like taking care of his every need—breakfast, lunch, dinner. I like doing those things." However, when it came to acknowledging that they too had unmet needs, they were tongue-tied. "I'm so out there taking care of him I've never been able to say, 'Hey, what about me?'"

Many believed they had to do "extra" to be loved. "In most of the relationships I've had with men, I've usually felt as if I cared more, loved more, worked more than they did. If I didn't give more, I was afraid I'd be left." "All these years I bought that it was my job to fix my husband's problems and take care of him."

In our discussions, Alice realized that in her relationships with men, as long as she cooperated with what they wanted and held in her contrary feelings, everything went smoothly. If she spoke up or—more accurately—blew up, they backed away. It seemed to Alice that men always got what they wanted, but she did not seem to get what she needed. Until now Alice had presumed that "that's the way it's supposed to be."

Alice first learned from her father, who did not believe in or allow outbursts, "to get away" from expressing her feelings.

Years later, in her marriage, if she expressed herself her husband would arbitrarily cut off all conversation. He told Alice that when she regained control of herself they could continue talking. Jim then would walk out of the house, leaving Alice alone with a "barrel of unexpressed thoughts and feelings." After a while, she gave up trying to express herself.

Anna came home from a demanding day at her office, tired and cold. She felt miserable and wanted a hug but could not ask for one. Her lover offered her a hot drink. Anna did not want that but could not ask for what she did want: to be held. Instead she said, "You won't give me what I want so I won't ask." Retreating from that volley, her partner changed the subject. That gave Anna a convenient excuse to blow up. "Although he's trying to show me he has my best interest at heart, I feel he's always changing the subject and not paying attention to my needs."

In therapy, however, we noticed that her wish to be held had totally vanished. Because she did not give a direct message about what she wanted, her chances of getting that were reduced. "If Joe hadn't been home, I wouldn't have expected anything. Since he was, I expected to be warmly welcomed. When that wasn't forthcoming, I felt so vulnerable that I couldn't ask for what I wanted. I was afraid he'd refuse."

While intimate relationships are deeply satisfying, they also stir incredible vulnerabilities that have to do with rejection or abandonment: feeling unloved. These feelings are so painful that it is typical for individuals to sandbag them rather than communicate such sensitive emotions. Strategies for concealment are further buttressed by female role conditioning, which rewarded women for developing their sensibilities to what other people are feeling while simultaneously instructing them to suppress their own needs to maintain harmony in relationships. Like Alice and Anna, the majority of women are unpracticed in asking for what they need. They have not developed an equitable balance between paying attention to themselves *and* to the people they love. Why is it that women's compassion, a precious resource, is bestowed on others at their own expense?

Problems

> You give up everything you want to keep men happy. It doesn't work.
>
> Alice

> How can I stand up for myself if I don't know I have a self!
>
> Kim

The first clue, by and large, to trouble in each client's marriage was her husband's affair with another woman. "I played by the rules in my marriage and I got trounced." Even though the husband's actions precipitated the problems, since it is a woman's job to make relationships work, and sexual satisfaction is the glue that binds the attachment, when their husbands had affairs these wives felt to blame.

Laura discovered soon after their son was born that Todd had been having affairs with other women. Although she wanted very much to keep the family together, it became impossible.

In therapy Laura reexperienced the profound rejection she felt when her marriage failed, as well as the guilt that she had not done enough to make it work. Laura wished she could have done better. "It's all my fault" still echoed in her mind. "I did something wrong because Todd was having affairs with other women. I felt insecure and unworthy. I couldn't hold this marriage together."

It was easier to blame herself than to accept that there had been problems. To acknowledge them meant facing painful decisions Laura did not think she could handle. The glass slipper had broken; Laura and her prince were not going to live happily ever after.

The majority of these women, who were 21 or younger when they married, had been programmed to expect that marriage, the traditional path to womanly identity, status, and self-esteem, would also provide them with both financial and emotional security. "I used to say to my husband, 'Tell me how to think; you're always right. You're so perfect.' I don't know if he got me to believe it or I chose to." In turn, each woman expected she would give generously and consistently to make the relationship succeed. "I felt the best way to make the marriage work was to give more and put myself last." "I see how badly he feels and I bury my own needs."[1]

Some women born in the 1960s demonstrate that this flawed conditioning persists. One 22-year-old woman, recently separated from her husband, declared in therapy: "I cared for a person who couldn't give it back and it was hard to realize that. I had trouble accepting that my dream of a man, a house with a picket fence, a child, and a dog wasn't going to happen."

Previously discouraged from acquiring the skills and capacities for knowing themselves and shaping their own lives, these women counted on their male partners to provide them with emotional well-being. "I've never been able to champion myself because I've always looked to relationships to do that for me." "I'm upset that I can still be influenced by John when it doesn't reflect what I believe I want for myself. Have I absorbed his ideas and feelings so much that I don't know which mine are?" Asserting her own emotional needs and staying with that while being in a loving relationship are major issues for every woman. "It's always what does he think I am, not who I am."[2]

After Alice learned that Jim had been sleeping with another woman she no longer felt the same love for her husband, even though they tried to repair the rent in their relationship. "I withdrew and turned inward. Something in me died. I was stuck and didn't know what to do."

Alice attempted to drown her pain with alcohol; she also slept a lot to get some relief from her despair. Neither tactic helped much. While hoping to figure a way out, she felt trapped. "I didn't know how to do anything different." Now, she understands she was depressed and angry; she did not know that at the time.

Alice had never considered taking charge of her life for herself. She did not know what she wanted and was unprepared to take care of herself, alone. She had been raised to expect that a husband would always be there to provide direction. It took Alice several years to find her own ground and the strength to assert her own needs; then she left her marriage. "I still don't know exactly how it happened. It was so scary. I feel like Jell-O inside when I do totally new things."

"All the things I might have done," cried Alice. She was bitter over those "wasted" years. "I lost the marriage and the dream. I wish there was some magic to wipe that all out; I don't want to get back into my feelings. I've spent the last several years hauling this around, isn't that enough?" While indeed angry, Alice found it even harder to acknowledge the helplessness and the lack of choice she experienced. She preferred to forget all that.

Like many divorced women, Alice was determined to be strong and independent. "I can't let on if it's too much. I can't yell for help unless I'm desperate." She had not yet accepted that each woman's emotional repertoire is complex and varied. It is natural for any woman to feel self-confident and still experience feelings of helplessness sometimes, to wish to depend on someone else and look forward to doing things on her own. The ability to comfort oneself is not minimized by nurturant attention from others.

Endings

Ending any intimate relationship results in feeling disappointed and sad, even though the ending might be desired. A loss is experienced. Often, that has a finality reminiscent of death. Very complex emotions are evoked. A period of severe distress is heralded. Everything comes into question. There are ample opportunities to reexamine oneself.

In addition to coping with their strong emotions as a result of the ending of their marriages, these women experienced a change in life-style that made money an ever-present concern. "I wish I had the economic stability to kick back a little. I miss the security of being married." The loss of the husband's income and erratic payments of child support immediately reduced most clients' standard of living. "The future looks bleak. It's such a struggle managing on my income." Moreover, since nearly every woman assumed the primary child care responsibility, their job options often decreased. The responsibility they felt for their children further exacerbated the pressures to provide for themselves.

While Laura moved to San Francisco in search of a better life, once here she became depressed and scared. She felt weighed down by the responsibility for herself and her baby. Could she make a life for herself and her young son? She had to learn how to do many things on her own. It was unbelievably hard. There was a long period of emotional numbness. "Everything was a blur. I didn't look at anything, I was just coping. I was angry with Todd and what had happened to us, and took it out on Michael." While her son's smiling face spurred her on, now she could acknowledge, "It must have been hell for him."

For a time, Laura thought her child would be better off with his father and considered sending Michael back to Todd. Accustomed to relying on her husband to supply what was required to feel worthwhile and to make the decisions that would shape her life, when Laura had to depend on herself she felt, "anxious, exhausted, and fearful, I'll fail."

Gradually Laura pulled herself out of her depression and began to handle her life; she found a job. Besides handling a bitter and protracted legal battle over property and child support payments, day-to-day living demanded consistent attention. Managing her money was a constant concern because Todd's child support checks were always late. Many times Laura felt pressured and lonely. With practice, she learned to juggle more skillfully the demands of a young child, a job, and a life for herself.

A factor sometimes overlooked and deserving attention is that for all of these women their divorce became a major catalyst, prompting them to grapple with taking charge of themselves and their lives; each woman had previously believed herself incapable without her husband's backing. These changes did not happen quickly or easily, yet few women gave themselves the credit they deserved for handling the turmoil of divorce. Despite the skill and artistry they applied to meeting the needs of their husbands and children, it was remarkable that they still discounted what they knew when it came down to using their expertise for themselves. "What do I want for myself? I'm afraid if I take responsibility I'll make a mistake." The women doubted their ability to provide for themselves. They were in the habit of believing men would do that better for them.

Isolated from Her Needs

The way to be loved is to take care of someone else.

Amy

I never thought when I was growing up and learning to take care of everyone else first, that could hurt me. Now I realize that it did.

Katherine

Many clients portrayed their partners as "emotionally stingy," self-centered, and unable to see beyond themselves. "When I'm feeling hurt I can't depend on John to help me, but if he's suffering he expects me to do for him." Very sensitive to their partners' distancing emotionally from them, several women described the isolation they experienced that exacerbated feelings in the women of not being worthwhile, a vulnerability they often have disguised. "My husband's unable to think about other people—me. He takes it all in and leaves me out of the picture, which reminds me of my father. Take from me. I'm the corn husk left over, discarded. I felt so lonely and distant from him."[3]

The very idea of directly expressing their own emotional needs immobilized these women in spite of the clamor of their own inner voices. They themselves were often frustrated and occasionally "screaming angry" with their partners' inability to "catch on." "I give to men without their asking; why do I have to ask for what I need?" It was safer to pretend not to notice their unmet needs than to call attention to them. "If I really look at things and recognize that I'm dissatisfied, I'll have to do something about it." However, they did not hesitate to judge themselves. "I need so much reassurance. I don't trust my responses to what's going on when my monster need comes into play."

Paula recalled how she had let Keith determine the pace of their relationship. She had not figured out what she wanted or needed because that might have resulted in conflict. Rather than speak up about her grievances, Paula kept hoping things would get better without her taking that risk. As a result of our discussions, Paula realized that when she wanted something badly—as she wanted this relationship to work—she denied what was unpleasant. She also ignored her own observations and feelings. Paula was fearful that if she expressed herself and really took a stand, Keith would do just what he did—leave her.

These sensitive issues between partners in intimate relationships continue to concern women. In therapy, women in their

20s also comment on the difficulties they experience with male lovers who are "self-absorbed." Although these women recognize that they are not getting their needs met, the anticipation of male disapproval keeps them silenced. They discount their own observations. "I've gotten in this really bad habit of thinking about him, not me, and I base my judgments on what he thinks and feels. I have to convince myself that I'm deserving."

Another young woman, a newcomer to therapy, complained to her lover that she felt unimportant to him. Afterward, she reported in therapy: "He made me feel insecure and dependent after we talked. Like I need to improve myself."

Tensions

> If I express my fury I don't know if Keith will be able to contain his. He might attack me.
>
> Paula

While the women's male partners were not physically abusive, several of them behaved in a manner that was intimidating and decidedly influenced the women. "Although I know he won't hit me, he can scare the hell out of you with his voice. It makes me very uptight and afraid." After an intense, angry outburst by her husband, one woman said: "He might as well have pummeled me. I was totally limp. I didn't care about anything."

When they dared to complain to their lovers, several women reported that the interaction left them feeling unhappy and belittled. "When I'm upset and he doesn't respond, the message I get is I'm not as acceptable as he is." "Whenever he and I have a difference of opinion, I always end up feeling on the defensive—like something is wrong with me. I'm a second class citizen."[4]

Socialized to regard vulnerable feelings as evidence of weakness within themselves and to depend on women to handle the emotional ups and downs of relationships, the majority of men are untrained both in directly stating their feelings and in the art of skillful listening. Many men express confusion; they presume they cannot comprehend or provide what their female lovers want. Most do not even try. Men, too, have complex feelings stirring within them for which they need to take responsibility. Distancing emotionally from women's demands or intimidating them with angry outbursts does not address the issues.

Either partner is capable of resorting to defensive, distancing maneuvers when unable to express what is really going on. Thus, within the context of a loving relationship, opportunities to find out if one's scariest feelings could be listened to and respected are sacrificed.

As one partner is able to voice and the other is able to listen, fundamental anxieties and common human vulnerabilities become more possible to accept. The ability increases to handle the sensitivities aroused by one's own feelings and to grow from the recognition that powerful forces underlie individual behavior.

The Paucity of Options

> Ralph intimidates me and makes me question my every motive. I don't feel like I have a right to fight back.
>
> Kim

Despite their training to keep their dissatisfactions silent, a few women became so angry that they struck their lovers when they felt especially misunderstood or frustrated by a partner's unresponsiveness. "It was very tense just before we separated. My husband wouldn't pay attention to me, and when I tried to talk to him, he'd turn away. One time, he drove me to lose control and I slugged him. Then, he grabbed me and restrained me."

These cases of uncontrolled outbursts of anger arose when the pain and rage aroused by emotional neglect could no longer be tolerated. These incidents demonstrate the depth of frustration and despair experienced by a woman when she cannot get the attention she needs to feel respected. "I feel erased when I'm not heard." It is to the men's credit that they restrained their own behavior and did not escalate these already stressful situations.

The complex undercurrents that can operate between partners go unaddressed when either person squelches her/himself or strikes the partner. Women and men both have lacked a working model for expressing vulnerable feelings and constructively dealing with anger. However, the training of women to placate men and suppress themselves to defuse potentially volatile situations further interferes with their acquiring the skills and strategies that are essential to tolerate one's own disquieting emotions while handling difficulties with a loved one. After her wedding, one woman reported that her father instructed her not to argue with her husband. "I should shut up and let him have his way. That's how women keep marriages together!"

By examining their training to discount themselves, suppress their self-expression, and avoid conflict, women can halt the disabling consequences of their role conditioning. "I'm trying not to go into the reflex: worry about him, make him happy, and forget about me."

Assumptions that one's actions might result in a negative response from one's lover need to be investigated; it is just as possible that a meaningful discussion could occur. "Getting what I want from my lover is a slow process—discussing and arguing, putting all kinds of things out there. There is also the fact of being willing to work on this, not resistant or stubborn. The end results are worth it."

Dealing day to day with the ongoing issues in an intimate relationship is an ever-changing process providing opportunities for both partners to be themselves, rather than each reflecting only what pleases the other. "It's a real equal relationship like I've always wanted. I want to depend on him, not be dependent on him. We're working on problem areas not trying to change each other." As the partners' ability to appreciate that each one is primarily responsible for her or his own satisfaction expands, both individuals grow. Their relationship acquires substance.[5]

Varied Challenges

Some of the women are in long-lasting first marriages, although the majority have been married and divorced once; several have remarried, and a few have divorced twice. Generally, following the dissolution of their marriages, the women became involved with other men; a few are living with those men now. Several women came out as lesbians and are currently in committed relationships.

Some of the few women who are single, widowed, or not in relationships talked about finding a relationship that works for them. Highly valued by our cultural belief system, this fundamental, strong desire for companionship keeps in balance the loneliness that torments each of us throughout life. "I never intended to spend my life alone." What happens between individuals in relationships is always being affected by these divergent, strong pulls. "I was in love and wasn't reading the signals at all. I didn't think there'd be more opportunities."

When absent from daily life, the benefits of a loving, sexual relationship are missed. "Everything is richer, fuller, and more fun with a partner." "I don't like living alone, I like having a man around." Since being unpartnered has never been a socially esteemed choice for women, it can be more difficult to tolerate. "I don't want anyone to think that because I'm single I'm lonely."

Until the present time, the high visibility of heterosexual relationships and the belief that marriage was *the* symbol for loving attachment squelched the possibility for other, equally satisfying intimate relationships. That one might prefer to be unmarried, or even to love another woman, was once inconceivable.[6] Moreover, the hostile reception that often awaits any woman who challenges social conventions influences her choice.

For many lesbians, for whom an intimate relationship provides the impetus for one of the women's coming out, additional conflict and anxiety have to be handled, since societal disapproval is often compounded by the withdrawal of affection and acceptance from one's family of origin.[7]

Similar experiences were reported by both women of color and Caucasian women when they brought home male lovers who were different in either skin color or religious or economic background.[8] The socially condoned intolerance of individual differences has infected most of us, distorting our capacity to appreciate individuals for who they are.

As these women and men exercise their right to choose and thereby expand possibilities for each of us, the absence of affirming family and social support places added strains on their relationships. The pressure on each partner to rely on the other to provide everything can heighten.

Additional Complexities

Additional complexities await two women in an intimate relationship. Because they share the same gender, the assumption that they are emotionally alike is heightened in each woman. Yearnings to be loved forever by the ideal mother, who will understand and nurture the daughter without her having to ask for anything, are reawakened in each of them. Thus, it can be even more problematic for lesbians to maintain their sense of self in a relationship than it is for heterosexual women.

As one attempts to carve out a more distinct identity, the other may exert pressure to restrain her. The fantasy of the perfect union is threatened. "I realize I want to involve my lover not just to blame her, but to take care of me." Difference heralds a rupture in intimacy and the potential of condemnation for being oneself. Ancient remnants are continually being reworked: Can I be myself and be loved?

Cynthia had difficulty standing up for herself when Joann opposed her wishes. To mollify her lover, she immediately amended her agenda. Later on, however, Cynthia realized that she resented her peace gesture and became distant. It was difficult to tolerate both her own and her partner's discomfort as she experimented with a new balance between them.

Once Cynthia distanced from her, Joann became anxious. Instead of acknowledging what she was feeling and her concern that Cynthia would reject her because she had taken a firm stand, Joann verbally attacked Cynthia.

Under that barrage, Cynthia agreed to work on this with Joann. However, once this was said she cried out: "I don't know if I can do this. It's more than I can handle."

Ellen bristled under the paucity of room to be herself. Her lover, Stacey, wanted Ellen to like what she liked, do what she enjoyed doing so they could both "be on the same wavelength." Ellen felt controlled by Stacey's demands but was afraid to express her annoyance; "It'll hurt Stacey's feelings." Instead, she swallowed her discomfort and tried harder to please her lover.

Most lesbian clients in relationships, trained like heterosexual women to expect their needs would be met through caring for their partner, had difficulty asserting their emotional needs. Concern rested more with pleasing the other than oneself. The heightened sensibilities in each woman to what the other wanted made individual assertion even more complicated.

Conditioning to demean and devalue oneself as an emotionally expressive woman further affected every woman. Even though these women yearned for intimacy with their partners, frequently they, too, lacked a good working model.

Tolerating Pain

For some lesbians, ending a relationship immediately brings the heart of their discomfort to light. There are usually fewer side issues, since they often do not share custody of a child or own property jointly, although that is rapidly changing.

Denise and Gwen came for several counseling sessions to ease the pain of ending their relationship. Denise was very distressed and angry. "It was too intense, too much togetherness. Gwen pulled out, leaving me to figure out the rest of my life." Filled with emotion, Denise felt very exposed. "I need to make closure, not keep options open."

Their pain filled the therapy room. It made Gwen very uncomfortable; past losses reverberated within. She tried to tell this to Denise, but Denise was unresponsive. Feeling discounted, Gwen retreated into silence. That triggered Denise's anger, and the two women began to verbally spar with one another. Their unbearable sadness was momentarily alleviated.

Denise wanted to express her anger. However, she sensed that Gwen would not be able to handle that, and held back. Gwen acknowledged that Denise's hunch was correct. Although she did not want to hear the anger, she also did not want to further distance herself from Denise. She felt very confused.

These two women had a difficult task, to be with a very disturbing collection of emotions and *just* allow them expression. No one could make this feel good. It felt awful.

In my counseling experience, lesbian couples are more able than their heterosexual counterparts to allow unbearable feelings a fuller expression. They are more able to tolerate the confusion and distress that always accompany the emotional upheaval of ending a relationship.

I wonder if this has something to do with three women being together, working, in the therapy room. Outside of the customary measures by which women and men tackle problems and judge one another, women establish their own standard. Sometimes, they listen more carefully and better tolerate each other's limitations.

Children: The Ardent Attachment

At the time of their divorce, many of the women who had children drew very close to them; some mothers even endowed their children with special powers. Unfamiliar with taking charge of their own lives, their children became that essential spark required to overcome the inertia created by the despair. Hesitant to take up the reins of her life on her own behalf, a woman did it for the children. "My child was my life raft; she kept me from abandoning hope." "My son was my project. I didn't have a replacement. I had to have someone to keep me going." Moreover, the father's absence from the child's daily life often intensified the attachment between the child and its mother.

A young mother who sought therapy six months after she separated from her husband had very similar concerns. She declared: "My child was my main focus. I was really low and petrified of being on my own. I needed my son to pull up my self-esteem. I couldn't do it for myself."

Some children became constant reminders to their mothers of what once had been good and bad in their marriages. "This real special person came from that mistake." "We had a baby together; it wasn't always shit." Several expressed how terrible it felt to raise a child without both its parents. The child was a continual reminder, "real sticky stuff," that having once "really loved someone you can't just make that love go away."

A few children could not return their mothers' affection. Upset and angry about what had happened and incapable of comprehending the complexities of the situation, they tended to blame their mothers for the unhappiness they experienced.

Walking out of her marriage miserable and confused, Alice felt she could not take care of anyone. She chose to leave Jessica with her father in the family home where "she'd always been." Alice thought that would be best for Jessica.

Several years later when Alice came to therapy, her first priority was to repair the relationship with her daughter. Even though unhappy at being treated like "a bad mother" and very hurt by Jessica's behavior, Alice wanted to demonstrate her caring and affection for Jessica. Jessica would make arrangements to visit her mother and then fail to appear. That was Jessica's way of telling her mother she was angry about the divorce.

After airing her pained feelings in therapy, Alice gained some perspective about what her daughter might also be feeling. She was then able to talk openly with Jessica and express her feelings and wishes. This enabled Jessica to do the same. The two of them began to experiment with a variety of visit plans that could respect both their needs. Two years later Jessica asked to come and live with her mother.

Amy was having trouble disciplining her teenage daughters. Only after she had separated from Peter and they shared the custody of their two children could Amy appreciate that subordinating her point of view to Peter's had affected her credibility in the family. "I was a good mother and made sure the children did what they were told. When the kids were small, I spent all my time fostering their adulation of their father. I reported their behavior to him. His word was the gospel. He got all the credit. Now, when I speak up I'm just crazy. I don't have any impact. I feel like a second-class citizen in my own family and I'm mad."

No matter what difficulties these women encountered in their intimate attachments with adults, they consistently tried to make the relationship with their children better. Sometimes they succeeded; sometimes they made mistakes. In contrast with their other relationships, they never gave up, and they evidenced an admirable determination. "I didn't give up with my daughter and now I can appreciate what I did do. I did something right." When a tricky problem was solved there was satisfaction. "I don't feel smug, but tremendously aware. There is joy and awe. I'm being responsible."

Aghast if there were problems, they generally blamed themselves: "Look at how I fucked up with my baby." Often their guilt, confusion, and anger were unbearable. Once in a while, if a mother could dare to say it, she felt very disappointed, even misunderstood by her child. "I make a window in time for my daughter, and she doesn't appreciate what I do." "I wish my son would perform better in school. It's hard for me to tolerate the discomfort of accepting him as he is."

They love their children very much and on rare occasions are furious with them, but usually they hold back their anger. A fervent desire to do better shines through it all. In part, the wish to improve this relationship is fueled by the desire to have with their children something they did not have with their own mothers. "It's so heavy to realize that what she gets from me *is* important. If she doesn't get it from me, who will she get it from?"

The wish to do better is further underscored by the profound programming of every woman to believe that a good mother is responsible for her child's well-being. Should the child have problems, that would reflect negatively on its mother.

Expanding Experience

Each child's move into increased independence, which is synonymous with adolescence, was a pivotal occurrence for both the child and its mother. Whether lesbian or heterosexual, unpartnered or in a committed relationship, the majority of these mothers experienced feelings of sadness and loss as their teenage children prepared to widen their realms. In general, accustomed to putting someone else's needs ahead of their own, the women acknowledged that they would miss no longer having "someone to do for."

Several women did not know what they would do now that they had no one else to take care of; it had been very important to have their children to come home to. Some would be totally on their own for the first time. "I can't figure myself out for myself. It's hard to keep myself on the straight and narrow. I have to have someone to keep me going and to check in with about my day."

Facing her son's departure for college, Katherine thought about her own mother, who did everything for others. "When everyone split, she did nothing. It's either everyone or emptiness. There was no positive activity for herself. If structure is provided by the job, kids, or partner, where is the parallel structure for your very own self?"

For two decades these mothers had calibrated every move to match their children's needs and demands. Suddenly, that sensitivity, the conditioning to be there, attentive and connected, would no longer be in such constant demand. At one time that provided a woman's primary source of satisfaction. Retooling might be complicated.

In therapy, as the women explored making different, more equitable arrangements between themselves and their offspring, anxiety was aroused. "It's making me anxious to set up a lifestyle of my own, to try on different hats. I just need to do it."

A very special connection was changing. This transition could feel like an ending; it was very sad. Both the child and its decisions would no longer be totally within the mother's control.

This important transition placed both these mothers and their offspring on their own. "The only person I have control over is myself." The balance was shifting. "It's time for myself. A chance to look at what I want to do—for myself."

Once they had investigated, expressed, and accepted the depth of their mixed emotions about these upcoming changes, all of the women were able to support their children's moves toward independence. They did not diminish the children's pleasure and excitement at moving ahead with their own lives. They were passing on a different set of experiences from those passed down to them.

This biological tie provides a model of permanence and resiliency worthy of keeping in mind. The women demonstrated a flexibility and acceptance of difference in the attachments to their children that was harder to sustain in other intimacies.

Other Changing Attachments

I want to mention that in the course of therapy surprising opportunities to reevaluate other significant relationships were often presented. For example, a parent's aging or sudden, serious illness could enable an adult daughter to work through more of her feelings about that relationship. For some, this became a special chance to express the sadness and anger about what had not happened in the past and move toward accepting what was happening in the present. "I want my dad and mom to stay strong and responsible. I don't want them to grow old and frail. It's so hard to accept that the people who once knew and did everything can't and don't anymore."

Several women have just begun to discover the specialness of female friendships. Accustomed to directing much energy toward their partners and children, many women had not developed other significant adult friendships. Their new experiences offer the promise of expanding patterns for intimacy between individuals.

CHAPTER 13

UNCOVERING
THE PAINFUL PAST

I want everything to be harmonious and it's not. It's hard to step out of those expectations. When I don't try to make things work out it feels cold and I make judgments about myself.

Jackie is representative of the many women who have developed extraordinary sensibilities for keeping harmony in relationships; these women pay attention to others and take care of their needs. For them, as for Jackie, it is second nature to allow the demands of a partner and/or children to determine what they want for themselves. They are unaware that taking care of the needs of others short-circuits knowing their own.

Furthermore, trained to believe that the assertion of their different needs would cause problems, these women squelch themselves. Often, both their mothers and their fathers, similar to Jackie's parents, are unable to provide models of individuals who express their different needs and appropriately handle whatever conflict might arise as a result.

Jackie's story unfolds in this and the following chapter. At 19 she married Paul and they had four children. During the years of her marriage, Jackie devoted herself to the care of her family. She believed it was her job to keep everyone happy. It had not occurred to her that such a goal might be unrealistic, impossible to attain.

After her youngest child started school, Jackie registered for classes at a junior college; eventually she moved on to a university program. Her relationship with Paul became strained.

Jackie graduated with a degree in health education and soon found her first job. This increased the tension between the partners even more. From the outset, Paul had not been in favor of Jackie's going to college; he did not like her new friends. Now he definitely did not want *his* wife to work.[1]

Troublesome Changes

Recognizing that the troubles in her marriage were serious, Jackie began to feel overwhelmed and anxious. These were unhappy, tense times. "When I broke out of the typical housewife role we began to argue. I felt more like an equal and became aware of a lot of anger." Conflict increased and Paul retreated. At first he refused to respond to Jackie's demands for change. Then he became silent and would not talk to her for long periods of time. Years later in therapy, Jackie associated Paul's retreats into silence with similar experiences with her father. "If he was annoyed with either my mother or me, my father'd retreat into silence which often lasted for a whole week."

Jackie suggested to Paul that they go for couple counseling; he refused. At that point she called me for individual therapy, hoping that by getting help for herself she could save her marriage. It soon became clear that Jackie and Paul could no longer agree on anything. Only later did Jackie become aware that the anger she felt at that time had been debilitating and very frightening. She had not wanted to feel it. "I was too caught up in surviving and didn't have as much insight into what was going on."

Jackie initiated divorce proceedings, which became heated in court as she and Paul battled over money and their house. A shared custody arrangement for the children was somewhat easier to negotiate. "I got what I wanted but I paid every step along the way." Relieved to be freed from the tensions that had mushroomed between them, the sadness Jackie felt at ending her marriage of 16 years was triggered primarily by the children's being very upset at the disruption of the family.

Many years later, reflecting back on this time, Jackie said: "Paul was one of a string of people who ignored my emotional needs. Even though it was painful to fight for what I wanted, I got it.

"If I look at Paul, my mother, and my father—I was doing what they wanted me to do. I did have needs, and when I put them out, I got squelched. I did something about that with Paul. I don't think there's remorse, it's more surprise: I married someone who didn't care about me."

With the divorce came a freedom Jackie had not experienced before; she had been accustomed to modulating her wants to comply with the demands of her parents and Paul. Now Jackie alone would determine her wants. While the notion of new possibilities often stirs anxieties, it also presents opportunities to discover different aspects of oneself.

The changing mores that had been in evidence in the San Francisco Bay Area for several years might have played a part in expanding Jackie's awareness of choice. About a year after the divorce Jackie realized that she was attracted to women and began dating them. Stepping outside the heterosexism of her conditioning, in a more supportive social environment, she was able to experience options that would have been unthinkable 16 years earlier. In therapy she found support for reaching out and making new alliances with women.

A few years later she met Pam. They became lovers. Pam moved in with Jackie, and their life together included juggling the demands of each woman's career with Jackie's responsibilities for her children. In time Jackie came out as a lesbian— first, to her closest friends and family; then, much later, at work. Several of Jackie's children were under 18 and she did not tell them the real nature of her relationship with Pam. She was very concerned that their father would challenge her custody of them in court.[2]

Pam was a successful, busy attorney whose job required frequent travel away from home. The women were apart for days, sometimes a week at a time. Jackie found these separations very trying. Each one was experienced as a final and total loss, as if her lover would never come back; or if Pam returned, she would not be the same. Even when it was possible for Jackie to travel with Pam, she did not want to go.

In therapy we investigated these reactions, and long-buried memories began to surface. Like Jackie, many clients are enabled to recall very early childhood events as they experience a growing acceptance of themselves and their own emotional responses. As the feelings surrounding early experiences are released, more recall is promoted. Sometimes while this is occurring, clients talk to family members, look at old family diaries and/or photographs; often they begin to dream more. Occasionally I have introduced art materials to help a woman reach back, prior to verbal skills. All this facilitates recall.

Reluctant Traveler

Although we traveled back and forth for a long time, I couldn't tell anyone how it felt. Since I was only sixteen months old that would have been very important. Being a nonverbal child is like being in a foreign country: you can't communicate.

Jackie was 16 months old when her father was drafted into the army to fight in the Second World War; he was absent from home for four years. Jackie's mother adapted to that dramatic change in their lives by joining the millions of other women who went to work during the war.[3] To provide for Jackie's care, she moved in with her widowed mother for part of the week. This new family of three rode back and forth on trolleys and buses as they shuttled between two homes, each in a different community. There was confusion, much movement, and far too many changes for Jackie. Her father had disappeared and her mother worked full time, often not returning home until Jackie was asleep. Jackie's grandmother replaced her mother as the primary caretaker. No one replaced her father.

Jackie remembered that during her childhood her mother had repeatedly told her: "You loved our moving around. You were always so excited to ride the trolley. You never fretted or complained." Much later, after questioning her mother for more details about the trolley and bus rides, Jackie exclaimed: "It was terrifying to go back and forth; you could lose someone. I could get lost! Didn't anyone care about me?"

During Pam's absences, Jackie felt very vulnerable: unloved and abandoned. She thought that if Pam really cared, she would not go on all those trips. When Pam returned home, Jackie was reluctant to tell her how vulnerable these absences made her feel and that she had missed Pam a lot. Instead, Jackie often became angry and the two women quarreled about some unrelated subject. Jackie's reticence to express her feelings made it difficult for Pam to appreciate what Jackie was experiencing. Hence, Jackie could not receive some of the understanding she yearned for.

In therapy she acknowledged that her feelings were out of proportion to the reality of the separation. We surmised that Jackie's responses were giving voice to feelings she had previously been unable to express about the disruptions that had accompanied her father's leaving home. While this opened a door onto untold chambers of memories and emotions, it took more than a year before Jackie could walk among the rooms, and several years before she could recognize what was in each one of them.

How It Was

> It's not the way I always thought it was. Me and Mom, close, taking care of each other, allied against Dad. It's easier to blame him for all that went wrong, but it's really Mom I'm angry with. She's not meeting my needs.

Even though Jackie's father was away fighting in a war and her grandmother substituted for Jackie's mother while she was on the job, Jackie had been told and believed that she had a happy childhood. In fact, she had prided herself on adjusting to her father's absence. While it is very frightening to question what one has always assumed to be true, Jackie did begin to wonder: "What about me?"

Early clues to very complex feelings included a dull awareness of discomfort and fleeting glimpses of sadness and anger. Anger was more easily expressed; it shielded Jackie from experiencing the vulnerability that accompanied realizing she did not like her father's abrupt departure and some of the changes her mother made, which included their moving back and forth between two homes. There had been too much to cope with.

A few weeks later Jackie had an image of trolley car tracks, which enabled her to express her dislike at having to ride back and forth between the houses. Then a dream made her feelings more explicit. Jackie hated riding back and forth. Also, she was very angry with her mother for abandoning her and going to work. A hint of sadness was quickly controlled. "I hate to travel. I had enough at two!" Sparse memories surrounding her father's return home, which primarily centered around the birth of her brother, Ed, provided additional clues to Jackie's unhappiness. She hated the baby; he took away the little attention she had received.

Another dream, in which a little girl was unable to hold her grandma's hand, jostled additional memories. Shortly after Jackie's father's homecoming, there were many changes. Her grandmother returned to her own home, and soon afterward her brother was born. Her mother's involvement with the baby intensified Jackie's feeling neglected.

Unhappy about all the changes, and feeling incapable of communicating her needs to her mother—"I can't tell her that I feel neglected, it makes me feel too vulnerable"—Jackie wished she could have gone to live with her grandmother. "Grandma would have known what I needed. I felt real protected and cared for by her. I was special to her." Jackie's face tightened and her body tensed up. Having originally learned that vulnerable feelings are best avoided by toughening up, she could not cope with the sadness now being experienced. "My family didn't cry easily. To feel a lot of emotion is to feel out of control. It's easier to be angry."

I appreciated that Jackie was angry with her mother, but I pointed out that now she was using her anger to retreat from her more tender feelings. Jackie acknowledged she felt empty, alone, and sad.

The Homecoming

> My father's coming home and I'm supposed to like that and
> be happy, but I didn't. My mother was depressed, maybe
> Grandma was too. She never liked my father and was pretty
> close to my mother. He came home and we were all depressed.
> No wonder I always blamed him for everything.

As memories continued to be unburied, Jackie questioned
her mother; she discovered that her father's homecoming had
created problems between her parents. During her husband's absence Jackie's mother had managed well, enjoying the independence afforded by both paid employment and her mother's
caretaking of Jackie. Jackie even recalled her mother's exuberance
when she came home from work.[4]

Nevertheless, with the end of the war and the return of the
soldiers, it was assumed that, like millions of other women,
Jackie's mother would automatically, enthusiastically, resume
the life she led before the war: at home raising a family and
caring for her husband. Meanwhile, every effort was urged to
reestablish men like Jackie's father in their breadwinner–head of
the household role. After all, they had suffered severe hardships
and traumas; it would have been "selfish" not to direct the most
attention to the men.

Typically, women's experiences were underappreciated.
Despite their participation as equals with men in the world of
paid work during the wartime years, they were invited to suppress their pride in their achievements. The reluctance and
resentment many felt at giving up their jobs and the help they
had with child care was discounted.[5] Alternative options for
women's peacetime employment were not explored, and many
became silent casualties as the tide pushed everyone to return
to conventional practices. It became virtually impossible to resist
the pressure to conform.[6]

Jackie's mother was one of those casualties. Unhappy and depressed, she felt uncertain about remaining in the marriage. Taking Jackie with her, she separated from her husband; however, divorce was not an acceptable solution, and the parents soon reunited.

Although Jackie's father has been dead for many years, we can speculate that he returned home eager to leave behind the experience of war and reconnect with his wife and child. Once the welcome quieted down, however, he, like many other returning soldiers, may have also felt a complex and painful series of emotions. Many servicemen found readjustment to civilian life perplexing and more difficult than they had anticipated. The abrupt transition from soldier and witness to the horror and devastation of war to being back home again, a civilian—husband and father—was not simple.[7]

The Strains of Reunion

I was raised in a matriarchy, all the men were away at war. When my father came back he expected to pick up where he left off, but he was a stranger. I was afraid of him.

We know that it was not easy for Jackie and her mother to fit her father back into the picture. While he was away fighting in the war, each of them had made her own adjustment.[8] The years apart had altered all of them, and undoubtedly her father also had difficulties fitting back into the family. Everyone had endured serious hardships; their reunion was strained.[9] "I think I looked forward to the homecoming. My mother led me to expect that it would be good, Daddy was looking forward to seeing me. But it wasn't good. It was hard. We didn't get along. The father I remembered was fun-loving and playful, this father was harsh and critical. We couldn't get back the old connection. I didn't fit his expectations. My mother didn't pay attention to me and Grandma went away too. I waited for my dad to do something to make it feel right, but he never did."[10]

This complex situation deserved continuous sensitive monitoring on everyone's part. However, the postwar exuberance of 1945 emphasized that the best way to handle the wounds left by the war years was to slip back into the usual routine as if nothing had happened: look ahead to the future. Such beliefs do not provide a model for communicating confusing vulnerablities.

Jackie's father, typical of most men of his generation, was not in the habit of directly expressing either disquieting or vulnerable emotions. He had been trained to presume that his wife and daughter would understand what he was feeling and respond accordingly.[11]

Since he was reluctant and unpracticed in declaring his needs, we know from Jackie's recollections that when she and her mother could not provide what her father needed, his angry silences told them that something was wrong. "He was a presence to deal with, not someone who fit into the family." By distancing himself from his feelings, Jackie's father also became unavailable to his family.

Jackie's mother, like many women, was also not very comfortable with her sensitive feelings. Furthermore, as is typical of women of her generation and unfortunately often true today, when Jackie's mother's needs clashed with her husband's expectations, she suppressed them and put on a "happy face." Her unhappiness was buried.

Even though acquiescing to both her husband's expectations and the cultural prescription for how a good wife and mother should behave, Jackie's mother became visibly depressed, Jackie remembered. "She went from a happy, independent woman to being a depressed, busy housewife trying to please everyone."

Without the understanding and acceptance that could come from the mutual sharing and respect for each person's difficulties

and different experiences, the complexities of this reunion remained unaddressed. In this most difficult time, each person felt
reluctant to communicate her or his pain. "In my childhood, feelings were not okay, they were something to be ashamed of. They
got you in trouble."

These parents were unable to be attuned to what their child
needed because they were unable to acknowledge that they had
needs of their own. That left Jackie to cope alone with her confusion and discomfort, two unhappy parents, and—all too
soon—a baby brother.

It Was Too Long

> People who go away don't come back or they come back so
> changed, they're unrecognizable. I changed too.

Concurrent with these therapy explorations, Jackie's 20-
year-old son decided to move to Boston. Their tender parting
at the airport stirred complex emotions in Jackie. She felt very
sad and was trying not to be angry. She wished that Pam,
who was away on a business trip, could have been home with
her.

Jackie was also aware that she did not trust that her son
would ever come back, but if he did, he would not be the same.
"It's my father's leaving. I counted on him, I needed him. When
he came back it wasn't the same." Becoming uncomfortable with
what she had just said, Jackie tried to change the subject. My
pointing that out helped her to continue.

"I'm angry now that he left. It makes me feel so helpless.
I don't want to face the loss of his going."

"How come you're so angry?"

"Because he must have meant a lot to me. I didn't want
him to go then and now I don't want to feel that." With tears

in her eyes Jackie continued: "It was too long. My mother told me he'd be back, but that didn't change my sadness. My mother must have been depressed and, if she was, I'd be too. I'm sad my father left. After about six months I guess my mother began to make a new life and we did all right. She liked her independence and freedom.

"It wasn't the same when he came back. The depression started again. Dad also may have been depressed. He had seen a lot of death and starvation. I remember his nightmares. He would wake up and cry out. We were all depressed. However, no one in my family ever talked about that. It wasn't allowed."

Jackie began to blame her mother for how events turned out. I pointed out that by shifting the blame, Jackie was distancing from her own feelings. Jackie acknowledged that no one was to blame. "It was very complex. Events were out of everyone's control." I agreed, but noted how Jackie was again avoiding her vulnerable feelings. "I feel so helpless and hopeless. I can't do anything about what's happened and I hate feeling helpless."

I Can't Tell My Feelings

My needs have to hit me over the head before I'll acknowledge
I have any.

Over many months, while always hesitant and generally guarded, Jackie continued to increase her recall of these complex, life-shaping events. We came to understand that forgetting about her father, minimizing his importance, had been her way to conceal the sadness and depression his departure had created. Becoming angry with her father buried those vulnerabilities still deeper, and Jackie was reluctant to reawaken them. "I'm left out and not getting my needs met, but I don't feel anything."

Retreating from the unhappiness this aroused in her, Jackie shifted to talk of her grandmother's departure once her father was settled back home. I pointed out that whenever she got close to her feelings about her father, she ran off—either to her mother or to her grandmother. Jackie exclaimed: "Maybe everything would have been different if he had been around those first five years. We could have known each other better and I wouldn't have had to deal with so many separations, attachments, and losses. Plus all that traveling back and forth. He deserted me. He killed a piece of me."

Jackie was modeling behavior highly rewarded by the belief system that dominates this culture: Don't show what you are feeling; manage. Act independent. These revered attitudes make it even more difficult for individuals to accept that prolonged life stresses generate vulnerable feelings. The hurt and neglect Jackie felt was artfully concealed by her angry, prideful stance. Behind that defiance lurked further exquisite sensitivities: "They'll all leave me. I'm not important and I can't risk showing my feelings because I'm dependent on them."

As Jackie's emotions gradually poked through her armor, she accepted more of her feelings and complained about the painful, slow therapy process. There are no instant results when uncovering years of deeply buried emotions. Although she had put together many pieces, Jackie balked at acknowledging their impact. A dream implied that although therapy was a mysterious process, it would be okay. That message was hard for her to accept. She wanted immediate answers, direction, and help.

Shortly thereafter, Jackie stated: "His leaving me when I was sixteen months old is the first wall. Then he comes home and it's not the same. I don't want to deal with all my feelings about my father. I felt rejected by him and disappointed that he couldn't make it better. I allied with my mother against him, fought with him, and felt oppressed by him—maybe he didn't love me anyway."

I stopped Jackie and wondered if she was aware of what was happening. She recognized that she did not want to mourn her father's departure and instead defended against her feelings by growing angry with him. She further distanced from the disappointment of their relationship by allying more strongly with her mother. Blaming him for what had happened protected Jackie from all those sensitivities. She wailed: "Oh, I don't want to feel all this. It's going to feel bad!"

Soon afterward, Jackie discussed her father's death many years earlier. There was much silence as she wrestled with her feelings. She was tearful, sad. Jackie connected this sadness to her childhood losses. "Somehow, it's my fault my father left. I did something bad and he went away. Now I know that's not true and see how the pieces fit together. I couldn't ask for what I wanted. I wanted my father to stay home, and he left. I was mad and upset, but my mother squashed that behavior. It was unacceptable.

"My father could have been more adult when he came home. That's pretty egocentric. He was suffering from the war. None of us got what we wanted. It's sad, frustrating. That's the truth."

CHAPTER 14

TAKING A STAND

I got an overdose of survival skills and an underdose of getting
my needs met. I dealt with all this by never being home.

The tension in the family following her father's homecoming
deeply affected Jackie, but she was unable to find an acceptable
way to express herself. "It was hard enough if you were clear,
but if you were confused—forget it. I went outside to play and
everyone thought I was happy." This detachment protected
Jackie from feeling, "I don't figure in here." She became quite
adept at roller skating. However, Jackie also learned to discount
her yearnings for more nurturant attention. "When I don't get
attention I stop trying and my feelings close off."

The neglect Jackie really felt became masked as she learned
to be hypervigilant to other people's emotional states. "If people
I'm close to become distant or depressed, I have to do something

about it." While taking care of the needs of others was insurance against being rejected, it also heightened Jackie's development of womanly sensibilities, thereby further distancing her from her own needs.

Although Jackie was encouraged to be physically active, her parents provided few opportunities for her to experience her emotions without concern about reprisal. She remembered being picked on and criticized by her father, who also frequently pressured her to do well at school. Preoccupied with the instability at home, Jackie did not like school. "If I didn't know something which would have been appropriate at my age, my father made fun of that." She was resentful and angry. "I didn't know what was expected of me and I couldn't find out. Somehow I should have known, but I didn't. Then I was hollered at."

Believing the tension in the family was hers to ameliorate, and uncomfortable with conflict, Jackie's mother tried to "keep the peace" by minimizing difficulties. She would secretly allow Jackie to do things her father would not permit; however, no one ever confronted him directly about how it felt to abide by his rule. "My mother was resistant to listening to my needs. She had the same problem. She didn't get her needs met and passed that on to me."

In girlhood, Jackie liked being rescued by her mother from expressing herself to her father. However, when she was 17, her mother could not help Jackie obtain her aspiration. When Jackie's father refused to financially support Jackie's going to a college away from home, she did not go. "If she couldn't get it how could I?" Investigating this more thoroughly revealed: "All my fears of his anger are hers. He never slapped me. All he did was raise his voice and everyone jumped."

When Jackie's wants interfered with what her father deemed appropriate, she was taught not to question his decision but to muzzle her wants. Those expectations were further reinforced by her mother's counsel: "Do it now before your father comes home."

Discouraged from expressing herself and taught to shun conflict, as many other daughters are, Jackie was deprived of gaining the self-confidence required to stand up for herself. She could not learn to tolerate the normal anxiety that accompanies self-assertion because she associated that anxiety with critical rejection. She squelched herself to avoid both unpleasant experiences and upsetting emotions. "I never let on when they didn't catch on. I gave up. Maybe I needed more encouragement, or I cut off my nose to spite my face. I wouldn't achieve for them. I wanted to depend on someone else. When it came to depend on me I couldn't see the way and I balked."

The Repetition

During most of the marriage, Jackie complied with Paul's expectations of how a good wife and mother should behave, mirroring the beliefs she had learned in girlhood. However, once she asserted her wish to go to college, Paul became angry. Because he was not in accord with what Jackie wanted, she was expected to relinquish her goal. When she did not, Paul exerted further pressure through his control of the purse strings. Although Jackie had made adequate child care arrangements for the younger children, he refused to pay for them. "He thought I should be home with the children."

As Jackie attempted to express herself and voice her long-neglected wants, Paul further devalued her achievements. "He told me that I was just going through a phase." Not only did making changes in their traditional relationship require a great deal of effort on Jackie's part, but as she made that effort, her husband undermined it. Poignantly, getting something that she wanted did ultimately result in the end of her marriage. That experience exacerbated Jackie's anxiety: expressing her wishes leads to rejection.

In the habit of accommodating to Paul's demands while keeping her own submerged, Jackie complied whenever Paul requested a change in the shared custody arrangements in the post-divorce years. Rather than point out that sometimes Paul was not keeping his part of the bargain or that his requests pressured the children unfairly, Jackie silently fumed. Not only was Paul kept unaware that his behavior was affecting the children, but the children were exposed to poor role models. They did not learn to speak up when their father ignored what was important to them. Sensitive to the sadness the children were experiencing because of their parents' divorce, Jackie believed she was protecting them by minimizing conflict.

Until we examined this in therapy, Jackie was unaware that she was repeating behavior originally learned from observing her mother interact with her father. Although a mother might be trying to protect her children from their father's insensitive behavior, she is inadvertently depriving them of opportunities to learn to negotiate with their father.

Much later, Jackie expanded her understanding of the tie-in between conflict and her sensitivity to rejection. We knew that her father's moody temperament and her mother's difficulties tolerating his distancing behavior influenced Jackie's discomfort with conflict. Now she recalled that when her father first came back from the war, she was squelched for showing her anger. "I don't know who was responsible for doing that, but it was a long time before I showed anger again." As soon as Jackie said that, she got very quiet.

"What just happened?"

"I anticipated some reaction from my mother. It occurs to me I was afraid she'd leave—she did once. Would my mother have stayed with my father if I hadn't been born? She was unhappy in the marriage. It would be scary if she was gone. My mother was the only constant person in my childhood."

The careful unfolding that characterizes the psychotherapy process enabled Jackie to unearth ancient wounds and appreciate how these wounds affected both her behavior and her ability to tolerate her emotions.

Expanding Awareness

Pam initiated talking about a vacation to Hawaii, and Jackie was reluctant to go so far from home. This reaction stirred more memories. "I don't want to leave my house because my dad won't know where I am when he comes back. I'll miss him." Unwilling to acknowledge the vulnerability this aroused, Jackie immediately shifted to reviewing the traveling she had done between her mother's and her grandmother's houses. By doing so, she demonstrated a well-established survival skill: When feelings are too intense to tolerate, get busy, move physically; interrupt the emotional tension.

Expressing the sadness she had experienced when her father departed aroused such sensitivities that it took many months before Jackie could go into this more deeply. One day, when she realized that it was difficult to express her sadness because her mother did not feel similarly about Jackie's father's departure, she came closer to staying with her feelings.

Much later, while recollecting her strong dislike of her mother's involvement and pleasure in her job, Jackie unearthed further sensitivities. "Once my father left, maybe my mother didn't want to be home. She could be free." With her father absent and her mother her only parent, it had seemed to Jackie that her survival depended on trying to keep her mother happy, further incentive to squelch her own sadness.

A dream later prompted Jackie to recognize that if she could have talked at 16 months she might have said: "Don't leave me."

"First my father left for four years, then my mother left daily. Some days she didn't come back. I immediately focus on the loss whenever I'm unclear about whether someone is coming back. I'm sorry for me as that little person my mother didn't understand. And the war, things could have been different. It's sad."

Continued discussions of the proposed trip to Hawaii enabled Jackie to make further connections. She realized that she was complying with the plan Pam presented, just as she had complied with the plan her mother presented. Not cooperating created too much anxiety: someone she loved might leave. "As a child, I didn't have the option not to go along with the game." Several months later Jackie was able to say, "A child feels like she will die when a parent leaves."

Jackie learned all too well that it was safer to accommodate to someone else's wishes than to express her own. Openly declaring her emotional needs put all Jackie's vulnerabilities on the line. "I can't stand up for myself because I'm afraid of the other person's response. If I push the limit and let on how much I don't like what's happening, I dread that I'll be rejected.

"Asking for something makes me anxious. I don't have enough self-esteem to ask, 'What about me?' If I ask for what I want and Pam doesn't also want it, I jump to the conclusion that the relationship will end."

The people Jackie originally depended on could not keep what was best for her in focus. That certainly was repeated with Paul and surely contributed to Jackie's reluctance to depend on Pam, despite the affection that Pam demonstrated for Jackie and the reality of the years they have been together. "If I didn't trust my parents to take care of a situation for me, that would spill over into not trusting myself or other people."

Reluctant to acknowledge these additional sensitivities because they increased her anxiety, Jackie belittled herself, discounting her own needs. "I don't deserve to have my needs met so I can't make them known. If Pam knew my real needs she'd be scared off." It took several months before Jackie could understand that not trusting herself when she experienced her emotions harkened back to the early experiences with her parents and the ways they had coped with the conditions World War II created in their family life.

Worry about the prospective Hawaii trip continued. This time it was the child care arrangement. As she spoke, however, Jackie realized that her anxiety had more to do with her own childhood. She now questioned her grandmother's caretaking of her. Her grandmother, whom Jackie had previously idealized, became a more complex person. She had a feisty temper and hollered a lot. "She was no substitute for my mother." Now Jackie thought that maybe she had not liked being left with her. "I told myself that I loved Grandma taking care of me as a way to avoid the pain of all those losses. Maybe it wasn't so great. I didn't like it."

Jackie put the pieces together. Worrying about the present child care arrangement was masking her sensitivity about what had been missing in the past: her mother's constant presence. "That makes me feel sad. I depended on someone who wasn't available."

Soon after, Jackie and Pam did go to Hawaii. It was a good vacation and Jackie enjoyed her trip away from home.

I Can't Get What I Want So Why Bother

Whenever it comes to doing something for myself I renege and don't finish. I'm afraid and I call it quits.

One day in therapy, about a month after the Hawaii trip, Jackie was having difficulty getting in touch with her feelings.

She became angry with me and said I was being critical. Examining this more carefully revealed that Jackie was feeling very vulnerable but had not communicated that. She presumed, however, that I would catch on to what she was experiencing and respond empathically—something she herself had done many times for others. When that did not occur, Jackie sandbagged her sensitive feelings by becoming angry with me. My inability to respond to what she had not articulated made me appear critical. Her anger then protected Jackie from further disappointment.

Decoding this had immediate application. Earlier that week, Jackie had become angry with Pam, who also had not appreciated Jackie's unvoiced feelings. Then, too, anger disguised more delicate emotions. Now Jackie could express what happened when she felt misunderstood: she felt worthless, abandoned.

These sensitive feelings were never expressed in Jackie's relationship with Paul because he, like her father, distanced himself from Jackie and relied on silence to stifle communication between them. Those tactics stirred Jackie's anger and provided her with armor against acknowledging her vulnerable feelings.

However, the expectation for partner understanding, which can be greater between two women, combined with Pam's willingness to talk over difficulties, heightened these instances of miscommunication between Jackie and Pam. Jackie then discussed them in therapy. These misunderstandings were reminiscent of very-little-girl experiences between herself and her mother. At those times, when Jackie's mother was unable to pay attention or was preparing to leave for work, Jackie felt lost and abandoned. She learned then that being angry and stubborn got her more attention than revealing her unhappy feelings. Now she could begin to see alternatives: "It's not appropriate to act ornery when I feel sad. I don't have to do that to get attention from Pam."

Jackie closed her eyes, and images reappeared of unresponsive babies from many of her dreams. It was upsetting to realize that she had closed down emotionally because her needs had been unmet. "I couldn't do anything different." Long ago, survival had depended on not feeling, and again Jackie felt numb. She was escaping from the hordes of unruly emotions bivouacked right outside of awareness. "Keeping my eyes shut has affected me. It's not like I'm in total darkness, but more like there's a veil over me. If I opened my eyes, it would be overwhelming. So it's happening slowly."

Never having learned to trust her own emotions as a reliable measure of what she experienced, Jackie became accustomed to allowing other people's responses to her determine the legitimacy of her needs and the veracity of her feelings. To mute her disappointment at not being able to obtain what she needed, Jackie detached herself both from the situation and from her emotions. "I can't integrate the idea that it's possible to have feelings that I'm not in control of." She went "outside to play."

Jackie tried to maintain that those choices had been good ones. Several times I pointed out that she had reported feeling miserable and misunderstood as a child, and that no one had listened to her needs. At first, Jackie continued to deny how bad that had been. Stubbornness was again totally masking her despair. Then Jackie stated that as she appreciated how hard it was to change these old patterns, she felt hopeless and abandoned and wanted to give up. Nothing ever worked out. "I've spent my whole life being angry with my father, walling off my love and tenderness for him. Am I afraid to find that closeness again, to realize that he was important to me and that I loved him?" After a long silence, Jackie continued. "Although I feel good when I remember, it also makes me feel helpless and vulnerable, powerless."

Through the sensitive attention afforded by the psychotherapy process, along with the constancy of my presence, Jackie was learning that she could sustain important relationships *and* reveal her vulnerabilities.

Changing

> This is affecting every aspect of my life. I need to work on it. I
> guess doing it is the only way to change.

Jackie often disliked the discoveries she made; they aroused painful emotions. What upset her most was realizing that in trying to keep her feelings about her childhood losses buried, she had developed a false sense of bravado. "It was just a facade."

Jackie had depended on her mother's presence to keep at bay all her overwhelming feelings about the changes she had to handle. However, when her mother was absent, Jackie felt anxious. "When is she coming back? I was thinking, how does this connect to loss, and I rationalized, she always came back."

The next day Jackie became aware that by concentrating on the loss, she had been retreating from her fear that her mother, like her father, would not come back at the end of the day and Jackie would be abandoned by both her parents. "I must have made something up so I wouldn't have to deal with the confusion around waiting for him to come home and he didn't appear. I felt pretty hopeless and out of control. I probably experienced those feelings a lot—four years was permanent."

I wondered if that might have had something to do with her difficulty in accepting her father when he came back.

"I wrote him off. He doesn't exist. He isn't coming home. Okay, he's dead. I don't deal with it anymore. I'm anxious. I think it's about who else am I crossing off? What if my mother leaves? Then I'm really abandoned."

World War II created special conditions that Jackie, her mother, and her father had to adapt to. Jackie's father's prolonged absence fighting in a war far from home intensified her dependence on her mother to provide the stability and nurturance essential to all children. While there is no equivocating about the importance of the mother to her child's security and happiness, Jackie's situation highlights factors our belief system prefers to ignore.

Often absent from the home for extended periods of time in activities sanctioned by society, including fighting in wars, many fathers are only intermittently present during their children's crucial developing years. Other fathers, although physically present, are often not emotionally involved with their children. This paucity of father participation deprives children of the experience of male nurturance. There is no question that this influences the quality of family interaction, decreasing opportunities for children of both sexes to observe models of men actively participating in the business of making family life work.

Moreover, our firm conviction that the mother's presence and responsible caretaking of the children is what is essential, further promotes our accepting as commonplace this detachment by men, ignoring and undervaluing their contributions to the family's well-being. Paternal deprivation has had serious consequences for all offspring. The persistent focus on the mother keeps this hidden.[1]

Knowing Herself

If I don't express myself here, where will I do it?

The job demands on Jackie, a health educator, have been accelerated by the current crisis about AIDS. Many people have been affected and a good deal of strong emotion aroused as emphasis on educating about sexually transmitted diseases and safer sex practices has increased. In continual contact with many community agencies and officials who plan health education programs, Jackie has found herself taking positions at meetings that would have been unthinkable five years ago. "I'm speaking up for what I believe. I'm not just sitting here quietly, like a good girl. I'm making my voice heard whether other people like what I'm saying or not." Not only is Jackie standing up for her beliefs, growing more adept at handling either colleagues' support or flak, she is also openly identifying herself as a lesbian.

Drawing on the many skills she has acquired over the years that directly relate to womanly sensibilities to other people's needs, Jackie is especially good at standing firm for the benefit of others. However, when it came to revealing her own needs one day at work, she was reticent.

A colleague wanted to talk to Jackie at five o'clock and she wanted to go home. She damned herself for having needs when other people were in distress. Having gained a reputation for being a willing, sensitive listener, Jackie found it hard to set limits on her time. Moreover, the ancient, tender sensitivity to being rejected if she did not comply with other people's demands resurfaced.

For the moment, it seemed as if Jackie had no choice. Either she condemned herself for not being a good, generous woman, or she had to sit through someone else's complaints when she wanted to go home. "I've always been available to everybody and when I set limits it's hard for them to hear me. I, myself, have to be very clear in my own mind because it's so hard to set those limits. When I define my own needs I feel like I'm rejecting the others."

"What do you make of that now?"

"I think I'm very sensitive to having needs because it makes me feel so vulnerable, and not getting my needs met feels like rejection. As a kid, it was quite a struggle if my needs were different from my mother's."

Jackie began to talk about her mother. I pointed out that she was shifting away from herself. "If I'm not available for others I'll be rejected."

I commented on this familiar female pattern. Many women anticipate a negative outcome when they have to declare needs of their own; to bridle that discomfort they focus nurturant attention on others and their own needs get submerged.

"If I'm not this mellow, nonassertive person, people won't like me. Yet I know that's not true. I've taken that risk before and it's been okay. I just thought, 'This will be difficult to change,' then realized, I'm doing it."

Keeping Herself in Mind

Still wary about relying on her emotions as trustworthy guideposts, Jackie waffled between experiencing her feelings and disregarding them. She was so much in the habit of downplaying her own responses and experiences for so long that it was difficult to recognize that both they and she were acceptable. This was especially noticeable around new challenges. Initially, Jackie mistrusted her emotional reactions and assumed that things would turn out negatively despite her many new positive experiences.

I suggested that she was clinging to this outmoded behavior to avoid her feelings about something in the past that had been too overwhelming to handle.

Jackie responded: "A lot of the time I felt abandoned and helpless. There was too much to handle so I went into this either/or system, a system of avoidance. Maybe that's why I hang onto the past. Like I hang onto the memory of my father originally being there rather than moving on to the homecoming and just going on from there."

I reminded Jackie that she had skipped away from her feelings of helplessness and abandonment.

"I can't avoid this, but I sure would like to put it out of my mind."

One month later, Jackie walked into the therapy room upset. The previous night she and Pam had had a serious argument. The reality of Jackie's childhood was that she experienced a series of events that made her anxious about whom she could depend on to take care of her needs. This made her very vulnerable to feelings of abandonment. One way to curb those painful feelings was to comply with other people's demands, especially her mother's. "By being compliant I thought I had some control over her leaving."

When she and Pam argued, Jackie would lose sight of the strength of their relationship and assume that Pam would not stick around if they disagreed; their relationship would end. When she felt this vulnerable, Jackie realized that she often wanted to tease Pam in mean ways to defend against her own sensitivities. "This is not very adult behavior; it's left over from my childhood. Dealing with hurtful situations kind of like my father dealt with us."

In the past, to assure her security Jackie acted tough, but "I really felt more vulnerable than I like to think I was." She did not acknowledge her emotional needs because she dreaded being rejected. Now Jackie realized that if speaking up for what she needed meant arguing with Pam, she was taking that risk. "Getting into conflict and standing up for myself has meant that ultimately I'd be abandoned. I'm trying to change that—and that's scary. I need to tell this to Pam and she needs to listen. We'll have differences—that doesn't mean I have to give in."

PART IV

RECLAIMING PRIDE

CHAPTER 15

BEING A WOMAN
A Continuous Challenge

When I deprecate myself, sell myself short, do favors for others at my own expense, I become angry and don't work effectively. Then I doubt myself further and feel even worse. It's all a tight knot, a black mass in my body, right in the center of my stomach. It hurts.

Anna

Whether these women are asserting their rights in the work force or speaking up for their needs in intimate relationships, they grapple with a vast range of contradictions that is women's legacy growing up in a patriarchal society. When they disclose still more vulnerable, personal concerns—their menstrual cycle variations, contraception dilemmas, sexual difficulties with a lover, discomfort with their bodies, or health problems—even more startling discrepancies emerge.

Throughout the ages, women's complex and awesome biology, a powerful reminder of their essential participation in the miracle of life, has created problems for them. Although a reverence for their procreative potential is proclaimed, all women are subjected to another reality: continuous degrading experiences solely because they are female.

Grave Distortions

From taboos that have stigmatized and maligned bleeding women, keeping them isolated from rightful participation in community life, to the vast literature about the female reproductive cycle, which would have us believe that menstruation is the first dramatic awakening of girls to their sexuality,[1] grave distortions deny women's reality.

Overwhelming disregard for the female body prevails. From unexpected betrayals by trusted males to the blatant misuse of women's bodies to advertise and sell products, each generation of girls is conditioned to be ashamed of their bodies: to ignore body sensations and sensual feelings. How can a girl learn to treasure, to be at ease with her body when it is so flagrantly abused?[2]

For many girls, even the pleasurable discovery of their own sexuality is not theirs to make. One out of approximately eight girls is incestuously abused before the age of 14.[3] In spite of significant contributions by both women's self-help groups and feminist research that has broken the silence about incest, the privacy and integrity of many girls' bodies is violated long before puberty, without thought for the long-lasting deleterious effects on them.[4]

Not only does this create mistrust of their bodies, but there is still more to contend with, lifelong repercussions to self-confidence and esteem. The few clients who, in therapy, reclaimed their memories of childhood sexual molestation reported that their confidence in themselves had been shaken, and they blamed themselves for whatever abuse they had endured. They were bad; they felt guilty and ashamed, terrified. "Even though I know I didn't have anything to do with this, it feels like it's all my fault."

These women felt intensely uncomfortable as their fragmented painful memories of childhood sexual abuse were unearthed. Several doubted and denied their remembrances. "Could I be making this up? I don't trust myself. No one will believe me." Denial had been the original protection against realizing the full impact of what had happened. "By saying it didn't happen I can make it go away." One daughter, in retreat from her disturbing collection of memories, dreams, and images concerning herself and her father, said, "I'm sure my father's done some terrible thing to me because I've been running away from him all my life."

Early Disregard of Their Bodies

Although direct genital contact was not the primary violation of body integrity experienced by most of these women as young girls, their bodies were handled and their privacy ignored. Most commonly, beginning early in girlhood (and unfortunately still reported by many women of all ages both in and out of therapy) nearly every client had been exposed to repeated sexual harassment either verbally or by direct physical touching of body parts.

Such behavior by fathers, relatives, neighbors, friends, teachers, and, later on, co-workers and bosses usually evoked very strong feelings. Because it undermined their confidence, the daughters were prompted to first question themselves rather than the behavior of men. In girlhood, they had rarely spoken of these experiences to other family members. They were ashamed and doubted their word would be believed over a grown-up's. Sometimes the adult had told or threatened them not to tell others. Mistrust of their bodies and themselves resulted.

The majority of the women recalled intrusive, unpleasant physical behavior, primarily by their fathers. A few were repeatedly abused physically until adolescence. For others there were sexual overtones to the handling that made the daughters even more confused. For the most part, they crammed their feelings down as they were tousled, pinched, hugged, tickled, "playfully" punched, or beaten.

While most of them strongly disliked what was happening, they felt powerless to make their fathers stop. They did not complain; besides, no one seemed interested to hear what they thought. One women noted that when she was uncooperative her father would restrain her physically and tickle her. His idea of fun certainly did not match hers.

Jackie disliked sitting in her father's lap and would get "real mad" when he held her there. However, she also felt guilty for not being nicer. When I asked if there had been any sexual fondling, she replied: "I'm clear, after I was six nothing sexual happened. By that time, the battle was on. He'd given up being my friend. My brother was born."

Occasionally, a woman became aware of even more delicate feelings that were difficult to disclose. She recollected feeling aroused while being molested. Even though she very clearly also realized she did not want the experience to continue, she recognized that she had not wanted it to stop. She felt ashamed and had not appreciated that her body was responding normally. "Something I knew was wrong felt good. I was a good girl and this made me bad. It took away my confidence." It was startling to acknowledge feeling pleasure in an experience that had also been terrifying.

No one ever complained that her mother had been too physically affectionate. In fact, the opposite was a more likely complaint. "My mother was always telling me to keep my hands to myself." These daughters wished their mothers had been more physically demonstrative. They yearned for, and were also guarded about, a woman's touch. The soothing that could come from being held by another woman opened the floodgates to the longings for nurturant attention.

To survive in a society that does not respect a woman's body, *and*, in fact, continually demeans her for being a female, conditions most women to suppress their nature and feel alienated from their bodies. Moreover, to secure love and acceptance under these disabling, unjust conditions, many women have acquired a collection of strategies whose sole task is to squelch and constrain themselves. "That part of me that is passionate and alive is large and wants to burst forth. But it's not allowed." A woman's body is her most definitive statement of her uniqueness. Any abuse of it is a source of painful confusion.[5] "I'm sitting on the couch and a body in an outrageous fifties-style polyester red print dress falls out. I hastily sit back down to keep it hidden. It doesn't look like me. I'd never wear a dress like that. But it is me. Dead."

More Humiliation

Within this complex web there exist still more demeaning experiences. During their recall of abusive sexual experiences in childhood, several women remembered attempted rapes during their late adolescence. The memories sometimes included being forcibly held down and threatened with physical violence. Rape or attempted rape by either strangers or men known to the women is another frightening, humiliating experience women are expected to endure quietly. In fact, when they protest they have often been made to feel responsible for its occurrence. What a confusing wound to one's dignity, to be blamed for being raped!

While each woman who talked about these experiences had extricated herself from the situation without being raped, virtually every client talked about a close friend, sister, relative, or co-worker who had been raped.[6] Additionally, several women had the painful experience of listening to their daughters describe encounters with men who abused them sexually either on the streets, at school, or on the job. The intense pain and anger these mothers suffered are feelings familiar to many women as they cope with the reality of sexual assault. These outrageous, repetitive reminders of woman's vulnerability because of her gender played havoc with each woman's emotions.

Menstruation

Although menstruation could provide each maturing girl with ample opportunity to become intimate with, and pay respectful attention to, the natural vicissitudes of her own body rhythms, the confusing contradictory messages that surround growing into young womanhood instead created discomfort and embarrassment for many women at the onset of their menstrual period. "When puberty hit, I didn't want to be a woman. I had all those negative images." Many were wary and uncomfortable with all the changes occurring in their bodies. "I resented my body. I was pudgy and my breasts developed too early."[7]

Only one woman praised her mother's handling of menstruation, "She did that well." More typically, very little information was provided and even less attention paid to menstruation by either the women's mothers or fathers. "My mother dealt with menstruation by leaving me a pad and belt, correctly laid out. That was it." "In my family there was a lot of denial of the physical. My father especially ignored clothes and appearance." The parents' silence demonstrated their uneasiness with discussing this normal physiological process. A few mothers, however, following the onset of their daughters' menses, did inform them about sex with men, primarily cautioning them about the dangers of sexual mistreatment and rape.

Regardless of their girlhood experience with their own mothers about their menses, all the women who had daughters shared a sense of celebration with their daughters as they commenced to menstruate. One woman, becoming aware at the time of her daughter's first menstrual period of the public absence of positive rituals for menarche, remarked, "We'll have to create our own."

As women manage their monthly bleeding, they also manage the natural rhythms of life that are both joyful and sad, predictable and outside of anyone's control. Functioning on rhythms of their own, menstruation, pregnancy, childbirth, and menopause are continual reminders that body processes are downright unruly at times.[8]

Menstruation is messy and sometimes can be physically painful. "Menstrual blood stains everything." It also calls up memories of earlier, awkward childhood experiences when bodily functions were impossible to control, when one soiled one's underwear and wet the bed. We do not like being surprised by our body's behavior, and we distance ourselves from knowing that we might not be able to control everything.

These biological events keep each woman in close contact with a broad range of vulnerable emotions that place her at odds with a fundamental attitude in our culture: shun vulnerability—it connotes personal weakness. Hale, hearty, fully functioning individuals—that is what we like.

Vulnerabilities frighten us, recalling the helplessness of early childhood. "My sister was very sick as a child and I perceive sickness as being weak and limited. So, when I'm sick it's hard to accept it as part of life." We reject reminders that we are fragile, capable of being disabled, dying at any moment, and have recurring needs to depend on someone else for caregiving.

This regular grappling with vulnerability and dependency sets women apart from men, creating moods and demands of its own. Trained to be sensitive to men's reactions, women find that their uneasiness increases with men's discomfort. Male sensitivity to losing control, being hurt—which the bleeding could symbolize—and becoming helpless and dependent is avoided when they equate menstruation with inadequacy in women. They thereby distance themselves from the vulnerability of being alive.

These attitudes are not confined exclusively to men's minds; they also exist in the cultural institutions that disparage women because of their biology, and overmedicate and misunderstand them. Vestiges of this belittlement fuel intolerance for womanly differences, interfering with their receiving the same respect that men command.[9]

Monitoring Subtle Changes

The therapy hour provided ample opportunity to witness the influence of menstruation on women's lives. These women often talked about menstrual cycle vicissitudes, their relief at not being pregnant, or their happiness at now being pregnant. Occasionally, the dismay of an unplanned pregnancy became central.

Although a few women were sensitive themselves about having sex while menstruating, when a male partner refused to make love at that time of the month, some women reported heightened sensitivity to their own body process. "Men don't like you when you bleed. They think it's ugly."

Frequently, they noted their abrupt mood changes, remarking that their vulnerable feelings were much more in evidence around that "time of the month." For those women who regularly censored their emotions this was a marked contrast. "During my period I feel yucky, needy, and insecure."

With the emphasis on youthfulness that dominates this culture, subtle harbingers of menopause elicited additional sensitivities for women in their mid-40s. "It's a struggle at my age and I'm frequently tired. I wish I was younger and in tiptop shape." A few women expressed their concern at becoming more limited as they aged; they might not be able to do all the things they now did. The prospect loomed of physical and health changes. "I've always seen myself as vital and strong and now I feel incapacitated one or two days a month by heavy bleeding." Older divorced or unpartnered women who would have liked to be in a relationship were especially concerned with remaining thin and attractive. "I need to lose five pounds. If I were still married I wouldn't be worrying about that." Menopause, like the onset of menstruation, heralds change. "My period is changing, nature is taking over. Makes me think about growing old. I don't like it, but I have to look at it."[10]

Other Body Issues

Not until it physically affects me do I take care of business.
                                                        Amy

Exquisitely tuned, the human body is remarkably sensitive to stress and emotional dis-ease; it is continually signaling what it needs. Although we are just beginning to appreciate the intricate connections between stress and physical ailments, we live in a culture that has conditioned most of us to feel uneasy about being ill. "What am I doing wrong?" For the most part, my clients ignored their body's signaling. This habit of ignoring their own needs was deep, in the very marrow of their bones. "How long will I endure a situation that's causing my body damage before I pay attention to what I usually ignore?" Frequently misinterpreting the cues, they did not respect the message until they were really hurting. "Can it be true that I've kept so much buried the only way it can come up is through body ailments?"

Anticipating judgments of inadequacy if they did not adroitly juggle their swift-paced lives with the demands of the job and loved ones, many of the women ignored their needs for relaxation and/or nurturant attention. "It's an emotional fight to take time for myself without having an excuse." Suppressed, these longings for nurturant caretaking often entered via the back door: as body pain.

Sometimes the first clue to overload that could be acknowledged was menstrual discomfort. "I should know that when I get cramps, I'm stressed." "My period is alerting me to let go of something. Too much is going on. I can't handle all the pieces."

In the same way, a sprained ankle, migraine headache, back pain, high blood pressure, grinding of teeth, or similar symptoms often was required before a woman recognized that nurturant attention was essential. "If I speak my needs I fear rejection. So, I act them out by hurting myself. Once you're disabled, help can't be denied."

A bad cold provided Melissa with the required excuse. Now she could grant herself the solitude and rest she desired but could not otherwise take for herself. As she talked, early memories surfaced. Being sick as a child had resulted in positive attention, "Even Dad was nice."

More Clues

My mind has clamped down on my body. The way I've been thinking really restricts how my body acts. I don't know if my body is sending a message or giving up on sending a message. My diet is lousy and I've been drinking too much.

Katherine

When women talk about their bodies, they touch a vast range of sensitivities that express discomfort with their natural endowments: physical appearance, body size, hair, size of breasts.

None of these women is fat and very few directly expressed concern about their weight. Nevertheless, in time I came to realize that when eating habits were discussed the persistent, early training to squelch themselves was in evidence. "I was really stuffing it way back down. If I was going to feel bad I'd rather feel bad about food."

In discussing her long struggle with weight, Sara recalled a poignant memory when she was a thin girl of seven. She watched her brothers eat the dessert she was denied. Her mother had instructed her to control her appetite.

Several women realized that their eating habits had been holding back reams of memories of previous times when they had felt bad about themselves, unloved, undernurtured. They had eaten to comfort themselves; sometimes it had not worked. "It feels rigid and cold to express my needs when other people have needs of their own. I felt frustrated and ate a lot. Then, I felt trapped."

While reviewing very troubled, unhappy times, several women recollected extended periods during which they ate and drank too much. "I was getting satisfaction from food because it sure wasn't coming from anyplace else!" "I don't know how I got through that year. There were long periods of numbness. I drank a lot of wine and smoked too many cigarettes."

In the hindsight therapy afforded, many women recognized that they had adapted to intolerable situations by drugging themselves and dulling their consciousness. Currently, none of these women has any difficulty in controlling either her food or her alcohol intake.

Continual instruction to pay attention to the needs of others who are "more deserving," and to regard one's own needs as evidence of weakness, results in the diminished capacity to perceive oneself as a woman worthy of attention and respect. "I feel it's so selfish to do for myself. I'm hiding that from everybody. When I have to do for myself, I can't. I can't hold onto it. I can't even see it—if it's just for me."

The problems are not with women's bodies but with stereotypical expectations that fail to affirm the amazing diversity that is womankind. This is vast, uncharted terrain because being a woman has always been trivialized. As each woman is more accepting of herself, she gains the wisdom and strength to handle adroitly both her life and her body's rhythms. That is the complex challenge of being a woman.

Long after therapy was under way, and without direct discussion, many women reported either joining a gym, pursuing some regular physical exercise, or enrolling in dance classes. Now happier with themselves, they began to care for their bodies in new ways. "I'm starting a routine at the gym and sticking to it—just for me. I'm developing more than muscle."

To keep working well, bodies and minds require attention and good care.

CHAPTER 16

SEXUALITY
Passion and Responsibility

These women were raised in an era that typically regarded sex and sexual feelings as something secret and private, not to be discussed. In fact, it was customary to stigmatize women who knew too much about sex. They were "loose," "slept around." A major presumption was that sexual feelings were dirty and bad, dangerous. They should be "held in check." Masturbation was shunned; it was a bad, shameful practice. Totally taboo, sexual feelings for other women never reached consciousness. The idea that sex was to be enjoyed was not even a consideration. That discovery would be each daughter's to make herself.

By and large, the women's parents, especially those who were Catholic, Jewish, or foreign-born, espoused beliefs about sex that were grounded in stern religious and moral values. "My parents were so busy locking me up they did not prepare me for being on my own." "In adolescence, whatever they said 'no' to, I said 'yes' to."

Most of these daughters were instructed that to be well regarded a woman should be modest, virginal, and unexpressive about sexual needs. That was how a man's respect and love was gained, which ultimately led to marriage. Each daughter was taught to prize her virginity, to "save it for marriage," despite a contrary reality. Some of them had been molested during girlhood.

Even though shrouded in mystery and misinformation, strong sexual feelings during adolescence were recalled. Curious and eager to find out "what it was all about," several daughters "did everything but have intercourse" with their boyfriends. Before they were 20, the majority had had sexual intercourse; several recalled their fear that their fathers would punish them if they found out about their sexual activity. "Being sexual is bad. I was taught to save it for marriage and I didn't."

Damned If You Do or Don't

When adolescents, these women were presumed to be naive about sex, whereas men were supposed to know what it was all about. This attitude invited heterosexual women to rely on their male partners for their knowledge and pleasure with sex; men would initiate them to lovemaking and set the pace for their sexual relationship. "I wanted my husband to take the initiative. That's what men do. I felt shy about leading, saying what I wanted."

Remnants of this attitude are present today. In therapy, some women in their 20s have expressed their discomfort with themselves when a male lover displays less sexual desire than the woman feels. "When he says, 'I'm not interested,' I feel it's my fault. I'm not desirable." Lack of familiarity with, and acceptance of, their own sexuality conditions women to be passive participators rather than active agents of their own sexual desire.

Moreover, living with the knowledge that sexual abuse and/or rape is constantly taking place prompts more cautious behavior in women; they bridle desire. Sexual feelings can just as often arouse fear as pleasure. This restraint of sexual feelings in women is an appropriate response to the fact that such restraint is underdeveloped in men. These harmful conditions train women to ignore the fullness of their own sexual appetite in order to safeguard themselves against sexual harassment and violence.[1]

Katherine's partner was convalescing from a long illness, and sex between them was minimal; she became aware of wanting more sex than she was receiving. During this period, Katherine made several interesting observations: it did not feel okay to be taking care of her own needs, and it was also difficult to be assertive about what she wanted. Moreover, when her partner was not fully participating in the sex, she devalued it. Her earlier training that sex is something a woman does for a man, not for herself, was evident. Katherine was feeling bad about something that should have felt good.

Additionally, because she wanted more sex than he could provide, Katherine feared John's censure and rejection. Her mother had taught Katherine to keep her sexual feelings hidden; they were bad. "If I'm wanting more, something must be wrong with me."

Such beliefs have so thoroughly undermined the validity of women's different sexual needs that many clients were not attuned to the rhythms of their own desire; they described feeling "tied up in knots" when they thought about sex. Similarly conditioned in girlhood and also often exposed to humiliating sexual experiences with men, some lesbian clients have also remarked on difficulties with sexual pleasure.[2]

Not only does an unjust double standard exist in society, but we have created divisions in our minds that support this inequality. Sexual activity that is acceptable and expected of men is castigated when displayed by women.

In this culture, men are rewarded for their sexual prowess even though it frequently creates danger for women. Men are the initiators of sexual passion and excitement, whereas women who demonstrate their passion by initiating a potential sexual encounter still face disapproval.

Dependent on women for the survival of the species—only their bodies can carry forth the miracle of life—customs are threatened when women demand to be respected as individuals distinct from their biological function.

Difficult, Delicate Terrain

The definitions of good sex are definitely oriented toward male experience, a quick, instantaneous turn-on with orgasm as the outcome. That narrows both the options and the opportunities that are essential for many women, whether lesbian or heterosexual, to experience the pleasure of sex, which can rest on a delicate combination of responses and "take hours to get just right."

Characteristically, these women applied far more sensitivity to satisfying their lovers than themselves. For the most part, when it came to voicing their own complaints, they were reticent. "I'm afraid of his reaction. He'll feel threatened, get mad, and tell me to go." "I feel dumb and foolish. It's hard to keep in mind it's his problem." Vulnerable to rejection by their partners, the women concealed that sensitivity by demeaning themselves for wanting something they were not receiving.

Primarily their complaints centered around too much or not enough sex: a too mechanical, hurried lovemaking style, or an absence of consideration for the woman's needs and pace. Many talked of wanting more cuddling and physical closeness, which did not necessarily mean reaching orgasm. Similar to heterosexual clients, some lesbians talked about feeling shy, having "hang-ups," and focusing attention on the partner's demands, which diminished the woman's own desires. "I agreed with her that sex wasn't all that important and we went without it for a year. Then she told me she hadn't been feeling attracted to me all that time."

Whether it was receiving what they desired or trying to express their different needs, several women recalled feeling belittled by their partners' reactions. "One time when I was enjoying myself, he told me he had been turned off for some time." Besides, women who openly enjoyed sex expected to be punished. "I went after this guy I wanted and now I might be pregnant. I can't have anything good and enjoy it. I'm punishing myself. I wanted too much."

A partner's lack of consideration for a woman's sexual needs hurt, as did insensitive feedback about performance. It went to the core of her sense of self. Several women withdrew to protect themselves from further pain. "If someone trashes your garden you don't just stand there. I pulled up my plants and ran." At times, whether the lover was a man or a woman, dissatisfying sex touched the deepest vulnerabilities. "I won't be loved if I'm myself." "Something is wrong with me that he doesn't want me more."

Poignantly, sometimes only through a new sexual relationship did a woman discover that something vital had been missing in her sexual functioning with her lover or husband. "I don't have a sex problem, I don't feel unhealthy sexually. The problem is who I relate to and how he taps into that." "In my marriage, I'd have sex with my husband and not be there. I hated that. Now it's so different with my lover; I'm there and she is too." Occasionally realizing that she could get what she wanted in the new relationship—and still feel good about herself— provided the incentive to question the original relationship. For several women this was the time to acknowledge and do something about the unhappiness they had lived with for years.

"Theoretically, I had my act together for a long time, but I wasn't happy."

As in many other instances when it came to asserting their own needs, the majority found it very difficult. "Sex is so important, yet it's hard to be my own champion in this arena." They rarely directly discussed their complaints with their partners. They did not anticipate a receptive, sensitive audience. No matter that this was a mutual problem, the woman always felt to blame. Worried and unhappy, she presumed that the problem was hers alone to work out. "I'm writing the agenda, both the questions and the answers."

Customarily, the discomfort and confusion that had existed either within the woman or between her and her partner was silenced. Outside and inside the therapy room, talking about sexual feelings and lovemaking was awkward and hesitant. If partners did talk, most frequently they debated about who was at fault rather than reveal their sensitivity to disappointment and the fear of being rejected.

By acknowledging that her needs for caring, sex, and love are not being met, a woman takes a first step toward halting this damaging disregard of herself. Asking, Is this good for me? Is this what I really want? demonstrates the importance of each woman caring for and loving herself. "I'm putting my mind to things, putting out more effort. It feels good to be doing something for myself."

In order to thrive, sexual satisfaction requires energy and sensitive attention. Sexual appetite in both women and men is affected by their many other daily commitments. Ever-changing, a mutually satisfying, respectful sexual relationship is dependent on the interface between *both* partners' desire and energy. The payoff is an abundance of good, pleasurable feelings for oneself—which also extend to one's partner. A deep sense of being loved and cared for is realized. To continue to have these benefits in a long-term relationship the partners must understand what is required to make their sexual relationship a continual source of satisfaction—to both of them.[3]

The Arch-Guardians

As we turn our attention to conception, one outcome of sex between a man and a woman, we notice that by and large, male partners have not shared responsibility for contraception but have remained aloof from this very important issue. While this detachment is familiar—we have already observed that men do not actively participate in the daily ups and downs that characterize intimate relationships and family life—this time something more is involved. Men are less interested in protection against pregnancy because it threatens their connection to the survival of the species.

Widespread use of the condom has never been strongly advocated among men, although condoms have been available since the late 1800s. Men's lack of active involvement in contraception has left it to women, because their bodies carry the toll of repeated pregnancies, to be arch-guardians of birth control. They carry the anxiety about becoming pregnant or ending up caring for a child alone; their lives and life-styles are often at stake, as well as their sexual enjoyment and spontaneity.

When women act on their right to choose whether to carry a pregnancy to term or not, they often have been censured. The men who have participated in making them pregnant have been singularly absent from this condemnation. Protected, they remain tangentially involved, their shared responsibility unacknowledged. The responsibility for, and the consequences of, birth control practices remain women's. Their bodies pay the price.

A Current Repetition

The manner in which education about safer sex has been directed at heterosexuals in the current AIDS crisis demonstrates the persistence of these social mores. If birth control is desired, women must take responsibility because heterosexual men do not. It is the women and not the men to whom knowledge about the condom as a reliable, safe, inexpensive, and easy-to-use form of contraception is directed. They are being instructed to carry condoms, learn how to use them, even be seductive in the manner in which they "help" their partner put on a condom.[4]

For many individuals this remains a very emotionally charged topic. Even though many women have accepted this responsibility, some of their heterosexual lovers were affronted when they took that initiative. Despite the lessons from gay men's experience with AIDS—silence is dangerous; knowledge and protection are essential for safer sex practices—it is astounding that society is relying primarily on women to take responsibility for protection.

By stating their interest in sex while articulating how and who will be responsible for protection from unwanted pregnancies and unsafe sexual practices, women are daily shattering the secrecy that has traditionally surrounded sexual mores. As more women speak up for what they want, the possibilities for changing these ancient patterns increases. Women and men both are responsible for satisfying lovemaking and its consequences.

The Pervasive Discounting

The medical establishment, which is overwhelmingly male, has often acted on convictions about sex and morality that further contribute to keeping women ignorant about their contraception options and the consequences of each choice.

Many women reported that their physicians, typical of the other men in their lives—fathers, lovers, husbands, and bosses, frequently did not take their complaints seriously and often were insensitive to the women's distinct physical and/or emotional needs.

A few women recalled that in the early 1960s when they asked for contraception information, their physicians refused to prescribe birth control pills: It was against their religious or moral beliefs. The doctors' private opinions overrode their professional obligation to disseminate information that would enable a woman to make an independent, informed choice. One particular client, the mother of several children, found herself once again pregnant before she was able to successfully challenge her physician's refusal to prescribe birth control pills.

The women reported that oftentimes their physicians assumed that they really knew what was best for the women without first exploring their situations fully. One woman remembered that when she went for a consultation about contraceptive choices, her physician suggested a tubal ligation. She had not asked for that, and his suggestion only made her more confused. "Even though I was having difficulties in my marriage, I wasn't real positive that I didn't want any more children."

When a woman contemplates making decisions that involve her body, her emotions intensify significantly. At those times when knowledge and sensitivity were most important, the women reported feeling dismissed, misunderstood. The hurried, brusque manner of their physicians sometimes was intimidating, and the women could get neither the information nor the encouragement that would have invited them to explore choices and make the best decisions. The doctors' seeming lack of interest discouraged some women from elaborating on their physical and/or emotional complaints. "I'm left feeling there's something wrong with what I want help about. There has to be a crisis, real and concrete. It can't just be because I want help."

Disappointment and anger with the attitudes and practices of traditional medicine led groups of women to band together in the late 1960s and early 1970s to form health collectives. These women began to teach themselves about their bodies; they also hired medical personnel who respected them and dispensed the kind of care they had been unable to obtain satisfactorily from private physicians. The Boston Women's Health Collective is a stellar example of caring, responsible health maintenance for women. They have written a first-rate, comprehensive book about women's health and well-being, *The New Our Bodies, Ourselves* (1985. New York: Simon & Schuster). The clients and I often refer to this book for clarification about reproductive cycle problems.

Determining Her Own Well-Being

Each time a woman distinguishes between sex for pleasure and sex for procreation, she expands her experience beyond the confines of the traditional female role. She also exchanges her conventional status as a compliant woman for her hard-earned right to determine her own well-being. When a woman chooses for herself, whether availing herself of contraceptive choices, enrolling in an exercise program, asserting herself on the job, or making her complaints heard to her lover, she is flexing brand-new muscles: affirming and empowering herself, persistently and courageously dealing with choice and change.

As women take charge of their bodies and therefore of themselves, stereotypical expectations are challenged. Each time this happens, conflict is generated. Others who do not share these enlarged perspectives become threatened. In turn, they attempt to penalize the women by demeaning them and their actions in preference to grappling with these complex issues.

Tender feelings coexist with these strong beliefs. Every time a woman makes the choice between whether to mother or not, she is making a complex emotional decision. None of this is easy. Like any other choice, this one can require much deliberation and arouse strong emotions. The wisdom of an individual woman's decision does not alter her feelings of sadness and loss, should she choose not to carry her pregnancy to term. Loss is integral to this choice.

In taking charge of her reproductive capacity, a woman proclaims the standard: Each child birthed is wanted. It is important that a woman have options without feeling that she has done something wrong.[5]

Hard Decisions

> I haven't appreciated the gap between my politics and my feelings.
>
> > Anna

Several women had an abortion during the time they were in therapy. A few had more than one; on one occasion, complications set in. Very early in the pregnancy it is sometimes difficult to remove all the fetal tissue and a second procedure is then required.

Some women recalled the dread they had experienced years ago when abortion was illegal and they had procured one, silently enduring a most painful, frightening, and humiliating experience. For a few, their lives were in the hands of someone they could not know and sometimes did not see. An ordinarily upsetting experience was exacerbated by the secrecy and danger.

Like Alice, a few women were very young when they became pregnant. Jim, whom Alice had known only a few months, did not want her to have the baby. Feeling helpless and confused, Alice did not know what she wanted. At that time, abortion was illegal, which made it even more frightening; it could also be very dangerous. Nevertheless, Alice tried to find someone who would terminate her pregnancy. Unsuccessful in her search, like many other women, she married her lover. Years later, in therapy, Alice said, "That mistake turned into a wonderful child."

Although the procedure itself is medically uncomplicated, an abortion stirs complex emotions. Feelings of helplessness, concern about handling the pain, and fear of losing control are common concerns women discuss in therapy as they contemplate terminating an untimely pregnancy. One woman counseled herself, "I want to be gentle with myself; I feel vulnerable."

Feelings of sadness are paramount as each woman deals with her special loss. Memories of other times when the woman had also felt vulnerable as she coped with either physical illness or intense emotional distress are reawakened. "It's hard for me to be sick. I get very depressed and I have been feeling lousy for thirty days."

On occasion, an abortion was the result of ineffective birth control. This was very upsetting. "What did I do to deserve this punishment? I haven't been forgetting to use birth control." "Sex with my lover isn't even fun—and I'm pregnant."

In preparation for the abortion, a few women handled their longings for nurturant attention by surrounding themselves with close women friends. Sometimes, guarded about showing her vulnerablities to her lover, a woman might argue over how the payment for the abortion would be arranged; neither she nor her lover was able to acknowledge her wish for tenderness.

Several women remarked that after the abortion their colleagues at work noticed their absence. Concern was expressed; they had been missed. Some noted that they received more attention on the job than they got at home from their lovers. Even though several women have other children, an abortion severs a fundamental, inarticulate connection to motherhood. Afterward, a few reported feeling depressed, empty: "Like I had nothing to show for myself."

Just prior to scheduling an abortion that also marked the end of her relationship with Joel, Miriam wanted emotional support from her mother. Their recent closeness had been very satisfying and she decided to telephone her mother, who lived in another city. Although Miriam felt their conversation went well, afterward she felt disappointed. She had wanted her mother to be strong and spontaneously offer comfort. Her mother, however, had been upset and needed some time to absorb the news. Before she could offer Miriam solace, her mother had to get some herself: she talked to her closest woman friend.

Several days after the abortion, which had gone smoothly, Miriam became upset. She wanted to stay in bed, sleep, and hide out at home. She became scared and depressed. Feelings she had not allowed herself to feel surfaced. For a brief moment, being pregnant represented the possibility of having a good, nurturing relationship in her life. While that wish might be unrealistic, it attested to a significant loss. Miriam felt very sad.

Six weeks later, after her period resumed, she remarked: "That bright red coal is receding. A cycle has passed. I feel better and more energetic."

Irrevocable Choices

After an extended period in therapy, several women in their mid-40s found the courage to talk about painful decisions they had made in their early 20s that were now irrevocable: aborting a pregnancy or giving a child up for adoption at birth. When those choices were made, each woman's circumstance was not right for choosing motherhood. Because they had gone against conventional mores, the women anticipated censure for choosing for themselves. To counter the judgments of others, they presumed they had to conceal their own ambivalent feelings, appear certain, strong, and able to carry on with their lives as if nothing important had happened.

Taught to be impatient with both unhappy and sad feelings, each of us has been trained to carry on and move ahead. We are discouraged from elaborating on what is unpleasant and uncomfortable; there is a deep reluctance to pause and take the time required to mourn significant losses. These women had managed to keep their complex feelings about these old decisions well concealed. The majority never had another child and stayed away from other people's children; it was too uncomfortable.

When these events were explored in therapy, some women still felt guilty: Had they done something wrong? Made a mistake? As the women accepted themselves and the validity of their emotional responses, it was possible to review these earlier decisions. Sometimes the absence of choice 20 years ago had prolonged a woman's unhappiness.

Once Marie began remembering, she reexperienced her disgrace and shame at having become pregnant without the benefit of a steady, supportive relationship. She had been sent far from home, cut off from what is familiar, to sit out her pregnancy. Her family was protecting its reputation. It was also understood that after the delivery Marie would give up her child. She could only come back home without it.

Tender Discoveries

Several years ago Anna began to have very severe abdominal pain. This eventually led to a diagnosis of endometriosis, a condition in which intrauterine tissue builds up and eventually bleeds into and accumulates in the pelvic cavity. For two years this condition was treated by medication, with poor results. After some deliberation, Anna's gynecologist recommended a hysterectomy.

Anna experienced great relief once the surgery was over. The intense pain that had plagued her for more than a year had now ceased. Nevertheless, Anna felt weak. She was dealing not only with the aftereffects of major surgery but also with a premature menopause as a result of her hysterectomy. She felt sensitive over the loss of her uterus and sad about the choice that had been made for her. "I can never have a child."

Low in energy during her convalescence, she found it difficult to allow herself to feel these multiple losses. Many months later, a good friend became pregnant. This reawakened Anna to her own loss. This time, better able to tolerate her unhappy emotions, Anna recalled a still earlier, painful loss.

Many years before, Anna had become pregnant when she felt very anxious and insecure. Uncertain about her lover's commitment, she decided on her own to have an abortion. While recounting these events in therapy, Anna became angry, an emotional reaction for her that customarily preceded revealing other, much more vulnerable feelings.

Anna had not appreciated that, because she was unhappy and lacked assurance about her life many years before, it had seemed impossible to discuss this situation with Joe. She had worried that he would become furious with her and leave; she did not think she could handle having a child alone. Thus, Anna hid from her lover both the fact of her pregnancy and her subsequent decision to seek an abortion.

Although wondering now how Joe would have reacted if she had told him, Anna also realized that she liked neither what she was saying nor what she was feeling. In her mind she associated having a baby with being vulnerable and dependent. "I'd be out of control like every other pregnant female and relying on someone else to make my decisions."

Anna did not like the mixed emotions she was feeling: anger, sadness, fear, confusion; she retreated from them by talking about Joe's anger. That shift enabled us to identify a familiar old stratagem. Concerning herself with other people's responses diluted the intensity of Anna's emotions. When this was pointed out she commented: "I've never opened this up before. It's like puncturing a pimple. Things are shooting out in all directions."

When younger, Anna had not wanted to be "ordinary," like every other woman. She had been adamant that she did not want a child; she even made fun of people who had children because that would make them immortal. She would not say that now. "I used to deride that bond, it wasn't worthwhile. It was easy and thoughtless. I wouldn't be special. I missed the opportunity to really connect to someone who would love me forever—who really cared. Now I'm physically cut off, forever. I could adopt a child but I don't think that's what I'm talking about. Even if I could bear a child I don't know if I would. I don't know what I want."

"Is it possible that you're doing just as you want but it doesn't feel okay?"

"I don't know if it gets resolved. Back then I was sure and right. I never looked into my feelings, and now I have an incredible sadness because I never figured this out."

Currently, when Anna is with some close women friends who have had babies without remaining in relationship with the fathers, she has strong emotional responses. Very old feelings are reawakening that had never been allowed expression. "They've been stored. That explains why those feelings are so large today." Anna is making important, tender discoveries that have to do with making choices and taking responsibility for them, not with having done something right or wrong. There were choices she could not take advantage of because they did not feel right to her at that time. Chastising herself for what she was unable to do demeans the wisdom of the choice she did make given her situation.

Surprisingly vehement feelings continued to erupt as we proceeded with these explorations. Anna had felt she was "killing the baby" because Joe did not want it. Her words startled her. She had not realized her feelings were that strong. Around the time of the abortion, she felt unacknowledged and rejected by Joe, who was very involved in preparation for an extended business trip to Japan. Anna herself had just started her own firm, was working very hard, and had little money. "I couldn't have a baby on my own. I wasn't even living in a good place."

"What did you feel when you found out you were pregnant?"

"Relief. Warm, nice feelings. Frightened."

"How come it's so hard to admit this?"

"I wasn't in any position to have a baby. It was inappropriate. I wasn't married. I didn't have a warm environment in which to talk about this then. If I had, I could have let go of all this and had the abortion. The yearnings are dangerous; they make me feel so vulnerable that I have to bludgeon them. Not only can't I say to myself, I want and it was right, I can't say it to anyone else either. What's important is that I was doing what I did because Joe didn't want it. Since I felt vulnerable and rejected I didn't tell him. I just presumed what he wanted."

Anna went home that night and asked Joe the questions she had been unable to ask many years earlier. He told her that if she had confided in him he would have talked her out of having the baby; he did not think they were ready for a child.

She queried further, "Suppose I wanted to keep it?"

Joe replied, "I would have been unhappy."

Then Anna asked what she previously had been afraid to know: "Would you have supported me?"

"Probably."

More courage: "Would you have seen me afterward?"

"I don't know."

Having a Baby

Imagine, you could have a child who is having fun.

Most of these women had children born prior to their coming to therapy. On occasion, a woman came into therapy pregnant or, like Carol, became pregnant with her first child while in therapy. This provided possibilities for exploring feelings that normally might go unvoiced.

Profound change was taking place both in Carol's body and in her life. At times she felt anxious, a normal response to such changes. Reasonable worries about handling the experience of pregnancy—which included the labor and birthing of her child—stirred feelings that were not easy for Carol to talk about: helplessness and fears about handling pain. "I can't tell you this. It makes me feel so vulnerable and sensitive."

Being pregnant also gave voice to other, old sensitivities. Overweight during her adolescence, Carol was again gaining weight, only this time it was because she was pregnant. Still, she felt bad about herself. "No one will respect me if I'm fat."

As we explored this in therapy, Carol acknowledged that being pregnant made her anxious, and she was comforting and nurturing herself by occasionally overeating. She very much wanted something she felt she had missed out on with her mother: a deep emotional bond with her child.

Further concerns: "Can I mother myself through this experience or will she shut me out as I did with my mother? Will I like it? I might be real angry at it for changing my whole life." Being pregnant is a vulnerable experience, much is changing, and sensitivities are aroused that require attention.[6]

There had also been some conflict between Carol and her business partner, who worried that the baby would change Carol's commitment to work. The two women talked about this, and since they are equal partners in their own business, Carol's job security was not threatened as sometimes happens to pregnant women.[7]

Carol gave birth to a girl. She felt exhilarated. The delivery went well, her husband was present, and she was able to ask for what she needed.

Mothering one's baby can offer new possibilities to remother oneself, to grow up a little more. In time, caring for Deborah provided opportunities for Carol to work out more completely some unfinished emotional business with her own mother.[8]

In Carol's eagerness to give her child what she had missed, it was difficult for her to accept the baby's crying as a natural experience. The crying meant to Carol that she was a bad mother. In therapy, I talked about the baby being a separate person, with needs and feelings of her own that might and might not be able to be satisfied by its mother. Carol reflected: "I hear you. If I couldn't fix what was broken with my mother, I can't fix it with my baby. Yet I resist hearing. It's as if I want to mother the baby in me by mothering my baby. It's hard to let go of those feelings. That makes me feel helpless, little. I don't like it. I want someone to come and fix it for me."

Months later, Carol reported that earlier that week, when she left her daughter off at the baby-sitter's house, Deborah ran right to the baby-sitter. Carol felt dejected, angry, "like I've lost her forever." After a few minutes, she recovered from those feelings and went over to her daughter with an important insight. "I can distinguish between Deborah's anger at me for going to work and my own feelings about my mother leaving me."

One day in therapy, Carol recounted Deborah's accomplishments. Taught to be modest, she became uneasy sharing an intimacy that ordinarily felt too personal to disclose: her delight at Deborah's brightness. "I was a bright kid too, but I don't think I was encouraged. I was boxed in. It's as if this is a part of me

I'm not supposed to express. I had to restrain and limit myself. A lot of the work of therapy has freed this up for me.

"My daughter has also given me a chance to love myself and enrich my life tremendously. I can love my little girl and I feel like I won't ever lose that again. I'm loving my children—my daughter and the child in me."

CHAPTER 17

ON HER OWN

The last four pieces of the jigsaw puzzle. You work, and work, and the last four pieces go in real quick. It looks easy at the end, but that's because of all the work that went on beforehand.

Anna

I have this image of a discus thrower making one full revolution, 360 degrees and flinging it off. That's where I am now.

Elizabeth

In some ways you never finish therapy. You never know everything about yourself.

Carol

Stopping therapy, like starting therapy, brings up its own unique collection of emotions. "The little girl in me would have liked to stay tied to you forever." "It makes me very sad. I'll miss

275

you a lot. I don't feel abandoned or deserted—just—I'll miss you. It'll be empty. That which was there is gone."

Primarily, the woman feels two very contradictory emotions: exuberance and sadness. It feels wonderful to be handling an expanded repertoire of emotions and feeling confidence and trust in herself, natural corollaries of emotional flexibility. "It's up to me, taking the risk and moving on." It also feels very sad to be leaving this special relationship and the special room where so much has transpired. "I feel like a kid leaving home. You really want to go and you really gotta go, but you don't want to."

Typically, as each woman prepares to end therapy, a period of time is devoted to summing up and reviewing what has occurred over the years we have been working together. Sometimes this provides an opportunity to explore issues that previously had been only tangentially touched on. Often, there is an awareness that troublesome issues are not fully resolved and may continue to feel uncomfortable. Not everything can be made better. "I'm aware that I still have some issues with men. I do count on them for a good sense of myself. I wish that I could provide that for myself." "I know I'm not going to fall apart when I get upset. I might shut down for a while. Being aware is very painful. It always has been."

Carol said: "Clearly I felt rejected on a lot of levels with my mother. It wasn't intentional, but she made me feel rejected because of her inability to do a lot of things—her personal limitations. She couldn't deal with her feelings so she couldn't accept mine. It's still sensitive. It feels unfair and limiting. I didn't have a pot big enough to grow in."

As therapy stopped, Melissa noted, "I'm really managing okay and eager to try it on my own." She was also aware that moving forward with tasks she had set out for herself aroused both excitement and anxiety. Although feeling eager and hopeful about what lay ahead, Melissa did express some fears about opening her own business. Once this was acknowledged, Melissa realized that she could talk over her worries with her partner. That felt reassuring. "Now I know that I can be anxious and confident simultaneously."

Anita spoke about the exhilaration that she experienced as she was handling some very complex life situations. It told her that she was ready to stop therapy. Then Anita reminisced about her first visit several years earlier. She recalled that I had listened and paid attention to what she had to say. "I'll never forget that. It was a turning point. I'll carry the image of you and the work we've done everywhere I go. That isn't stopping because therapy is stopping."

Elizabeth is moving out of the state. After six very productive months, therapy will stop. During this time, Elizabeth has mourned the sudden death of her husband and expressed much grief. In one of our final sessions, Elizabeth remarked that she has learned "Everything is impermanent, good things as well as bad. I've got that on a gut level."

In the final meeting, Elizabeth expressed her satisfaction about all that she had accomplished in six months. She also acknowledged her sadness at parting. Then she smiled. A moment later, she said, "I interrupt the sadness by thinking about coming back." I commented that her smile is interrupting her feelings. Elizabeth responded, "A very intimate relationship is—just cut. I feel the grieving and then stop it by thinking, 'I can come back.'"

An Immense Journey

I've learned so much here and I've done so much myself. I'm not sure I'd have done it without this process. I feel like I really

know myself and am in charge of my life. Considering where
I came from that's an immense journey. Unbelievable. We've
made a lot of progress together, done a good job. I know it's
not been easy.

Carol

I have the uncanny feeling that what we are doing is affecting
the rest of my life.

Anna

Saying good-bye arouses ancient, tender feelings and memories of previous, painful separations. This provides us with yet
another opportunity to heal these wounds. "I have a tendency
to cast leaving in the form of summer camp. Maybe I don't know
any other way, or all leaving experiences are restructured to fit
into that one. Only this time, it doesn't make sense. I need to
let the feelings out of the jail I've put them in. They can't grow
and change that way."

Old, scary feelings become transformed into poignant
realizations. Something important is ending. People who have
shared much will stop seeing one another. "In leaving here I
leave a lot of expectations and take on a lot of responsibility
for myself. It feels great and sad. It's hard to put this into
words. I can't pretend about you and I can't pretend about
me. I understand that I have to be my highest authority. That
doesn't mean I can't ask for help or support—that's different
from the childish wish that someone else will be there who
always knows." "Therapy changed my life. It has been a very
important process for me, and I feel grateful. It's like a gift
lots of people never have. Now, I feel excited to do it on my
own."

Sometimes in working through the feelings aroused by stopping therapy and ending the relationship with me, fresh anxieties
about being their own measure surface for some of the women.
This usually emerges disguised. For instance, a woman might

check out if I will be available at some future time, should she want to return to therapy. Or, a woman might presume that I have some plans I have not disclosed to either move away or stop working. As these issues are explored, each woman finds another chance to state her concerns about being on her own. She is growing more accustomed to managing a new, natural combination of emotions: excitement and anxiety. "There will be times when I wish I could come here and talk, to work things out. I won't be able to do that. It's not that I couldn't come back. What you get is what you give up: the opportunity to say, now I can handle this myself."

This issue was especially poignant for Elizabeth. "Jeff left without consulting me. You could do that too." I wonder aloud if her focusing on my being available is a way to avoid deciding what she wants for herself. Elizabeth then focused and declared, "I want to stay in touch by mail until I decide if I will return or not."

A Parallel

Stopping writing this book has many parallels with stopping therapy. A process that has become very familiar to me and central to my life for several years is now complete. I have worked hard at accomplishing this task. I definitely have learned many things. I, too, feel the combination of exhilaration and anxiety that the women describe as they are about to walk out of the therapy room for the last time. A special relationship is ending. I feel sad. A space is created where previously none had existed. As any large undertaking comes to a conclusion, each of us is presented with an opportunity to pause and realize that partings and endings are very delicate moments.

Summing Up

Standing in the doorframe ready to exit, I, like the client, am motivated to sum up. This postpones the ending.

The experience of this particular group of women in therapy makes explicit that accommodating to a belief system that does not value women as highly as men significantly disadvantages women. Survival in this unequal, culturally condoned arrangement demeans all women, stifling self-expression and blunting their full development. Disabling conditions deprive women of their equal share of what is fundamental to self-esteem.

Furthermore, these conditions trivialize women's emotional reality, teaching them to mistrust their capacity to manage themselves. This lack of positive regard has had important reverberations. It has kept women dependent on imitating the standards acclaimed by men. Many women have been encouraged to look to men to provide what only a woman can provide for herself: respect for her own experience, which promotes trust and confidence in herself.

The conditioning to accommodate to the status quo to ensure loving acceptance, further conditioned women to adapt to stereotypical expectations and back away from differences, conflict, and anger. They have been taught to believe that personal aspirations significantly interfere with happiness and family harmony. These convictions have seriously deprived women of the varied tools and necessary skills to put their own, different objectives forward: to negotiate a path in the world that reflects their distinct qualities.

To make and sustain the changes that promote women's well-being, each woman must keep in mind that the pursuit of knowing and actualizing herself can, at times, be difficult, lonely, and unapplauded. The way is arduous, up and down. In fact, it is more than likely that she will be discredited as she challenges the dominant values of the culture by asserting her demands for equality, opportunity, and respect. Correcting the imbalance that has always existed between women's needs and public acclaim of them is a large task. It is important to make alliances with both women and men who share this vision.

To keep their varied objectives center stage, women must learn to tolerate uncomfortable situations and prepare for the strategizing that is required both to stand up to unfair practices *and* to introduce values of their own. The deeply embedded presumption that to get her own needs satisfied a woman must first meet the needs of everyone else keeps many women focused on paying attention to other people's well-being. They have not realized that in doing so, they often sacrifice their own.

Each time a woman pushes the frontiers of her experience beyond the known boundaries both in the intimate world of personal relationships and in the paid-work arena, she is loosening deeply entrenched stereotypical expectations.

Each time a woman expands her options beyond the limitations of her role training, she is contributing to the present-day collection of self-affirming female role models. She is establishing her hard-earned right to reach her full potential. "I feel really good—terrific—to be saying all this, and what's best, it doesn't feel like I'll lose it. I don't feel it will all disappear, like holding a rainbow in your hand. This is all over—light—instead of darkness."

As each woman expands her repertoire of choices, balancing her own well-being with respect for the well-being of others, she moves the self-knowledge gained in the therapy room into the world beyond this room. An appropriate, essential next step.

NOTES

Inscription Page

1. Griffin, Susan (1978). *Woman and nature: The roaring inside her.* New York: Harper & Row. p. 176. Reprinted with permission.

Introduction

1. Robbins, Joan Hamerman, & Siegel, Rachel Josefowitz (Eds.) (1985). *Women changing therapy: New assessments, values and strategies in feminist therapy.* New York: Harrington Park Press. Original copyright held by Haworth Press, New York, 1983.

Chapter 4

1. Caplan, Paula (1981). *Barriers between women.* New York: Spectrum Publications. Chernin, Kim. (1981). *The obsession: Reflections on the tyranny of slender-*

ness. New York: Harper & Row. Dinnerstein, Dorothy (1976). *The mermaid and the minotaur.* New York: Harper & Row. Flax, Jane (1978). The conflict between nurturance and autonomy in mother-daughter relationships. *Feminist Studies, 4*(2), pp. 171–189.

Chapter 5

1. "Society gives mothers the task of teaching daughters to be nurturant and self-sacrificing; as they themselves are supposed to be. It is a natural outgrowth of this situation that, as part of her training in responding to the needs of others, the daughter of a lonely and insecure mother will be taught to meet the mother's needs as well. Insofar as the daughter tries to meet those needs, ... her own needs for nurturance go unmet. Thus, the daughter grows up feeling inadequately nurtured. When she becomes a mother, she will have unmet needs and may turn to her own daughter, hoping the daughter will meet them." Caplan (chap. 4, note 1), p. 17.
2. "By placing sole responsibility for nurturing onto women, that is to say for satisfying the emotional and material needs of children, society reinforces the notion that to mother is more important than to father. Structured into the definitions and the very usage of the terms father and mother is the sense that these two words refer to two distinctly different experiences. Women and men must define the work of fathering and mothering in the same way if males and females are to accept equal responsibility for parenting." Hooks, Bell (1984). *Feminist theory: From margin to center.* Boston: South End Press. p. 137. Reprinted with permission.

Chapter 6

1. "Those who did not engage in denial but could see things for what they were became convinced that their only safety resided in escape. While up to a point in their mistreatment they had been willing to suffer rather than give up all they possessed, they came to realize that giving up almost everything dear to them, including all material things, was a small and necessary price to pay for mere survival." Bettelheim, Bruno (1979). *Surviving and other essays.* New York: Alfred Knopf. p. 88. Reprinted with permission. Copyright held by Bruno and Trude Bettelheim as trustees.

2. "From 1933 until the beginning of the war—for over six years—the Nazis were more than ready to let the Jews go; as a matter of fact, they tried everything to get rid of the Jews, provided they left all their belongings behind. But no country, not excepting the U.S., let more than an entirely insignificant trickle immigrate to it. The justification was again based on denial: things were not all that bad for the Jews; the Nazis did not really mean what they said, etc." Ibid., p. 89.

3. "The feeling of guilt and a special obligation are irrational, but this does not reduce their power to dominate a life; in more ways than one, it is this irrationality which makes them so very difficult to cope with. Feelings which have a rational basis can be met with rational measures, but irrational feelings, more often than not, are impervious to our reason; they must be dealt with on a deeper emotional level." Ibid., p. 27.

4. "The resulting 'conspiracy of silence' proved detrimental to the intrapsychic well-being of survivors and to their familial and socio-cultural integration. Not only did this conspiracy intensify the survivors' sense of isolation and mistrust of society, but it also formed yet another obstacle to mourning. In contrast, other survivor-parents welcomed the conspiracy of silence because of their fear that their memories would corrode their own lives and prevent their children from becoming healthy, normal Americans. But the children grew up in painful bewilderment: they neither understood the inexplicable torment within their family, nor their own sense of guilt." Danieli, Yael (1981). Differing adaptational styles in families of survivors of the Nazi holocaust. *Children Today, 10,* 6–11.

5. As adult children of survivors of the Holocaust began to share their experiences, some important commonalities emerged. Although some parents would be very emotionally detached—unavailable—more typically, these parents drew their children very close to them. Many of the children reported that their moves toward independence and autonomy aroused anxiety in the parents; separation reactivated the parents' losses. Adapting to the stresses of survivorship created issues for both parents and children. They each carried some excruciating sensitivities. For further exploration, see Bergmann, Martin, & Jucovy, Milton (Eds.) (1982). *Generations of the holocaust.* New York: Basic Books. Epstein, Helen (1977). Heirs of the holocaust. *New York Times Magazine,* June 19, pp. 12–15, 74–75. Levine, Howard (1982). Toward a psychoanalytic understanding of children of survivors of the holocaust. *Psychoanalytic Quarterly, 51,* 70–92. Rose, Susan, & Garske, John (1987). Family environment, adjustment, and coping among children of holocaust survivors. *American Journal of Orthopsychiatry, 57*(3), 332–344.

6. "The children are helpless in their mission to undo the Holocaust both for their parents and for themselves. The sense of failure is often generalized

as, 'No matter what I do or how far I go, nothing will be good enough.'" Danieli (chap. 6, note 4), p. 9.

Chapter 7

1. Claudine Vegh also attended a summer camp organized for Jewish children in France immediately after the war. "I never dared tell any of these children that my mother was alive. In any case nobody would have asked; the subject was taboo, absolutely taboo. When I came home from that camp, I had the impression that my life would never again be that of a child; something inside me was shattered; I only realized it at that moment." Vegh, Claudine (1979). *I didn't say goodbye.* New York: E. P. Dutton. p. 27.

2. "It is almost universal for a child of a survivor family to grapple with the conflict of whether one should dwell on the Holocaust or whether to forget it." Kestenberg, Judith, & Kestenberg, Milton. The background of the study. In Bergmann & Jucovy (chap. 6, note 5), p. 44.

3. "When a world goes to pieces and inhumanity reigns supreme, man cannot go on living his private life as he was wont to do, and would like to do; he cannot, as the loving head of a family, keep the family living together peacefully, undisturbed by the surrounding world; nor can he take pride in his profession or possessions, when either will deprive him of his humanity, if not also his life. In such times, one must radically re-evaluate all of what one has done, believed in, and stood for in order to know how to act. In short, one has to take a stand on the new reality—a firm stand, not one of retirement into a private world." Bettelheim (chap. 6, note 1), p. 257.

Despite Bruno Bettelheim's sensitive writing, his use of only the male pronoun would make it appear that *only* men face horrendous dilemmas when the family is under siege. Although the influence of patriarchal values on the Jewish family is well known, what has scarcely been acknowledged was the contributions during these trying years that women offered in each family, as painful choices were made, or not made. Claudia Koonz, a feminist historian, enlarges our understanding: "Within many families, however, it was the wives who felt the impending disaster and often overrode husbands' objections. In a society where fathers ruled their families this was an unusual reversal." (p. 366). "On the surface, of course, women exercised little overt influence…. There was no conception of divided authority…. But more often than not, the mother made her wishes known covertly." Koonz, Claudia. (1987). *Mothers in the fatherland: Women, the family, and Nazi politics.* New York: St. Martin's Press. p. 370.

4. Danieli, chap. 6, note 4, p. 9. "Survivorship also seems to entail a vague but very special responsibility. It is due to the fact that what should have been one's birth right: to live one's life in relative peace and security—not to be wantonly murdered by the state, whose obligation it should be to protect one's life—is actually experienced as a stroke of unmerited and unexplainable luck. It was a miracle that the survivor was saved when millions just like him perished, so it seems that it must have happened for some unfathomable purpose." Bettelheim (chap. 6, note 1), p. 26.

5. "A friend once said to me: Not to talk about the past is not to blot it out, on the contrary, it is perhaps to try and preserve it in the depths of one's being, like a secret which cannot be shared ... the only possible legacy when you have only a blurred image of your parents, and not even a photograph to help retrieve that image." Vegh (chap. 6, note 1), p. 30.

6. Claudia Koonz makes note of the fact that even though the situation for women—opponents or victims—differed in important ways from that of men, their history cannot be told apart from that of male comrades or family members. "To pull women out of that context skews their experiences." (p. 311). However, she also reports a conversation with a woman resister, Kathe Popall: 'The women were ... everywhere in the whole resistance. Many worked in silence their contributions scarcely noticed.... Without the women ... the men's actions would have been inconceivable.'" Koonz (chap. 7, note 3), p. 339.

Chapter 8

1. Soon after the entry of the United States into World War II, all Japanese-Americans along the west coast of the United States were ordered by the government to leave their homes. They were sent to hastily assembled camps to live for the duration of the war.

Chapter 9

1. In an interview in the *San Francisco Chronicle*, Daniel Levinson, a psychologist who has studied men's life patterns, said this about women: "Everything in society supports men having an occupational dream, but for a woman, there is still a quality of going into forbidden territory. There is more anxiety. Though it's very important for men to marry and have a family, the big difference is that a man feels he is taking care of his family by working.... when a woman marries,... the question of her further individual develop-

ment is ambiguous.... Either she is going to become an independent person with an identity of her own, or involved in love, marriage, and family. The sense of one or the other is very strong." *San Francisco Chronicle*, September 24, 1987, p. B4.

2. "The horrific effects of gender inequality may include not only brute violence, but the internalized control of women's impulses, poisoning desire at its very root with self-doubt and anxiety." Vance, Carole (1984). "Pleasure and danger: Toward a politics of sexuality. In Vance, C. (Ed.). Pleasure and danger: Exploring female sexuality." Boston: Routledge & Kegan Paul. p. 4. Reprinted with kind permission by Pandora Press, imprint of Unwin Hyman Ltd.

3. "Women—socialized by mothers to keep their dresses down, their pants up, and their bodies away from strangers—come to experience their own sexual impulses as dangerous.... Sexual abandon and impulsiveness acquire a high price, since women must think not only about the consequences of their sexual actions for themselves, but also about the consequences for men, whose sexual 'natures' are supposedly lustful, aggressive, and unpredictable." Ibid., p. 4.

4. "Women inherit a substantial task: the management of their own sexual desire and its public expression. Self-control and watchfulness become major and necessary female virtues. As a result female desire is suspect from its first tingle, questionable until proven safe, and frequently too expensive when evaluated within the larger cultural framework which poses the question: is it really worth it? ... passion often doesn't stand a chance." Ibid., p. 4

5. "Sexist ideology brainwashes men to believe that their violent abuse of women is beneficial when it is not. Yet feminist activists affirm this logic when we should be constantly naming these acts as expressions of perverted power relations, general lack of control over one's actions, emotional powerlessness, extreme irrationality, and in many cases, outright insanity. Passive male absorption of sexist ideology enables them to interpret this disturbed behavior positively. As long as men are brainwashed to equate violent abuse of women with privilege, they will have no understanding of the damage done to themselves, or the damage they do to others, and no motivation to change." Hooks (chap. 5, note 2), pp. 75–76.

Chapter 10

1. Degler, Carl (1980). *At odds: Women and the family in America from the revolution to the present.* New York: Oxford University Press. Foner, Philip (1980). *Women and the American labor movement: From World War I to the present.*

New York: Free Press. Giddings, Paula (1984). *When and where I enter: The impact of black women on race and sex in America*. New York: William Morrow. Wertheimer, Barbara (1977). *We were there: The story of working women in America*. New York: Pantheon Books.

2. Degler (chap. 10, note 1). Harris, Mark J., Mitchell, Franklin, D., & Schechter, Steven, J (1984) (Eds.). *The homefront: America during World War II*. New York: Putnam. Copyright held by M. J. Harris, F. D. Mitchell, & S. J. Schechter.

3. Shirley Hackett, interviewed by Harris, Mitchell, & Schechter, stated: "Many women went right back into the syndrome with which we were brought up—the quiet wife. The man's the boss, and you do what he says even tho' you've been on your own for several years." Harris, Mitchell, & Schechter (chap. 10, note 2), p. 230.

4. "The swift closing of many war industries literally left millions of women unemployed overnight. Their efforts to continue their employment in non-traditional jobs were largely unsuccessful ... women employed outside the home after the war usually had to settle for low wages, for working on the assembly line, or as a cook, dishwasher, waitress, or secretary. Many became full-time homemakers with the intent of being happy wives and mothers...." Ibid., p. 238.

    "When the war ended ... competition had been keen and the resurgence of the old anti-feminine prejudices in business and the professions made it difficult for a girl to keep or advance in a job. This undoubtedly sent many women scurrying for the cover of marriage and home.... During the war, women's abilities, and the inevitable competition, were welcome; after the war they were confronted with that polite but impenetrable curtain of hostility." Friedan, Betty (1963). *The feminine mystique*. New York: W. W. Norton. pp. 185–186. Reprinted with permission.

5. "I never knew a woman, when I was growing up, who used her mind, played her own part in the world, and also loved, and had children." Ibid., p. 75.

6. Paula Giddings reflected on the findings in a 1972 study by Cynthia Fuchs Epstein. (Positive effects of the double negative: Explaining the success of black professional women.) Giddings noted that in virtually every instance, black women professionals (unlike most of their white counterparts) "grew up in homes where their mothers were doers.... Many ... were in professional or semiprofessional occupations themselves." According to Giddings, Epstein's study found that these black mothers encouraged achievement almost without exception, and their daughters had a tremendous sense of confidence in themselves and their abilities. "One physician recalled that her goal was to be a nurse but her mother encouraged her to be a doctor." In contrast, white families had more ambivalence about their daughters becoming overeducated and thus having difficulty finding husbands. "One can speculate that although some black women shared these anxieties, their

life expectations generally were different from those of most white women. Black women expected to have to work, whether married or not. They didn't often think of their careers as 'supplemental' to those of their husbands." Giddings (chap. 10, note 1), pp. 332–333.

7. "In my generation, many of us knew that we did not want to be like our mothers, even when we loved them.... Strangely, many mothers who loved their daughters ... did not want to see their daughters grow up like them either.... But even if they urged, insisted, fought to help us educate ourselves, even if they talked with yearning of careers that were not open to them, they could not give us an image of what we could be. They could only tell us that their lives were too empty, tied to home; that children, cooking, clothes, bridge, and charities were not enough. A mother might tell her daughter, spell it out,'Don't be just a housewife like me.' But that daughter, sensing that her mother was too frustrated to savor the love of her husband and children, might feel:'I will succeed where my mother failed, I will fulfill myself as a woman,' and never read the lesson of her mother's life." Friedan (chap. 10, note 4), p. 72.

8. "Over and over, they matter-of-factly recounted the symptoms of depression: sleep loss, anxiety, fluctuations in weight, a constant lack of energy, and decreased sexual desire. When I asked how long they had experienced these symptoms, most shrugged and said they were used to them and really didn't know." Milwid, Beth (1987). *What you get when you go for it.* New York: Dodd, Mead. p. 206.

9. "Women learned never to show publicly that the going was rough. Intent on disproving the 'hysterical woman' stereotype, for the first few years they kept their feelings to themselves. Despite their anxiety and cumulative exhaustion, the women were determined not to let on. As I listened to individuals repeat the same cycle, I saw the more desperate they felt, the more they denied." Ibid., p. 43.

10. "Women who had emulated men for years said that the pretense hurt them psychologically and caused instability in their personal lives. By stepping back from the pressures and reassessing their larger goals, they are able to make choices more effectively and to feel their identities return. They have concluded that the only sustaining way to cope as a woman is to be who you are, refusing to pretend that you are someone you're not." Ibid., p. 237.

Chapter 11

1. "Professional women are entering the work place in escalating numbers, and, once inside, are unlikely to leave. Economic necessity forces mothers

to return to work. Equally important, the pride women take in their professional accomplishments is so much a part of their identities that few would toss it aside. Unlike the era of Rosie the Riveter, today's co-ed work world is a permanent fixture." Milwid (chap. 10, note 8), p. 237.

2. Beth Milwid describes a profound "loss of innocence" that women experienced 10 years ago after coming into the work world. Their "exaggerated expectations" and "glamorized notions" were shattered as they met the realities of business. "They had to see for themselves what fathers, husbands, boy friends, and sons had been feeling for decades but rarely sharing directly." Now, the professional women she met "appreciate the complexities of problems in the real world. They recognize the pressures they take home at night are not unlike the pressures that men have felt for years. Above all, they realize that mixed in with the disappointments and disillusionment, there is joy to be found in stretching one's mind and achieving one's goals." Ibid., p. 216.

3. On January 20, 1988, the *San Francisco Chronicle* (p. 1) reported a "landmark legal settlement" between State Farm Insurance Company and the women who challenged that company's discriminatory practices. Women had been given false information and discouraged from applying for sales agent positions, which paid 4 to 10 times more than clerical work. This suit had been in process since 1974; it was estimated that 85,000 women could be counted among the potential pool of candidates for over 1000 sales agent positions that were filled by men between 1974 and 1987.

4. "All was hushed for announcements:
'Take only what you can carry...'
We were made to believe our faces
betrayed us.
Our bodies were loud
with yellow screaming flesh
needing to be silenced
behind barbed wire."
Mirikitani, Janice (1987). *Shedding silence*. Berkeley, CA: Celestial Arts. Breaking Silence, a poem. p. 34.

5. Conrat, Masie, & Conrat, Richard (1972). *Executive order 9066*. Los Angeles: California Historical Society. Davis, Daniel. (1982). *Behind barbed wire*. New York: E. P. Dutton. Hosokawa, Bill (1969). *The quiet Americans*. New York: William Morrow. Forty-six years later, in August 1988, Congress voted to apologize to each Japanese-American survivor of the internment camps and to pay each individual $20,000 in reparations. "A federal commission created in 1980 concluded that the relocation was based on wartime hysteria and racial prejudice rather than on any evidence of a genuine national security threat." *San Francisco Chronicle*, August 5, 1988, p. 1.

6. "The sense of being debased human beings was inescapable for a people being guarded night and day by soldiers up in towers. As one Nisei put it, 'This evacuation did not seem too unfair until we got right to the camp and were met by soldiers with guns and bayonets. Then I almost started screaming.'" Weglyn, Michi Nishiura (1976). *Years of infamy: The untold story of America's concentration camps*. New York: William Morrrow. p. 79.

7. Michi Nishiura Weglyn points out that although the recovery of Japanese-Americans has been good to remarkable, the bitter evacuation legacy of rejection and social isolation during the war years have left scars of varying degrees on ex-inmates. Despite outward appearances, these scars have not entirely disappeared. In fact, they have created psychic damage that has been described as "a deep consciousness of personal inferiority, a proclivity to non-communication and inarticulateness, evidenced by shying away from exposure which might subject them to further hurt.... summed up by one Nisei activist, 'We were like victims of rape. We felt ashamed. We could not bear to speak of the assault.'" Ibid., p. 273.

8. Yamada, Mitsuye (1981). Invisibility is an unnatural disaster: Reflections of an Asian American woman. In Moraga, Cheríe, & Anzaldúa, Gloria (Eds.). Watertown, MA: Persephone Press. *This bridge called my back: Writings by radical women of color*. See also "Generations of Women," Mirikitani (chap. 11, note 4), pp. 10–16.

9. "I had grown up in such an isolated world that it was hard for me to recognize difference as anything other than a threat, because it usually was.... But sometimes I was close to crazy with believing there was some secret thing wrong with me personally that formed an invisible barrier between me and the rest of my friends, who were white. What was it that kept people from inviting me to their houses, their parties, their summer homes for a weekend? ... There was something here that I was missing. Since the only place I couldn't see clearly was between my own eyes, obviously the trouble was with me. I had no words for racism." Lorde, Audre (1982). *Zami: A new spelling of my name*. Trumansburg, NY: Crossing Press. p. 81. Reprinted with permission.

10. Jan Faulkner describes a process of armoring that is acquired in early childhood, and more "highly developed among people of color because they are more stressed by the mark of oppression." Armoring includes "specific behavioral and cognitive skills to promote self-caring during direct encounters with racist experiences...." One main goal being to "exercise more selectivity around the amount of energy used to deal with racist encounters." Women in interracial relationships. In Robbins & Siegel (Introduction, note 1), pp. 196–197.

In *Zami*, Audre Lorde discusses how her parents, who came from Grenada to the United States as adults, dealt with "the crushing reality" of American racism. They considered it a "private woe." "My mother and father believed they could best protect their children from the realities of race in America and the fact of American racism by never giving them name, much less discussing their nature. We were told we must never trust white people, but *why* was never explained, nor the nature of their ill will. Like so many other vital pieces of information in my childhood, I was supposed to know without being told." Lorde (chap. 11, note 9), p. 69.

11. "We were told
    that silence was better
    golden like our skin,
    useful like
    go quietly,
    easier like
    don't make waves,
    expedient like
    horsetails and deserts."
    Mirikitani (chap. 11, note 4), p. 33.

12. Milwid quotes one of her interviewees: "There's a lot of change going on, and people are looking at their old roles and trying to see what adjustments to make. They have to, because it's real clear now to everyone—the old stuff doesn't work anymore." Milwid (chap. 10, note 8), p. 203.

13. Beth Milwid asserts that gender inequalities need not be the focus of future workplace struggles. It is time to turn our attention and energies toward reordering and restructuring workplace priorities. She cites informal alliances that are emerging, within all types of organizations—alliances that support the "common beliefs and moral commitments" shared by men and women,... "based not on gender, race, or age, but rather on talent, mutual respect, and values." Ibid., p. 123.

14. In January 1987, in the case of California Federal Savings & Loan Assn. *et al.* v. Guerra, Director, Department of Fair Employment & Housing, *et al.*, the Supreme Court upheld a woman's right to pregnancy leave without jeopardizing her job security. In March 1987, in the case of Johnson v. Transportation Agency, Santa Clara County, CA *et al.*, the court acknowledged that women have been significantly underrepresented in certain job categories in the labor force. Therefore, it upheld the Transportation Agency's plan for improving its hiring and promoting practices by increasing the measurable representation of women and minorities on its staff.
    In November 1986, the San Francisco Board of Supervisors amended Section 314 of the City Planning Code. Also known as the San Francisco Office-Hotel Affordable Child Care Ordinance, this legislation imposes a child care condition on building permit applications. It is clear recognition that business must share with government in responsibly providing affordable child care

in close proximity to the workplace. Working parents, mothers especially, are a vital and permanent part of the labor force. In January and February 1987, the Family and Medical Leave Act was introduced into the United States Congress (HR 284, HR 925, SB 249). Individuals often forced to choose between family and work responsibilities would be provided job security when facing a medical emergency. Childbirth, adoption of a child, family health emergencies for oneself or, for example, one's aging parents, and the serious illness of one's child are some of the emergencies cited in this proposed socially responsible legislation.

Chapter 12

1. "The psychological, economic, sexual, and physical dependency that women have on marriage within a patriarchal framework means that getting married represents a personal and social achievement for the woman, whereas for the man 'it belongs to his personal life.' Marriage for a woman therefore has represented not merely one factor of her life among others, but *the* achievement, a 'career' in itself, the foundation of her personal and social identity." Washbourn, Penelope (1977). *Becoming woman: The quest for wholeness in female experience.* New York: Harper & Row. p. 81. Reprinted with permission.
2. "The young girl is trained to wait tamely for the future to happen to her.... Many women's entire lives are consumed in waiting not only for the promised man but for the hetero-relational promised land.... Waiting can be fatal, however, for it breeds a passivity and discourages risk-taking. Ultimately, it convinces women that they are not responsible for their own futures." Raymond, Janice (1986). *A passion for friends: Toward a philosophy of female affection.* Boston: Beacon Press. pp. 178–179. Copyright © 1986 by Janice Raymond. Reprinted with permission by Beacon Press.
3. *San Francicso Chronicle,* October 19 & 22, 1987, published excerpts from a new book by Shere Hite (1987). *Women and love: A cultural revolution in progress.* New York: Alfred Knopf. What was as interesting as Hite's report, which corroborates what heterosexual women have been saying in therapy about their experience with men, were two adjacent articles. Each one, written by a woman, took exception with the findings and cast doubt on the validity of the experiences of the interviewees. One journalist said, "they had such nasty things to say.... If they always sound like this, it's no wonder men don't listen to them." The second article reported a request by a sex educator for additional studies—one on couples who get along and another

on the mothers of these sons who become "mean and insensitive in the love-making area." p. B 5.

The absence of attention to men was remarkable while what the women reported was discounted. Hite's subjects were challenging stereotypes and making people uncomfortable. Significantly, neither reporter asked: Why is it that men behave this way? What can *they* do to change? We continue to demand a high level of flexibility from women whereas men sidle right on by, repeating time-worn patterns. Men are not taking responsibility, nor are they being held accountable for the part they play in maintaining these dissatisfying arrangements.

4. "Victimism ultimately negates Self-definition and Self-responsibility in the world. When women do not define themselves beyond the role of sufferer, then women will settle for the world as men have made it. There will be little inclination to create a different world. It makes women world-sufferers rather than world-makers.... Women's commonality is reduced to our shared oppression." Raymond (chap. 12, note 2), p. 184.

5. "Separating and coming back together is never a finished process.... We must keep in mind that neither separateness nor merger is the desired outcome, movement back and forth between the two is the real goal." Burch, Beverly (1986). Psychotherapy and the dynamics of merger in lesbian couples. In Stein, Terry, & Cohen, Carol (Eds.). *Contemporary perspectives on psychotherapy with lesbians and gay men.* New York: Plenum. p. 71. Reprinted with permission.

"Each may bully, threaten, seduce, or cajole the other into taking responsibility for his/her partner in a futile attempt to deny and evade the burden of separateness and ultimate responsibility for oneself." Karpel, Mark (1976). Individuation: From fusion to dialogue. *Family Process, 15*(1), pp. 65–82.

6. "After twenty-two years of marriage, I felt like a stranger in my skin; I was emotionally empty. I'd been ignoring my feelings, year after year. Patching up a relationship in which neither of us was happy or satisfied.... Finally we were divorced.... The realization that my life was half over finally helped me to accept my lesbianism." Roberts, Nancy (1986). A gift to share. In Adelman, Marcy (Ed.). *Long time passing: Lives of older lesbians.* Boston: Allyson Publications. p. 94.

"I'm a born-again lesbian, not one of those fortunate ones who have known since puberty that they love women. When I was growing up I never heard the word 'lesbian,' never knew there was anything other than heterosexual sex, and prior to my marriage I had never had a lesbian relationship.... I was married for seventeen years; I've been happily divorced for twenty." Frances Lorraine, Born-again lesbian. Ibid., p. 197.

7. "The illegitimate status of lesbianism means that the relationship exists in a hostile environment.... The outside world recognizes no boundaries

around the relationship. It does not exist as an entity. Family, friends, co-workers may fail to treat the couple as a couple, ignoring their status in major and minor ways that a heterosexual couple rarely confronts. This lack of external recognition causes the couple to pull closer for survival. They must mirror their relationship for each other since they will not find it reflected outside of themselves." Burch (chap. 12, note 5), p. 58

8. Jan Faulkner has noted that a major concern for women in interracial relationships, is the "day-to-day negative encounters they experienced in and outside the home ... usually in the form of a 'racist' confrontation questioning the rationale of their mate selection." Often, these women also experienced "a loss of network support from family and friends." Faulkner, J. Women in interracial relationships. In Robbins & Siegel (Introduction, note 1), p. 196.

Chapter 13

1. Psychologist Samuel Osherson, reporting on his work with men, expands our appreciation of what Paul might have been going through but could not communicate. "To understand the true impact of wives who work, we must set the phenomenon in its broader context as a substantial change in family life. Often wives begin work or return to work, for example, as their children become more grown up and independent. I believe there is a general experience of male vulnerability at midlife, especially in light of the growing autonomy of wives and children at that time. Both those changes in family life reveal men's disguised dependency on their families." Osherson, Samuel (1986). *Finding our fathers. How a man's life is shaped by his relationship with his father*. New York: Fawcett Columbine. p. 83.

2. Researcher Terrie Lyons found very few differences between lesbian and heterosexual mothers. She reported, "The only major difference we found between the two groups of mothers was the lesbian mothers' concern for loss of custody of their children.... The possible discovery or disapproval by ex-husbands of their affectional preference was a further area of concern for the lesbian mothers. This fear of disclosure and consequent challenge of custody caused many mothers to be circumspect about the details of their lives both to their children and their ex-husbands." Lyons, Terrie. Lesbian mothers' custody fears. In Robbins & Siegel (Introduction, note 1), p. 233.

3. "Prior to World War II women comprised twenty-five percent of the American labor force. By 1944, the peak year of female wartime employment, they constituted thirty-six percent of the work force. In those years 5 million women joined the fourteen million others who had already found work out-

side the home.... As the country's largest labor reserve, women were actively recruited by both government and industry." Harris, Mitchell, & Schechter (chap 10, note 2), p. 115.

4. "Whether in office or shop the wives loved their jobs, they loved the new friendships it developed, but most of all they loved the feelings of creativeness and power and independence they never had been able to derive from housework." Pratt, George K. (1944). *Soldier to civilian: Problems of readjustment*. New York: McGraw-Hill. p. 173. Copyright 1944. Reprinted with permission.

5. "Most women ... thrived. They enjoyed spending and saving the money they had earned and the sense of economic independence that came from receiving a decent wage. They gained self-confidence from the new skills they acquired and satisfaction from the work accomplished. At the end of the war many surrendered their jobs with great reluctance." Harris, Mitchell, & Schechter (chap. 10, note 2), pp. 117–118.

6. "What happened to women is part of what happened to all of us in the years after the war. We found excuses for not facing the problems we once had the courage to face.... Women went home again just as men shrugged off the bomb, forgot the concentration camps, condoned corruption, and fell into helpless conformity.... There was a kind of personal retreat, even on the part of the most far-sighted, the most spirited." Friedan (chap. 10, note 4), pp. 186–187.

7. "The men who returned were not the same persons who had entered the service a few years before. Their wartime experiences, ranging from the trauma of battle and war wounds to the regimen of military discipline, had affected them profoundly. Their loved ones knew only that war had changed some of the men in ways difficult to understand." Harris, Mitchell, & Schechter (chap. 10, note 2), p. 219.

8. "Those who had stayed at home were also changed by their experiences during the war. Women who had managed their affairs without the help of their absent husbands, or who had worked beside men when jobs were plentiful and labor scarce, were unwilling to begin or resume a career as a homemaker and a subordinate partner in a marriage. For these reasons not all homecomings were joyous occasions." Ibid., p. 219.

9. "All returned soldiers pass through a period of disillusionment as an inescapable part of their total problem of civilian adjustment.... disillusioned about their home town, their jobs, about their freedom from military restrictions, but most of all about their families and friends." Pratt (chap. 13, note 4), p. 123.

10. "Another problem confronting the returned serviceman with a family is the renewal of his relationship with the children. Sometimes, he can slip back into the old relationship with little trouble, but in other cases his absence

may have done something to the feelings of the children that will require the utmost patience and tact to restore." Ibid., p. 175.

11. Marjorie Cartwright, a woman interviewed by Harris, Mitchell, and Schechter, is quoted: "I think most of the men at that time were more emotionally inhibited than they are now. Men were taught to be brave and tough and not to complain or cry. Don't show emotion. Don't let your feelings out. You have to be big and strong. Men in those days could not confide how they felt especially after all those years of military training where they were taught to do things automatically and ignore their feelings." Harris, Mitchell, & Schecter (chap. 10, note 2), p. 226.

Chapter 14

1. Samuel Osherson has written a fine, poignant book about the deprivation sons experience as a result of the emotional unavailability of their fathers. Osherson deals very sensitively with the wounds in men that they have been trained to hide because there has been a lack of male models who reveal their vulnerabilities. He also point out that the family participates in "protective denial," mother and children often colluding with the father to protect him from "emotionally challenging family subjects.... Father's vulnerability becomes a taboo, fearsome topic in this system." Osherson (chap. 13, note 1), p. 26.

Chapter 15

1. "In our culture where marriage and childbirth are so delayed,... it is hard for a ten-year-old girl to appreciate that she is now a biologically mature female. With menstruation comes the possibility of pregnancy; yet that too is seen immediately as a liability rather than a potential joy.... The young girl knows that she is now a sexual being, but the reality of her body and her emotional and social being are out of joint." Washbourn (chap. 12, note 1), p. 8.

2. "How we feel about our bodies has much to do with how we feel about ourselves. And how we feel about ourselves has everything to do with being unempowered, with being unresponded to—except in the domain we are assigned, our bodies—and with feeling that our survival rests on pleasing them, the others. As long as our options are restricted, no women will ex-

perience her body as her home, but rather as her meal ticket." Munter, Carol. Fat and the fantasy of perfection. In Vance (chap. 9, note 2), pp. 228–229.

3. Russell, Diana (1986). *The secret trauma: Incest in the lives of girls and women.* New York: Basic Books. p. 74.

4. Two important early feminist contributions raised awareness about the reality of childhood sexual abuse. Their titles alone suggest the potency of the secrecy that has surrounded this subject. *The conspiracy of silence: The trauma of incest* (Sandra Butler. 1978. Volcano Press). *The best kept secret: Sexual abuse of children* (Florence Rush. 1980. McGraw-Hill).

5. "I know no woman—virgin, mother, lesbian, married, celibate—whether she earns her keep as a housewife, a cocktail waitress, or a scanner of brain waves—for whom her body is not a fundamental problem: its clouded meaning, its fertility, its desire, its so-called frigidity, its bloody speech, its silences, its changes and mutilations, its rapes and ripenings." Rich, Adrienne. (1976). *Of woman born: Motherhood as experience and institution.* New York: W. W. Norton. p. 284.

6. "One out of every three females now alive in the United States will be raped at least once in her lifetime." Colao, Flora, & Hunt, Miriam. Therapists coping with sexual assault. In Robbins & Siegel (Introduction, note 1), p. 205.

7. "Our feelings about menstruation are the image of what it is to be a woman in this culture. While menstruation and the fear of revealing evidence of loss of body control bear possibilities for humiliation for women of which men are not aware, it is humiliating to be that sex whose voice and presence carry far less significance. It is humiliating to speak the same words as a man and have his heard, and not yours. It is humiliating to feel invisible when God gave you a body as solid as his." Friday, Nancy (1977). *My mother/myself: The daughter's search for identity.* New York: Delacorte Press. p. 130.

8. "To regard menstruation primarily as an unfortunate nuisance that now can be handled largely through better sanitary products is to treat female sexuality as an unfortunate burden or weakness which can to a large extent be overcome and thus ignored. This solution is very prevalent in our society, and it implies an inability to integrate the female body structure into the process of identity formation. This lack of self-acceptance and trust of the body stems from being unable to experience any value in female sexuality." Washbourn (chap. 12, note 1), p. 14.

9. Despite the facts, women continue to be maligned because of their biology. Studies done in the early 1920s established that dysmenorrhea did not cause a significant loss of work time or efficiency. In fact, Department of Labor statistics for 1980 support that thesis. "Women only lost three hours of work per person that year" (p. 40). "To the extent that the literature exists, it cannot support the notion that menstruation interferes with women's ability to

work. Yet the theoretical framework underlying most of the extant research is built upon the premise that menstruation negatively affects women's functional capacity." Harlow, Siobán D. (1986). Function and dysfunction: A historical critique of the literature on menstruation and work. In *Culture, society, and menstruation*. Olesen, Virginia, & Woods, Nancy F. (Eds.). Washington: Hemisphere. p. 46.

Psychiatry has recently pushed women a step back. The latest *Diagnostic and statistical manual of mental disorders* (DSM-III-R), 1987, published by the American Psychiatric Association, proposed a diagnostic category, Late Luteal Phase Dysphoric Disorder. This category would link severe menstrual symptoms that could result in temporary impairment in social or occupational functioning, with mental illness. This diagnosis is included in the appendix of the manual "to facilitate further systematic clinical study and research." Placement in the appendix instead of the main text was a concession made by the APA as a result of protests in Winter 1986, and Spring 1987, by feminist and other therapists and mental health practitioners, many of whom use this manual.

10. "In Western culture, with its strong emphasis on female youth and beauty, the menopause is seen as a time of decline and loss of status for women. Belief in 'progress' and in the taming and changing of natural forces makes us willing to alter women's hormonal levels in mid-life. The menopause is viewed as a medical event—even a disease process—which requires treatment and careful medical follow-up.... Today, as millions of women reach their forties and fifties they are seeking new approaches to the menopause. They want to replace the negative stereotypes of the menopausal woman with a realistic and positive outlook. This new viewpoint will flourish as women learn more about how to live through the changes of middle age with maximum health and equanimity." Greenwood, Sadja (1984, 1989). *Menopause, naturally*. Volcano, CA: Volcano Press. pp. 3–5.

Chapter 16

1. "As long as I lived afraid of what I would discover about my own sexuality and fantasies, I had always to wait for another person to discover and 'give' me the material of my own desires. Every time we have been afraid of our desires, we have robbed ourselves of the ability to act. Our collective fear of the dangers of sexuality has forced us into a position where we have created a theory from the body of damage done to us.... By recognizing the danger of our circumstances, we have said, 'There is no way to be a woman in this culture and be sexual too.' ... We have accepted a diminished

set of alternatives and become paralyzed by the fear." Hollibaugh, Amber. Desire for the future: Radical hope in passion and pleasure. In Vance (chap. 9, note 2), pp. 406–407.

2. "Virtually all lesbians have had heterosexual experiences and much of this has been quite negative ... associated with no pleasure, with inauthenticity, even with a sense of being exploited. This early conditioning can remain as part of a lesbian's sexual response ... long after she relates only to women and cognitively views sex quite positively. Early anti-gay attitudes, similarly, can linger long after a gay woman has come out. Further, many lesbians denied their sexual orientation to themselves for extended periods of time by repressing their sexual (but not emotional) attraction to women. Again, the tendency to repress sexual desire may remain despite a heartfelt wish to be sexually active." Nichols, Margaret (1987). Doing sex therapy with lesbians: Bending a heterosexual paradigm to fit a gay life-style. In The Boston Lesbian Psychologies Collective (Eds.). *Lesbian psychologies: Explorations and challenges*. Urbana: University of Illinois Press. p. 254.

3. "In an on-going relationship sexual desire is usually not so automatic, nor is it capable of conquering and overcoming fatigue, tension, or normal preoccupation with everyday affairs. And yet the typical couple assumes their sexuality will continue to function in an automatic fashion, and they consign the role of sexuality in the relationship to something that should occur, without planning, paying attention, or forethought, at the end of the day, just before falling sleep.... We pay less attention to our sex lives than we do to maintaining friendships, to planning meals, to physical exercise. It goes against the grain of all we have learned, and our cultural expectations to place this kind of priority upon sex, and it is particularly grating to us to plan for sex; it feels mechanical to us. But our sex lives suffers from the myth of spontaneity." Ibid., p. 257.

4. "Making condoms sensual also helps make them attractive. If a woman buys four or five brands and says,'Let's try them all and see which one we like best,' that would be almost irresistible." Chris Norwood described a film made for a teenage audience in which three teenage girls are talking about the use of condoms. Not only are teenage boys not shown having the slightest interest in this, but no simple statement is made about safe sex being a shared responsibility between the individuals engaging in lovemaking. Norwood comments that the point at which a woman feels she is becoming "single-handedly responsible for two people's health, and the man is not being gracious or cooperative at all, may be the point at which she decides not to proceed with the relationship. After all, millions of men throughout the world use condoms routinely. It shouldn't be such a big deal." Norwood, Chris (1987). *Advice for life: A woman's guide to AIDS risks and prevention*. New York: Pantheon Books. p. 49.

5. "All of us would prefer to see fewer abortions. Most of us want to see the decrease come from better education and contraceptive methods rather than coercion. We would like to see our respect for individual rights fully include the right of a woman to make free and informed decisions over her own body and future. It is the woman who experiences the responsibility and the hazards of bringing life into the world, and it is she who has the most information about whether she, hopefully with the help of the child's father and others, can properly support this life." Braude, Marjorie. The consequences of abortion legislation. In Robbins & Siegel (Introduction, note 1), p. 89.

6. "Pregnancy and birth also involve *real* physical discomforts. The modern stress on the ability of the mother to control the amount of pain she experiences during labor through relaxation, breath control, and education of her attitude toward her role in the birth process suffers sometimes from oversimplifying the nature of the experience. Pregnancy and birth *do* involve physical and psychological changes that are intense, sometimes painful, often frightening. The normality of these changes and our need to understand them fully should not blind us to the fact that pregnancy and birth are indeed a life-crisis for a woman because she must come to terms with the fears as well as the joys and attain a new understanding of herself." Washbourn (chap. 12, note 1), p. 100.

7. Despite the Supreme Court ruling, January 1987, in the case of California Federal Savings & Loan Assn. *et al.* v. Guerra, which upheld a woman's right to pregnancy leave without jeopardizing her job security, women in other states often have been dismissed from their jobs as a result of becoming pregnant. The employer's assumption that motherhood and job responsibility are incompatible serves to disadvantage women, some of whom are summarily dismissed with no mention of the pregnancy. In December 1987, the National Organization of Women began championing the cause of just such a woman employee in New York State.

8. "Pregnancy offers a woman the chance to wrestle with her relation to her mother, her identity with her, and her distinctiveness from her. It is a chance to find a unique style, a new perspective on herself as a woman in her procreative role." Washbourn (chap. 12, note 1), p. 107.

INDEX